Also available at all good book stores

9781801500630

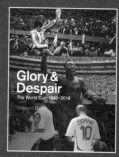

9781801501248

9781785316470

9781801501170

9781801501255

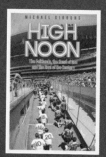

9781785317828

9781801500913

9781801500937

9781801500975

THE
CORNERSTONE
COLLECTION

Stuart Quigley

THE
CORNERSTONE
COLLECTION

Sculpting the Premier League's
Past, Present and Future

First published by Pitch Publishing, 2022

Pitch Publishing
9 Donnington Park,
85 Birdham Road,
Chichester,
West Sussex,
PO20 7AJ
www.pitchpublishing.co.uk
info@pitchpublishing.co.uk

© 2022, Stuart Quigley

ISBN 978 1 80150 123 1

Typesetting and origination by Pitch Publishing
Printed and bound in India by Replika Press Pvt. Ltd.

Contents

For my dad and my mum, who gave me the words.

For Bry, who gave me all strength to carry on.

For Baz, who put up with me every time I'd had too much to drink and helped make all of this a reality.

For Matt, Bill, Barber, Dave, Chris and Mike. Without you this process would have been so much harder. I owe you all.

For everyone I've ever had a drunken conversation with.

For a game that brought us all together.

Introduction

FOOTBALL DIDN'T get me until I was nearly ten years old. Which is to say I didn't get it. Hopeless when it came to playing (some things never change) and completely shut out from this world that I barely understood. Slowly, that shifted.

It feels like so many who grew up during the 1990s have an identical experience. Competing to finish sticker books. Watching games on Teletext. Learning to play *Sensible Soccer*, then endless nights of *Championship Manager*. As time moved on, what was once a passion became an obsession. Whatever I knew, there was always more. Whether it was Serie A on Channel 4, stories of players and teams gone by well before my time or the few occasions a year – without Sky – that I could sit down and watch a full game. Each 90 minutes was its own, yet all of them belonged to something bigger.

Throughout my teenage years into adulthood and from watching games on TV to experiencing them in real time; from having to sit alone and absorb the madness unfolding to being in either a packed stadium or drinking establishment and sharing in those moments – making memories that will last forever.

I am – unashamedly – a complete football romantic. Stats, facts and figures all intrigue me but the humanity is what excites. There's no questioning the wider sanity of pinning all one's hopes on 11 men kicking a ball around every week, just an embrace of the emotions that take us along the way.

English football is more than just the confines of the top division since 1992; that's not when it was invented. Over the course of the last 30 years, the Premier League has taken all those who supported a team within it on a journey, some good, some bad. Some have lasted decades, others just a matter of months. Within the pages of this book I hope to have told them all.

Most of these stories are very familiar, others less so. Choosing the players you're about to read about wasn't easy. Every fanbase will be able to nominate someone I've missed, which in part is the beauty of it. This wasn't about going back over the greatest players to have ever played within the Premier League, though that's part of it.

It's not just about their goals or their trophies but rather the things that shaped them, as well as the league itself. Shining a light on where football has been over the last three decades and where it's going.

This is for anyone who loves the game anywhere near as much as I do. Regardless of who you support, we are all fans.

1

Wayne Rooney

CERTAINTY IS a trap. Conversational camouflage over a black hole of opinion. Some are all too eager to jump down this particular void of stubbornness, carrying with them nothing more than either bad or blind faith and personal bias. The light at the end of this particular tunnel vision lies within an objectivity that is difficult to muster within the moment. Even within that, it defies reason that the most gifted English player of his generation requires a second opinion. Accolades of a certain distinction shouldn't need further investigation. Abandon all hype all ye who enter here.

Aside from the great partisan divide, football demands an ever-increasing instant insistence in regard to consensus. It doesn't make sense to appraise someone's place in history before they've even become it. Like so much when it comes to opinion, there's no exact science. But there does need to be an accepted baseline. Nobody in their right mind could ever put down a playing career that consisted of five English top-flight titles, a European Cup and half a dozen other major trophies. The gripe with Rooney, once you move past the realm that one can exist, is that it's not more.

As is so often the case with footballers, what initially propels them forward can ultimately lead to their undoing: potential.

Used as an arbitrary, imaginary line drawn not once but repeatedly, for every set of subjective eyes watching. The idea that learning and success are both aligned, while reasonable in theory, soon turns sour once one fails to coordinate with the other. For Rooney, this appears to be especially harsh given the frequency with which the records tumbled so very quickly. Bursting on to the scene in such a way, it would have been nigh-on impossible for anyone to keep up with the perpetual motion machine that was the English media. Therein lay the ultimate source of his perceived failure.

Certain players have a buzz even before they've taken to the pitch. To say that things were different in 2002 than they had been before in regard to those on the verge of the first team is to exaggerate slightly,; however, media has played a part in bringing to a boil the hype for a new generation in such a way as didn't happen before the saturation of the game on TV. An ever-increasing showing of youth prospects as they make their way along their early careers as broadcasters scour even deeper for a particular narrative makes for a greater expectation. Everton fans didn't believe, they *knew*. Buzz around the club grew as Rooney's breakthrough in the first team drew ever closer. They were privy to an advance screening of a phenomenon. When the wider world saw him, his A-List status would be confirmed almost instantly.

For all the prestigious highs reached in a career, there were none quite as seismic as that first. He scored a multitude of winning goals over the course of his time in the Premier League. None lit the touch paper quite so spectacularly as that which he scored at Goodison against Arsenal in October of 2002. He had made his debut some two months prior, playing in every game of Everton's season to that point barring one. Those who remember it do so with him doing it in an instant; being summoned off the bench by destiny rather than David Moyes.

Ten minutes was all he needed. Of all that stands out in retrospect all these years later, it's his first touch which underlines everything else that is to come, both in terms of this game and forever onward. Richard Wright's booming goal kick bobbles in and around midfield, resulting in another indiscriminate poke forward by Thomas Gravesen. Football at this point generally evaporates, the battle between defender and forward so commonplace it could be mistaken for code. Rooney's control of the ball does what the goal itself will, and opens up a world of possibilities. The turn to face goal is effortless, the finish exquisite. With one strike of a football he would be tethered to the future. Whatever happened from here on in, tomorrow had found its main character.

Everton's joy was also their struggle. Developing and unleashing this kind of talent soon led to the conundrum of how they were going to hold on to him. The two years that followed produced almost as many yellow cards as goals and for all the skill and technique that was very clearly there, it became more and more of an inevitability that his career would be more fulfilled elsewhere. What's more, the need that came down from boardroom level to cash in and push him in the direction of Chelsea illustrated part of the problem at Goodison Park during the 2000s. For all the good work Everton were doing in building a team that would very soon go on to challenge for the top four, there would always be the need to sell to buy. With that – along with some behind-the-scenes negotiations with Newcastle in order to inflate interest – he got his move to Manchester United following the conclusion of Euro 2004.

Given the anticipation for Rooney's debut, it would have been hard to meet expectations. He exceeded them to a level that even the most ardent United fan would have struggled to predict. Completing his hat-trick before the hour mark, there was very little doubting the promise that lay ahead. The future appeared to be set in stone for a player who would not be held back from success. This was in contrast with the fortunes of his team as threats to United's dominance became plural. After a previously unheard of two years without a title, it was clear they would have to adapt.

Alex Ferguson made but one signing in the lead-up to the 2006/07 season, which paid dividends in terms of the team as a whole. Michael Carrick being the only signing that summer didn't capture the imagination, but with a strong defence, a dynamic attack and an ageing midfield it made the most sense. In among that team, a collection of world-beaters, two stood out who were at the very top of the game. Combined, they struck fear into the hearts of every defence they came up against. Few could contain them. Together they were part of the same unstoppable force. Under the surface, however, they were two very different people.

Playing for the same club does not exclude treading different paths. At the time they were together, only one of them had to shake off the tag of having no end product. Even after an international dispute the two put everything aside in order to win. It was never a competition between the two of them, until Cristiano Ronaldo moved on and made everyone an opponent. His devotion to marginal gains and the player he became at Real Madrid was at odds with a force of nature who made things happen. Rooney did everything he could, scoring goals at a rate and with such impact that his place at the top of English football was assured. Yet somehow a team-mate went on to bigger and better things.

Not all of it revolved around Ronaldo, yet it most definitely began in Portugal. Before Rooney's move from Goodison to Old Trafford, just as that initial hype was about to peak, there was a prodigious performance against Croatia as England beat them 4-2 at the European Championships. A few months before he put Fenerbahçe to the sword on his debut, sharpening that particular blade on the international stage put Rooney front and centre of a so-called golden generation. Except, unlike the doors he was able to unlock for Manchester United, things were never quite as simple when it came to playing for his country. It wasn't for a lack of trying; so many of his Premier League peers never quite lived up to their billing when it came to the international stage. None of them quite suffered quite the same punch to their reputation, regardless of standing.

The World Cups that were to be in Rooney's prime both ended with a very specific infamy. In 2006 he was lucky to avoid being chased by a rabid English media that had shown previous for making scapegoats of Manchester United players, with their focus being all about Ronaldo's wink rather than a more than questionable red-card-earning stomp in the quarter-final. By 2010 a lot had changed, none of it in regard to disappointment. England's eventual defeat to Germany may have been marred by a lack of goal-line technology that may or may not have made a difference but it was a game earlier on, during the group stage that elicited widespread condemnation.

To say the mood in the camp was tense is to slightly undersell it. By all accounts no one was having a great time, such was the strictness with which head coach Fabio Capello regimentally marshalled the squad. Coming off the back of a draw with the USA in somewhat inexplicable terms put a certain amount of pressure on the next group fixture with Algeria. What proceeded to happen was one of the most non-eventful 90 minutes that has ever been played out. Not quite detrimental to the point of permanently damaging the chances of emerging through the group stage, still the England fans in attendance very clearly voiced their disapproval. As frustrated as they were, an equally exasperated response from Rooney was captured by the cameras, 'Nice to see your own fans booing you.'

One sentence – uttered in the immediate aftermath of a deeply unsatisfying performance – does not condemn Rooney to anything. Not least because he was right. The process of booing at full time has always remained a peculiar one, especially when it is so performative. Everyone has the right to express their emotions at any given time, fair and true. It doesn't achieve anything, however. Certainly not at this level.

England underachieved, given the talent they had during the 2000s, that much is reasonable. As part of this unfulfilled legacy, an unwarranted black mark grew into existence.

Despite a storied career that saw him tear up the record books, butting heads with an equally legendary manager over a period of years was part and parcel of an ever-changing landscape. Even during times of unprecedented success, there were those who crossed the boss only to find themselves close to the exit door. Transfer requests, protracted contract discussions and much more. Of all those who ever took on Sir Alex during his time, Rooney may very well be the only one to engage in such a battle and remain at the club.

The struggle that existed within the corridors of Old Trafford during the latter stages of Ferguson's reign only became more important once there was a vacuum. Mythical though Rooney had become, his role at this point had become akin to forever rolling a stone uphill only for it to fall down again. A team that had been rinsed clear of its ability to go again, the surgery that was required became terminal. For as bad as David Moyes and Louis van Gaal had it, things would have been a lot worse were it not for the ever diminishing returns of a player who found himself having to plug more gaps.

Time catches up with the best. Those who burst on to the scene in such a way are rarely those who disappear without a trace. Moving into midfield gave a spark of new life both in terms of Rooney's latter-stage Manchester United career as well as a final chapter for England that saw him wildly adrift in a 2-1 humiliation to Iceland during Euro 2016. Rejoining Everton might perhaps in another world have added the perfect epilogue for a player who the Goodison faithful once saw reveal a t-shirt saying 'Once a Blue, Always a Blue'. Ten goals in the 31 games that he did play – including a sensational hat-trick against West Ham – wasn't necessarily the ending that many had envisioned. Right to the very end, the potential of what might have been overshadowed what was.

Going to America felt like one move too many. Calling it a day after returning to Everton satisfied the biographers and completionists; still there was more football to play. Even with the less than impressive gaze through which MLS is viewed from European shores, there was still enough time to produce what might – after everything else – be the definitive piece of play of his career. A last-minute corner with a side trying to find a winner so much that they send the goalkeeper up. Once the ball breaks a certain way a goal is all but certain. When it comes to percentages however, Wayne Rooney never gave up on anything.

In the US they call it hustle, chasing down the one player who was about to hit an empty net before him. Clutch means something very different. To pick out a ball from the halfway line that would allow a forward at the other end to score and win the game, that's on another level entirely. Every aspect of that play highlighted a different part of one of the most gifted English footballers of all time. The desire to win it back, even when it wasn't his responsibility or the moment didn't really require it. Alone it would have been enough. To follow it up with the perfect technique, there are so very few who have that kind of all-round ability. That was Wayne Rooney.

Even after it's over, it's never really over. Coming back over the pond in the middle of the 2019/20 season and joining a Derby County side in desperate need of help in their quest to get back to the Premier League, it wouldn't take long before the task changed. Then the job changed, from player to manager. After that the job became impossible. It's astonishing that a player who saw it all and did it all can find themselves in an unprecedented situation. Even more so, there's an end point here that for once won't affect his reputation. Whatever happens to Rooney the manager, nothing can compare to the conviction that was put upon him after that first moment. Judgement comes after, not during.

2

Ian Harte

EXPECTATION EXISTS only to set the boundaries from which the exceptional can break free. There's a difference between playing a position and the result of doing something different within that remit. Convention very quickly becomes unnecessary when the alternative – regardless of how flawed – soars above. That which we've seen before we'll see again. However conventional, the lure for something different entices. The really special players don't fully fit into any specific label, regardless of where those assumptions may lie. They are forged out of fate and made to play out their careers knowing that what makes them special will ultimately be their undoing.

Of all the clinically defined roles to have changed over the years, it is full-back that has seen – and continues to see – the wildest swing. For the longest time it was just about competency. Helping the centre-halves, making sure that the defensive shape was compact and then maybe on a rare occasion if the circumstances called for it there would be the opportunity to link up with the wide midfielder. Prevention above all else, with the focus more upon the defensive end than anything at the other end of the pitch. As the 1990s rolled on and positions became less fixed and more illustrative of a starting position, a revolution of this role was both forthcoming and inevitable.

The catalysts for change came – if you can distil it down to just its most basic tenets – from Brazil. Cafu and Roberto Carlos were seen as so far ahead of everyone else but also somewhat of an anomaly. Their all-round play while spectacular was unlikely to be replicated anywhere else, both domestically or internationally. But it planted a seed, one that grew at a remarkable pace. Fast forward another 15 years or so and Dani Alves made them both look like dinosaurs. In between those two points, the blueprint for what was to become the full-back position was written.

Domestically it was as ever a different story. For the most part of the modern era it has been dominated by Ashley Cole, with a smattering of Leighton Baines in terms of both sheer talent coupled with number production. There's also the Gareth Bale experience that went in the other direction. As for where we are now, things have reached something of a tactical impasse with the obvious outliers plying their trade at Anfield. If nothing else, Trent Alexander-Arnold has changed the conversation around the modern full-back. The idealistic tug of war that's broken out into an arms race between rivals for the position for England is an extreme conclusion to both the ever-demanding numbers that are required and the standard being produced. If ever the complicated nuances of positional discord can be undone with a single phrase it is thus. The end justifies the means.

Such is the delicate balance within team setup these days, it's easy to think that defenders who contribute are a liability at the back. This is something of a false projection because their overall play is factored into any system. More or less everything you see is by design, not that a manager has sat there and watched someone bomb on in behind the space left behind and not bothered to do anything about it. The primary job for any position has always been the same and it will never change, no matter how much the minutiae around it continues to fluctuate. It's not even as if these debates are anything new. As the 20th century drew to a close – before Cole, Baines and Alexander-Arnold – there was another Premier League full-back who broke the mould, associated much more for his goalscoring prowess than what he did going the other way. Ian Harte wasn't the first, nor the last – but he was a point in time along the way as things began to change forever.

Leeds United began the Premier League era as reigning champions of the English top flight. Teams of this size and repute can be haunted by their history but no side has ever been written out of it in such a way. Harte came over from Ireland in 1995 to join a club that was going through some changes but still contained at the very least one familiar face. Keeping family close – especially when moving away – is a key factor in being able to adapt to new surroundings. Most players don't have a family member already in the team. With his uncle Gary Kelly there off the pitch for familial comforts and also present in playing terms, it set the stage. Like most things at Elland Road at the time, however, it wasn't until the decade drew to a close that things really started happening.

George Graham was a world away from the whirlwind, free-flowing side that is associated with this time period, so it's hard to conceive on face value that it would be his assistant who would facilitate all that would come next. The sheer volume of young talent coming through at Leeds meant that whomever did take the job would find himself access to a bounty of assets and despite numerous attempts to fill that vacancy differently, David O'Leary rode the wave of fearless attacking football all the way to a permanent position in the manager's hot seat. An intrepid season could have blossomed even further, save for a not so good run in the winter that put paid to any further progress. As they marched on into spring and beyond, Harte began to take centre stage, showcasing quite literally a game-changing asset. In addition to all his attacking intent during the play, it was set pieces where he really came to life.

Dead-ball situations make all the difference. They can define a player as much as the results of them come to represent the game itself. Having the ability to influence proceedings in such finite moments can be something of a superpower. Being able to change the game speaks volumes for those that play in that specific role. Posing that kind of threat from left-back opened up a whole new world of possibilities. Harte's career had the sprinkling of that particular stardust and he was on his way to the very top. Scoring the opening goal in a World Cup play-off against Iran from the penalty spot set a particular tone. With the Republic of Ireland, Harte was on top of the world. With Leeds he was about to be front and centre of a most remarkable European odyssey.

Competing for trophies captivates a fanbase and makes all the bad times feel insignificant. It allows a team to become more than just the sum of their parts and gives them a chance of making history. Whether it comes down to a particularly favourable cup draw or just having a group of players capable of taking on anyone. If the domestic trophies are to be a journey then their continental equivalents are an adventure. From travelling to far foreign lands and pitting yourselves against the very best that other countries have to offer, there's nothing that comes close to both the prestige and excitement that comes with a run in Europe.

If there is such a thing as a complete performance, it would be hard pressed to beat that which Ian Harte put in during the 2001 Champions League quarter-final. Deportivo La Coruña were the reigning La Liga champions but they were put to the sword with a succession of set pieces, all of which derived from one very specific boot. Winning 3-0 at Elland Road with Harte opening the scoring and setting up the other two, this was as high as it got for Leeds in many different respects.

As rapid as the rise had been, the fall was much quicker. Savouring those European nights became a distant memory and clinging on to Premier League status replaced it within the blink of an eye. Harte scored the second goal against Arsenal in 2003 in a decisive game for both clubs, the 3-2 victory both ensuring Leeds' safety and handing the title to Manchester United. To

THE CORNERSTONE COLLECTION

avoid relegation given the circumstances was to halt an inevitable slide. As false dawns go, the behind-the-scenes financial black hole into which Leeds were being plunged meant there was never any chance of a reprieve. As much of a foregone conclusion as things were at the end of the Ridsdale era, the real surprise would come next.

In terms of Spanish heritage, Levante aren't necessarily near the top. At the point Harte signed on the dotted line, they were entering only their second stint in the top flight. It seems as surreal now as it did in 2004 that Harte scored their first goal of that season. What makes more sense is that it was an expertly dispatched free kick, as so many of his strikes had been. At a time in which very few British players plied their trade abroad, this was a breath of fresh air even before he hung around to play in the Segunda División for a season.

What happened next both sets up and encapsulates the life of a footballer, coming back to familiar territory in 2007/08 for a Sunderland side that even the manager Roy Keane would barely recognise. Harte played his last meaningful minutes in a 7-1 defeat to Everton. There are always these periods at the end of someone's career when even the fans of those involved would struggle to picture the man in the shirt. Stints at Blackpool and Carlisle did little to suggest anything other than the end was nigh. In spite of all expectations, there was one last hurrah to be had.

After signing a player from the league below – even given Harte's previous reputation – there was no sense of what was about to come for Reading. The feeling was one of deflation, having sampled Premier League football prior and not being able to recapture that momentum. They needed something extra and the consensus was that it was unlikely to come from a division below. It was an underestimation of epic proportions. Reaching the play-off final in his first year only to lose to Swansea, there may have been a sense of an opportunity missed. To follow that up with another tilt at the top, an even better campaign, was to blow all of that out of the water. For a player who had signed from League One, his usefulness all but disregarded, playing himself into the Championship Team of the Year and being a pivotal part of a comprehensive promotion was as heroic a last act as they get.

As a late-2000s refresher, Reading were promoted in 2006 with a record 106 points. Following on from that their first season in the Premier League under Steve Coppell garnered an eighth-placed finish. Both remarkable feats are forever underappreciated. By the time Brian McDermott returned them in 2012, the Premier League was very different. The evolution that had begun during the late 1990s was now so far ahead that attackers had devoured the space left in behind. The likes of Eden Hazard weren't around before Harte moved to Spain. If there were questions regarding the defensive side of his game some years prior, the answers given in 2012/13 were particularly harsh. As such, the Royals' second stay in the top division was even shorter than their first.

Time moves at an even constant, as a result of which everything else is in a hurry. It didn't take long for a flawed, albeit tactically gifted player at his position to go from one of the biggest assets in the league to being left behind. The problem with making an impact is that it quickly becomes the norm, and not long after that what was once innovation gets left behind. Even in those fickle wastelands, there should always be a reminder of those that paved the way.

3

Charlie Adam

NOTHING HAS quite so many top-level plateaus as sport. Football itself is filled with milestones that in turn reveal more obstacles behind them as things go along. Debuts – that were once the be all and end all – become about establishment. Simply playing isn't then enough anymore, it's about playing at a particular standard. In a practical sense it means however far up the ladder anyone goes, it's never quite far enough. What makes it worse is that this process doesn't even have to be self-inflicted. However considerable the achievement, there's always someone waiting for the failure.

Criticism comes from everywhere. Some of it is well-intentioned, most of it is ignorant malignance. The theory goes that you can prove those people wrong. Knuckle down and put in the work – both on the training ground and on the pitch – and they'll somehow be won over. All this in a world where opinions are both inflexible but become solidified well before there's the required information at hand.

Every season starts with a blank slate. Except even within all the unknowns there's so much that has all but been decided. Teams are judged without the requisite evidence and players both new and old are assigned stat lines. Sometimes these assumptions are within a reasonable plane of plausible reality, sometimes not.

Before a ball has been kicked, the perceived predictability of what is about to unfold renders the whole process infinitely more stale. Fighting against the tide of expectation shakes everything up. A single team under the right circumstances can create some real waves.

By 2010, the top flight in England had gone through certain phases. Long after its rebrand in 1992, there were periods of adjustment that had finally begun to settle. The teams at the top had altered their approach and become more ruthless in a variety of ways; those at the bottom had changed in a more definitive sense. Within that there was a certain protocol from the teams coming up into the league anew. During the early years the hierarchy was clearly defined but teams didn't really care too much about it. Over the years and as the money grew, it's not that the prestige of the league increased so much as their financial might. In these circumstances, a team came along that defied all convention. In the high-powered, media- and money-driven world of the Premier League, how did Blackpool fit in?

They were outcasts from the off. Talk often turns to teams coming into the Premier League and just being happy with their day out. Acknowledgement of any achievement often lends itself into the realms of condescension; this often happens in the cup competitions but the language surrounding Ian Holloway's 2010 team was just as nauseating. Predictions veered from the disrespectful to outright ignorance. The assumption was that they were down before a ball had been kicked. Relegate them now, save everyone the time and effort. But that's the thing about what Blackpool did, as well as their eventual fate. In the end they fell but for so long they flew so high. In the face of those denouncements and the idea that they had nothing to contribute when in actuality they really were a breath of fresh (seaside) air.

Some players do a great job in setting up success. Theirs is the job to pass the torch, especially when it comes to promoted teams. Often those who finished one season aren't able – through opportunity or talent – to perform in the same way a second

THE CORNERSTONE COLLECTION

time. Charlie Adam made the step up look easy. To even get into that position in the first place involved one of the more prevalent cliches in Championship football. They timed their run of form to perfection while circumstances elsewhere fell into their favour. The number of teams that have risen to the Premier League through the play-offs having capitalised on a late run of form is almost certainly lower than has been suggested in the past. Still, these platitudes exist for a reason. Momentum means a lot on the surface when it comes to achievement. Whether or not it's a particular driving force, it's better to have than not.

With Newcastle and West Brom having the automatic promotion slots locked up between them, for those immediately below in the play-off spots it was a case of playing a long game. Once third became the highest realistic finish for Nottingham Forest for example, there was less of a need to win those games at the end of the season as there might otherwise have been. Blackpool, meanwhile, had emerged through a rough spring period that pushed them to go on one last run to try and snatch that last play-off place. After losing to Newcastle, there was now very little room for error.

Billy Davies's decision to give his first-teamers a break opened a door. Seven points in their final three games got Blackpool to a place where they could go through, all kick-started by a 3-1 victory over Davies's Forest.

Adam from the penalty spot was something of a recurring theme over the course of his Blackpool career. In the space of a month there were two that really sent them on their way. That first started a process that could end at Wembley, the second ensured they would be able to get there in the first place. Forest again, Bloomfield Road again, Adam again. A 2-1 defeat in the play-off semi-final first leg would no doubt have left Davies rueing the idea of giving Blackpool a lifeline but at the same time there was still another game to play.

Blackpool winning at the City Ground was never on the cards, which summed up the contempt that Ian Holloway's team had for expectations. DJ Campbell cut Forest apart that night in a 4-3 success (6-4 on aggregate) and closed the number of games they needed to win to just one. Cardiff stood in between Blackpool and a place in the Premier League. The Bluebirds were on the cusp themselves, having also been to an FA Cup Final two years previously. During this time they were always in the mix when it came to big games. For some teams, the play-offs can become an unbreakable hurdle. Others are able to make it look like a breeze. For a match that went back and forth and was eventually decided by the odd goal in five, it's not that this was a clash between two of those types of teams; yet that's how it finished. At the very least, it was an incredible first 45 minutes.

Cardiff scored within the first ten minutes having already hit the bar. Adam levelled things up with a free kick right into the top corner shortly afterwards. Three more goals followed as Blackpool came from 2-1 down to lead 3-2 even before the half-time whistle had gone. Inevitably in a game with such stakes, the action tightened up when play resumed. Chances for both sides to add to the scoreline were spurned right up until the unthinkable became reality. Having been completely unfancied at the start of the season, the idea of Blackpool getting out of the division wasn't too out of the realm of possibility. Rather than going down, however, they were going up.

There's only so much one man can do alone. The idea of a one-man team is something that has propped up many a drunken argument between rival fans for the sheer contempt it holds for everyone else. This kind of bitterness is usually levelled at the top teams, more so to pull at the ego strings of those higher up. When it comes to teams at the bottom of the table, it's more about valiant efforts that just didn't quite match up. Whatever anyone thinks about Adam, it's fair to say he couldn't have done more for Blackpool in their solitary season in the Premier League.

Given the amount of responsibility on his shoulders, especially as things became increasingly difficult during that second half of the season, it would have been so easy to express that burden on the pitch. Partly due to the nature of the manager, none of it ever felt like a slog. Too many teams before or since have treated the Premier League as though it's a necessity. The money may be good but it's not everything. Their ownership at the time might have used this period rather cynically, which is about as neutral and nice as what could be said about the Oyston family at the time, but it went against everything that team stood for. Blackpool were fun. They got in the ring and threw punches, unafraid of being knocked out like so many others. At the very least, they took it to the final round and to the scorecard.

Old Trafford. There can be no worse enemy fortress to try and ransack in order to secure survival. Across the course of the previous 37 games the dream had played out. When Manchester United took an expected lead, that might have been that. Defying expectations to the very end, Adam equalised before half-time. One more free kick to give the away fans something to cheer about. When Gary Taylor-Fletcher put them ahead in the second half, those voices emboldened. It didn't last long. Anderson tied the score before a cruel Ian Evatt own goal finally opened the trap door. As things transpired, an equaliser at this point would have seen Blackpool go down courtesy of a single goal and so the most unlikely of turnarounds was needed. Michael Owen added a fourth for Manchester United late on, ending any hope of one last hurrah. Making it until the last ten minutes of the final game was not bad for a team written off before a ball was kicked.

The Blackpool adventure having finally come to an end, there was no doubt that Adam would remain a Premier League player. Liverpool had looked to make a move earlier on that year but continued to offer unsubstantial bids. By July the two clubs had come to an agreement and having beaten the Reds home and away that previous season, he would now line up alongside them. It was a summer of upheaval at Anfield, with large amounts of money also being spent on Stewart Downing and Jordan Henderson. This was also off the back of a hefty figure being laid down for Andy Carroll. The departure of Rafael Benítez and being restrained by the financial mismanagement of the previous ownership had cost Liverpool their place within the top four. Given what he had shown at Blackpool and in terms of his set-piece delivery alone, Adam in theory ticked boxes. Football isn't a theoretical game though and what worked at Bloomfield Road never quite clicked at Anfield in spite of the players around him.

Kenny Dalglish's sacking in 2012 was as glowing an illustration of where the game had gone at the very top. Going to two cup finals and winning one of them – in spite of Adam's wild penalty against Cardiff at Wembley – would have in days gone by, guaranteed more time. In some cases it would have been held up as one of the more important seasons in a club's history. Not for Liverpool. Failure to qualify for the Champions League, including a truly wretched end to the Premier League campaign, meant that rather than be given another chance, the decision was taken that King Kenny was to be scrapped and a whole new project had to begin. Brendan Rodgers came in and Adam went out.

The shape of a career when it is all said and done can look very different to that it appears to be in the moment. A single season at both Blackpool and Liverpool compared to six at Stoke City and yet the strength of feeling is that they were all about the same. With the first two there were positives and negatives at almost opposite ends of the scale. Plaudits and relegation traded for disapproval and a trophy. At the Britannia Stadium, for the most part there was that happy medium. Joining the club for what was the final season under Tony Pulis, the groundwork had already been laid. Five straight seasons in the Premier League was enough of a safety blanket to look ahead rather than behind. Mark Hughes arrived, making it his mission to mould Stoke into something different.

At first there was a great deal of promise, both in terms of their overall league position as well as a gradual upgrade in levels of ability. Bojan Krkić, Marc Muniesa and Ibrahim Afellay all came from Barcelona to ply their trade at the Britannia over the next few years and even if there was limited success within the performances of those players it helped on an aesthetic level in turning over a new leaf. It was more than just a Catalan influence; Xherdan Shaqiri and Marko Arnautović added another layer of style to proceedings. Three consecutive top-ten finishes underlined the improvement. Two years later, Stoke were relegated.

Going from being a battle-hardened team of fighters to a team of better players that couldn't be bothered became the accepted reasoning. In actuality Mark Hughes began to rely more and more upon the defensive ethos of old as the years went on, most notably during a League Cup semi-final at Anfield in which Stoke had Liverpool beaten but failed to go for the killer blow and eventually lost on penalties. From there the progress in terms of expansive football became mitigated. By the end of the 2016/17 season even the impact of their once fearsome home record became less and less effective. The warning signs were there.

When disaster strikes, answers are demanded. Learning from mistakes is very different from being absolved of blame. Hughes left in January 2018 with Paul Lambert coming in to arrest the slide. Unable to turn draws into wins or create any kind of momentum, Stoke's relegation was confirmed with one game to go before the end of the season. Long after the dust had settled, there were comments made to the media about certain members of the squad that year, most notably Shaqiri.

For a player who had received plenty of flak himself, these words felt quite sour, especially given what happened when Adam had chances to contribute himself. An unfortunate but ultimately costly red card against Everton before a golden opportunity to give Stoke a much-needed three points at home to Brighton spurned from the penalty spot. In the beginning of his days in the Premier League, it was up to Adam to do everything.

During this dismal ending there was nothing at all he could do. Lots of players go through tougher times towards the end of their career. Very few have such highs that they are so heavily associated with like those days at Bloomfield Road. Charlie Adam was never the most fashionable of players. His career in the top flight became a magnet for overreaction. Immediately incredible, latterly lamentable.

4

Heurelho Gomes

NO MATTER what happens, redemption is never far away. Forgive me gaffer, for I have sinned. Absolution – in a football sense – requires very little. Fortunes can be turned around with the swing of a leg. The striker who misses will have another chance, likewise those who misplace any passes along the way. As ever, goalkeepers have different rules that they have to play by.

An existence in isolation with the scales forever tipped against them. Even within these parameters they can never do it on their own, being at the mercy on both ends of in-form strikers and inept defenders alike. For them as much as anyone watching on, there is more than a small amount of faith involved. Losing all belief in just one person over an entire 11 can become crippling. Especially someone whose entire role is based around propping up everyone else.

Goals come with their own reckoning. The inquest begins immediately and there are usually a multitude of suspects. Removing the possibility of any actual skill involved from the opposition team – which rarely happens in these moments of retrospection – a guilty party or two will be singled out. Often, even in the pursuit of condemnation alone, there isn't much more that could be done save for small details. It's in those instances where mistakes are plain to see that judgement becomes much more punitive.

Being right doesn't tangibly matter anywhere near as much as it feels. First of all when it comes to football so much of it is subjective and circumstantial that arriving at these conclusions is much more difficult than those that are so assured of their superiority. Even having the correct answer won't change anything in the grand scheme of things, which is where the frustration must lie. As if everyone around, while sharing in this deep despair, is ultimately blind. Such visions of a splinter which, when removed, would solve everything tend to oversimplify a more complex conundrum. It's when everyone but the manager can see it, things confound even further.

After Heurelho Gomes signed for Tottenham Hotspur he was laughed at. Derided by the club he had just joined for stating his ambition was to win the Premier League. That goal may have died very soon after his opening interview but the laughter never fully went away, except those at White Hart Lane that weren't finding the funny side anymore. The summer of 2008, in which he signed, was meant to be a new beginning, the start of something special. Capturing the League Cup just a few months prior and beating both Arsenal and Chelsea along the way, this was supposed to be a new dawn. Juande Ramos had begun the process of bringing Tottenham up the hill only to dramatically come tumbling down again.

Settling into new surroundings, especially when there is any kind of culture shock, takes time. Gomes found himself playing in a new team in a new country with a different kind of pressure and everything going wrong around him. Earning himself the nickname 'The Octopus' during his spell in Holland, getting his head around it all took a back seat to trying to get his hands on something. One clean sheet in the first eight and a total of two points was enough to seal the fate of Ramos. Among the six defeats in that early part of the season, a challenging Aston Villa came to White Hart Lane and took all three points. Not only was it a bad result in the short and long term, for these were two sides that wanted to be jostling for those Champions League places at the end of the season, but also the way in which Ashley Young scored Villa's second was a concern. Picking the ball up in midfield with an ocean of space in which to turn and drive forward, for all the criticism the outfielders will have got, the subsequent shot should have been nowhere near powerful enough to get through. By the time Ramos was shown the door, some six months after Gomes came in on an impervious reputation, the goalkeeper was never quite seen the same way again.

New managers tend to want to change things up, especially in a team where things weren't going well. Even if Tottenham were only in a temporary turmoil, Harry Redknapp was always one to to put a stamp on his own squad. Were there not already enough to make his mind up, a costly mistake against Fulham in November led to the manager's first defeat as they were attempting to turn things around. Two months later, Carlo Cudicini joined on a free and at face value that might have been it. There was the thinnest sliver of a lifeline, owing to the fact that the former Chelsea man was cup-tied for the upcoming League Cup Final. Gomes stepped in as Spurs looked to retain the trophy against a dangerous, albeit rotated, Manchester United side. That the game would remain scoreless throughout and be decided on penalties gave a tangibly sudden chance for the Brazilian to redeem himself given everything that had gone before. It was a goalkeeper who walked away with both the trophy and the man of the match award that day: Ben Foster. The two would meet again.

Trust is incredibly easy to lose and infinitely harder to gain. After the League Cup Final at least Gomes was starting that road back. Such is the fickle reality of the position, having an injury at the start of the following season allowed him to come back to a degree of affection. What adds to that particular cause are saves of a stature that defy the laws of physics. When Tottenham travelled to Portsmouth in the autumn of 2009, the only factor of note was meant to be the inter-club connections between the two, as well as the return of Redknapp for the first time since leaving the Fratton Park club a year prior. In a game full of chances, Spurs winning 2-1, what grabbed the attention was a stunning one-handed save.

Reaction saves can at times feel like a glitch in time. When hit correctly, the ball appears in long before it ever reaches the net only for something to get in the way. When Younes Kaboul's sweetly struck free kick was deflected from the right-hand side to the middle, it was in. Gomes had already committed himself; there was no way back. Reaching out an arm, somehow he still managed to palm it over the bar. Afterwards, Tottenham legend Pat Jennings likened it to Gordon Banks's iconic save against Pele in 1970.

Following this up with a critical performance against Arsenal at home only added to the growing sentiment. With Spurs two goals to the good, Gomes played his part. Twice he denied Robin van Persie with increasingly acrobatic saves, before pushing a Sol Campbell effort on to the post as the intensity increased. Despite being eventually breached by Nicklas Bendtner, the game finished 2-1 and Tottenham had their first victory over the Gunners in over a decade. Just days later Spurs completed a particularly satisfying double by beating Chelsea by the same scoreline with the Brazilian again showcasing his shot-stopping ability. Gomes had battled his way back and earned the plaudits he was receiving, going some way to regaining all the trust that had dissipated in those complicated beginnings. All of that effort, only to lose it all over again.

Gomes and Gareth Bale have very distinct paths even within the time they played together. Both needed to find a new lease of life at Tottenham. While one was making saves and blunting strikers, the other began making opposition goalkeepers look like fools. Their dynamic splits at almost the very same time: October 2010, the San Siro, against European champions Inter Milan. Spurs would ultimately lose this Champions League group game but it wouldn't feel like it. Cut apart and conceding in the second minute, Gomes's misery was compounded by giving away a penalty and being sent off very soon afterwards. Inter Milan's goalscoring did not stop in a rampant first half which saw them go in at the break four goals to the good. If the first 45 minutes belonged to one side, the second belonged to Bale and him alone.

When Peter Crouch laid the ball off to him inside the Tottenham half, the first instinct might have been respite, simply keep the ball and prevent the damage from getting worse. Bale thought otherwise, driving at the Inter defence and carrying it all the way, not before leaving Maicon for dust as he blew by him rapidly. The run was good, the finish better. From a tight angle on the left-hand side of the penalty area, Bale cut it right the way across goal and into the opposite corner. At 4-1 there was a modicum of pride back. Though it was perhaps too late, the trick was repeated again as the game went into added time. Javier Zanetti, who struggled to keep up with Bale for the first, was again powerless to stop the Welshman from rifling into that same corner. In a flash, Aaron Lennon was running at a staggered defence once more and his pass to Bale once again produced an exquisite finish. It was Bale's hat-trick – he had also scored just moments before the goal – and the score was 4-3 with seconds left on the clock. Though Spurs weren't able to finish the job, there was no doubt a star was born that night. As for Gomes, his precarious reputation was very much on the way down.

With a league campaign undergoing serious repairs, even before Bale's heroics it was always going to be Europe that would be Spurs' saving grace that season. Going back over to the Italian capital to dump out AC Milan in the round of 16 meant a quarter-final with Real Madrid. Once again they would be down to ten men, Crouch's two yellow cards in quick succession putting Tottenham up against it even more after having already gone a goal behind in the first leg. They were still in the tie right up until the hour mark. Emmanuel Adebayor doubled his tally and Ángel Di María curled one spectacularly into the far corner. Cristiano Ronaldo's fourth rubbed salt into the wounds. Though the strike was clean, it was saveable. Any attempts at a rousing comeback in the second leg were similarly dashed by an even more glaring howler. This time the ball was struck straight at Gomes, who rather than catch it, gloved it away to his side and was forced to helplessly back pedal in a futile attempt to stop it from going in. Whatever part luck had to play, during this period it was having the game of its life against the Brazilian.

Goal-line technology never caused the same kind of arguments that expanded video replays would go on to evoke. Even so, during the early 2010s there was still a delay in implementing something so simple. Tottenham were on the receiving end of the kind of mistakes that helped usher it in quicker. In a game that would help decide whether Chelsea would win the title or if Spurs could get back into the race for Champions League football, the home side came out on top with a particularly fortunate roll of the ball. Frank Lampard's effort from distance went through Gomes's legs as he bent down to pick it up. Having this time successfully scrambled back to retrieve it off the line, the errors this time were from the officials. With the goal given, Chelsea went on to win 2-1. This wasn't a final straw as such but it was the end of the road. The end of the season saw Spurs out of the Champions League places and Gomes frozen out completely.

Subtlety isn't something that was ever really associated with Harry Redknapp. Bringing in a 40-year-old goalkeeper in the summer seemed to indicate that he was very much in the mood to move on, regardless of how good Brad Friedel had been over the years at Blackburn Rovers. A frustrating loan away to the Bundesliga for Hoffenheim in which Gomes barely played due to injury meant a fate worse than ridicule. Forgotten about with a career completely stalled, Gomes packed his bags and readied himself to return to Brazil when the call came. Instead the path to recovery would begin in the Championship. A journey of faith and of second chances, leading back to the Premier League and beyond.

Consistency is seen as the key to security. The convenience of knowing what's likely to come next based on a regularity of what's gone before. Watford have had a disregard of this concept. From 2015 onward their perseverance in standing outside of convention when it comes to turnover makes them a case study in ruthless ambition. With ten managers in seven years and a multitude of players coming in and out of the Vicarage Road dressing room, they certainly cannot be accused of standing still. Yet with all the interchangeable faces that came and went, there have been those that earned their places within the affections of the Watford fanbase. Gomes is very much one of them.

The 2014/15 season was an erratic affair with notions of winning the Championship outright in November giving way to an acceptance of playing in the play-offs before a late run saw them run away with automatic promotion once more. Only the final day saw Bournemouth snatch top spot but ultimately all that mattered was that they were heading back to the top flight. Priorities changed for Watford just as they had Gomes. No longer being relied upon in flashes like he was at Spurs, he thrived on being called upon more often and was able to showcase some more of the shot-stopping prowess that attracted Spurs in the first place. Quique Sánchez Flores put together the first of a succession of Watford teams that would surprise their Premier League counterparts, all the while doing just enough to keep them away from the threat of going down.

When it came time to being replaced at Vicarage Road, things were nowhere near as volatile as they had been earlier on in his career. Despite having the captain's armband, Marco Silva switched him out in January 2018 before making a move for Ben Foster that summer. A squad in harmony is one that performs at a level capable of achieving more than the sum of its parts. A team is just that and with goalkeepers, even though two players are both vying for the same position, they in turn have to keep each other sharp in spite of the established order. For everyone else in training, there is that chance – form and ability permitting that they'll be able to take to the field together. Gomes and Foster were able to form that kind of relationship and it in turn helped the Brazilian get the one thing few footballers get the chance to do, which would have never been on the cards previously: to say goodbye properly.

It started as standard rotation. Through the early rounds of the 2019 FA Cup, Gomes took his place in between the sticks against Woking and Newcastle as these are usually the only chances second-choice goalkeepers get. As the games went on and the momentum from each round began to pick up pace, the story changed. Gomes made it known that at the end of that season he would be retiring, which by proxy meant that wherever Watford's FA Cup journey ended would be his last game. After the quarter-final win over Crystal Palace at Vicarage Road, there were tears in his eyes for the last time he would ever play there. Under normal circumstances some teams and managers might have put their first-choice goalkeeper back in for the semi-final but Foster made it clear that he wanted Gomes to play on.

Wembley for the semi-final meant at least if this was to be the end, it would be on a grand stage. All the hope of making it further looked lost at half-time though as Wolves took a two-goal lead. When Gerard Deulofeu came on with 25 minutes to go, the final was so far away with so little time left. His wonderful effort brought the game back to life before Troy Deeney's 94th-minute penalty sent the game into extra time. Deulofeu's second goal was enough to send both the Watford fans and Gomes himself crazy. Whatever happened next, they had at least made it all the way.

What came next was vicious and unrelenting: Manchester City 6 Watford 0. The harsh realities of football all came to bear. Winning the FA Cup would have been the perfect way to sign off but there's only room for so much sentiment in football.

Getting there in the first place was to be enough. For Gomes, the day itself was a culmination, not just of the run they had been on over the past six months but of a player who became a figure of fun only to find a club and a fanbase that fitted. A man of faith, looking for salvation.

5

Nwankwo Kanu

TO THOSE on the pitch and everyone watching, football gives. Whether it's the realisation of a dream or to come together as a community, there is prosperity wherever you look. Players are in the unique position of being able to requite those blessings. Because of their experiences and the tenderness within them as a whole, they reach out beyond the game.

Charity has many different guises and small gestures can indeed make a big difference. When it comes to giving back however, less is not more. Going above and beyond in this regard is to truly do something special. Playing it forward from humble beginnings, making a difference in the scoreline to changing the world. Nwankwo Kanu brought happiness to many throughout his career but it could have all been so different.

Retirement from professional football is a gradual process that reaches its inevitable conclusion even after the body can no longer perform. The decision to call it a day is so often taken out of the hands of the professional. Having to face that possibility at the age of 20 is a much more jarring prospect. Even at this point, Kanu had already done so much: a three-time Dutch champion and Champions League winner with Ajax, as well as being a key part in Nigeria's triumph at the Atlanta Olympics immediately preceding an astonishing diagnosis.

Leaving Amsterdam for the San Siro, medical officials at Inter Milan discovered a heart condition. At once, all of that which was to come, disappeared.

When reaching for a reality that isn't there, it's more about the moments that did happen rather than those that could replace them. Kanu was one of a kind. There was no feasible way to replace what he was able to do, even if the events themselves somehow matched up to how they played out. So much of the conversation around football is based on comparing players, whether it be their style or the roles that they perform. This oversimplification of ability incorrectly assumes there are only a handful of ways to play. Had Kanu retired at 20, there would have been so much that ceased to be. Primarily what would have been lost was the spirit he played with. That which the game is meant to be.

Life-changing experiences have ripple effects that move out in different ways. It's never just a single life that is affected. Outside of an immediate circle, in this instance there are so many who have benefitted as a result of an individual response to a personal crisis. Formed in 2000, the Kanu Heart Foundation helps African children with heart defects gain the medical assistance they require. Football and charity go hand in hand so often with various different organisations born out of the beautiful game giving something back. For Kanu, this appears more important than anything he could have done on the pitch, of which, from the moment he arrived in the Premier League, there is so much.

After the operation, getting back to a place where it would be safe to resume his career was going to take some time. Over the course of two and a half seasons in Milan he played only 20 times. Arsène Wenger had been closely monitoring the situation and with other clubs stalling on a transfer given the conversations surrounding Kanu's health, the Arsenal manager made it very clear he was wanted at Highbury. A paltry £4m saw the deal done. A world away from the incredibly lavish introductions that players are now given via social media, in front of the hotel that he was staying at Kanu and Wenger stood for photos to announce his addition to the squad. If the media aspect of his arrival was low key, his impact on the team was very much the opposite.

Football and contention go hand in hand. In addition to the rules that govern it, there is a separate unwritten code of conduct. Because of their ambiguous nature, these are judgement calls made in the heat of the moment. This all came to a head on Kanu's Arsenal debut in the FA Cup in January 1999. When the Sheffield United goalkeeper put the ball out of play for a throw-in so that Lee Morris could be attended to by the physio, consensus would dictate that Arsenal would simply throw him the ball back. Contesting this action wasn't really in the script and so it surprised everyone when Kanu did in fact chase down Ray Parlour's throw and emerge with the ball. Laying it off to Dennis Bergkamp for a winner incensed the opposition and put Arsenal in a potentially tricky scenario, technically having done nothing wrong but having gone against the spirit of the game. Sportsmanship in the professional realm is a very precarious concept and so Wenger offering the Blades a replay seemed more than courteous. Controversial though it may have been, it's certainly not that much of a stretch to say that this kind of proposal might never happen again.

It would have been easy in a sense for the media to attempt to portray Kanu as a villain. His jovial presence flew in the face of all that. Once the goals started to flow he managed to win over more than just the Arsenal fanbase. The Gunners were just starting to gel not just as an opposition force in regard to the teams around them but as a real footballing unit too. Over the next couple of seasons, Wenger's team became such an enjoyable team to watch because of the way they approached games making it hard not to appreciate them. Kanu remained a likeable figure throughout his time at Highbury even if his playing time did diminish over the years as Arsenal were reaching greater heights.

There is one thing they will always remember and be thankful to him for.

There are a lot of concepts in football explained by simple terminology but become rather large threads when unravelled. Technique is one of those things. In short it's how you control the ball and what you do with it. Long form, it underpins an entire career. There are some goals that stay with you, long after the fact. Some even resonate despite there being no connection to either the respective clubs or participants, such is their quality. Kanu's hat-trick against Chelsea in October 1999 would have been heralded as spectacular even if what capped it off had been a tap-in. Instead he treated the Premier League to a moment of genius.

Down by two goals at Stamford Bridge with 15 minutes to go, victory was a long way away. The first goal wasn't pretty but it didn't need to be. Marc Overmars scuffed a shot from outside the penalty area that, as an attempt on goal, failed miserably. As a pass it was absolutely perfect. Kanu had just enough time to turn and poke the ball into the left corner. Remarkably, ten games into the season, this was the first goal Chelsea had conceded at home. There would be more to come. Overmars was involved again in the equaliser, this time more conventionally. His low cross along the ground just about evaded the sliding outstretched boot of a defender, to which Kanu could now take a touch into the space he had vacated and slot home for an incredible quickfire double. With enough time still on the clock for a winner, Kanu was saving his best for last.

Ed de Goey must have replayed what happened next in his mind a million times. When Albert Ferrer's ball forward was blocked, good fortune allowed it to break down the left wing. With no one there to challenge Kanu, the Chelsea goalkeeper ran out to meet him. In a flash the ball was whipped away from de Goey and he was on the floor. Even then, they were both basically on the touchline and plenty of defenders were back. He wasn't about to score from there. Oh but he was. Kanu curled it around and above Marcel Desailly and beyond Frank Leboeuf to cap off both his hat-trick and an astonishing turnaround.

At a time in which Arsenal were going from strength to strength, Kanu was never far away. His playing time began to dwindle by the 2003/04 season but he still played a part in the squad that made history. Regardless of how diminished his role was, his place among the supporters' affections was assured. Kanu played with a smile and the good nature of his attitude that was so infectious. Coupled with the ability he had, he was able to bless the game with his influence, if not his direct presence. Saying goodbye to those at Highbury after an unbeaten season meant finding a different challenge. From being invincible at one end to needing a great escape at the other.

Christmas in the Midlands, West Bromwich Albion with nothing to celebrate. Bottom of the table, facing the very serious superstition of the fact that no team had ever survived the drop from the Premier League having been in this position before. West Brom had history with relegation and would have a future with it too. Yo-yo clubs, not quite good enough for the top tier but more than good enough to get out of the second; the Baggies were their pioneer. Going down was factored into the forecast at The Hawthorns, which meant one very vital thing. They weren't afraid. Teams before and since find themselves stuck in a mess and press the panic button; for Gary Megson and his team this was just business as usual.

Contributions aren't limited to hat-tricks, last-minute winners or the kind of skills that make the crowd roar. It's about being there week in and week out in training, operating at a level that everyone else feeds off of. Having a wealth of experience and being able to pass it on isn't something that happens on the pitch. West Brom had a group of players at the time who were solid pros but nothing on the scale of Kanu's stature. That kind of excitement and anticipation goes from the stands to the dressing room, even if a direct impact is harder to see. It all matters.

With increasingly limited playing time during the second half of the 2004/05 season, Kanu's on-field contributions were a couple of goals, one of which came in October against Bolton Wanderers – West Brom's only victory before the end of February. A combination of dogged efforts from March onward and the form of those around them led to a remarkable final day full of possibilities. Four teams all had the chance to save themselves with any number of permutations available. Dubbed 'Survival Sunday', West Brom, having had the most work to do, simply managed to do what those around them couldn't.

Norwich were first to go, their hopes absolutely shattered by a 6-0 defeat at the hands of Fulham. Southampton had their hands full with Manchester United and despite taking an unlikely lead they succumbed 2-1 to a late Ruud van Nistelrooy winner. That left Crystal Palace, who were on course right up until the end. An equaliser for Charlton would also be enough to condemn the Eagles so long as West Brom managed to win. Two goals to the good thanks to Geoff Horsfield and Kieran Richardson, those last few moments were an agonising wait. Kanu came on in the dying embers with little more than stoppage time to go; he would not be the last person to get on the pitch at The Hawthorns that day. Upon the final whistle there was an outpouring of emotion on a mammoth scale. The flood of fans on to the pitch captured a feeling; Richardson himself being hoisted up into the air and the look of amazement on his face summed up another. In the end it didn't matter who did it, what counted was that they did it.

Moments like that don't come around often. In between those rare instances of pure bliss, anguish fills the gaps. After such a remarkable escape West Brom were never out of the clutches of relegation the following year. A complete reversal of fortunes saw Kanu responsible for more in terms of his performance from a personal perspective but results were not good enough from the team as a whole. There was at least one notable result in the form of a 2-1 victory over Arsenal that saw him haunt his old employers and was also the first time the Baggies had come from behind to win in the Premier League. Eight years into a beloved Premier League career and some 13 years after coming to Europe from Nigeria, there was little expectation for a third act at all. Let alone one so magnificent.

As anecdotes go, it does its job. Harry Redknapp's description of how Kanu joined Portsmouth and all the circumstances around his everyday health were – and remain – fantastic media fodder. Comedic licence aside, Kanu was serious business for Pompey right from the beginning. Propelled by an explosive start to the season that even saw them top the table in the early stages, six goals from his first seven games demonstrated how unwise it was to ever write off someone with such ability. Up until this point Fratton Park had always been a tricky place for visiting teams but in 2006/07 it became a fortress. Of the top six that year, only Chelsea were able to emerge victorious. Coupled with wins over Manchester United and Liverpool, this was a real confirmation of their ascendancy over the last few years. The next stage involved winning a trophy.

Cup runs take on a life of their own. As the games go on the momentum builds. There's a reluctance to get carried away too early but all it takes is one victory for fans to convince themselves they have the touch of destiny about them. Getting to the semi-finals in 2008 and being the only Premier League team remaining only added to that. With minimal effects of the pressure of being the overall favourites, Portsmouth had to seize this opportunity and Kanu ensured they would be returning to Wembley. Yet again being able to get one over on his old team-mates from West Brom, his solitary strike took Pompey one step closer still. Playing against a Cardiff City side who had finished 12th in the Championship seemed like a straightforward task. Every game Portsmouth had played so far along the way to the final had been won by a single goal. Kanu completed the pattern and Pompey had their first major honour since 1950.

Some moments in time are worth freezing. The knowledge of what was to come for all those involved at Fratton Park not withstanding, being 2-0 up over AC Milan holds up as something of a pinnacle. After Kanu had essentially fallen over to add the second that night, from there – for the club as a whole – the only way was down.

The speed with which things go wrong is inversely proportional to how long it takes to get things right. With a major trophy in the cabinet and the prospect of European football on the horizon, it should have been a time for celebration. Redknapp's departure may have taken the wind out of Portsmouth's sails, but they were on choppy waters even before that. Being unable to pay the players' wages as early as October meant the writing was on the wall. Boardroom upheaval, the likes of which barely seems believable in terms of a deal to buy the club that lasted just six weeks, the aftermath of which eventually led to Sulaiman Al-Fahim being jailed for stealing the money used for the purchase in the first place. He wouldn't even be the only Portsmouth owner to go to prison in the immediate future. Both the FA and the EFL have been found wanting when it comes to the people they've allowed into the higher offices of football clubs over the years, with Portsmouth having been at the wrong end of these transactions more often than not.

Kanu stayed beyond Pompey's demotion to the Championship and was even technically still on the books as they entered League One. His high wages were weighing down the club to such a degree that releasing him from his contract was the only option. Still, it did not make up for the money that hadn't been paid. At first attempting to go through the courts, eventually with the state of Portsmouth's finances being so desperate, he released the claim on the £3m he was owed. A truly sad end to what had been a career full of such joy.

As the world got smaller, the 1990s helped bring African football to the masses, from Cameroon and Nigeria on the international stage to Liberia having the best player in the world in George Weah. For Kanu and the Super Eagles, he will forever be remembered for a star-making performance at the 1996 Olympics. His goals against Brazil in the semi-final were worth their weight in gold, which they were then able to claim against Argentina in the final itself.

As far as the Premier League was concerned there were those who came before. Tony Yeboah, Lucas Radebe, Bruce Grobbelaar and Peter Ndlovu were all held in high esteem. There was also a rich heritage going forward as clubs around the league embraced players from all over the continent from Didier Drogba and Yaya Touré through to Riyad Mahrez, Sadio Mané and Mohamed Salah. Nwankwo Kanu was a winner. He won respect and admiration wherever he went, along with a few trophies. Since retiring, his work off the pitch has done so much for so many. So too does his work on it.

6

Oleksandr Zinchenko

THROUGH DEVELOPMENT players emerge, and over time so too does their character. A lifetime of work just to get to the pitch doesn't even necessarily mean on the training ground either. That's just it, it's an accumulation of everything. The oft-cited football cliche of being more than the sum of the parts means more than putting a team together, it's about rallying together a group of people that all have completely separate upbringings; be that in a football sense or otherwise.

Among the many balls in the air that managers have to juggle is the idea that they have to prepare for the distant future as well as the here and now. Finding the formula for winning now is complicated enough, let alone trying to conceive and construct it all over again for tomorrow. Few are afforded the luxury. It's why it's important that those with the deepest pockets are able to spend money when necessary but also bring players through from the academy as well. It's the least they can do.

Potential might be the most open-ended term used in football. That delicate balance between hope and expectation, youthful enthusiasm and being in over your head coupled with the instant demands of the Premier League means that it's difficult to know when is the right time to give them a shot.

It's a leap of faith that is only occasionally rewarded.

Academies are the lifeblood of any football club. Even global powerhouses should look to showcase what there is available on its doorstep. Clubs exist as an extension of that community and to turn away from that would be to do a disservice. Looking towards the future has, however, become a global sifting process. In doing so a couple of things have happened. Primarily there are the players from very different backgrounds who now have a pathway through to the biggest clubs in Europe. On the other side of the coin is a perceived narrowing of those same opportunities to more local talent.

As the prospective pool rises, the window for that chance closes. The fear with this dynamic – and something that has become ever more prominent as the first teams in the Premier League have become more cosmopolitan – is that clubs will become unrecognisable from their roots. Borders and birthplaces play out very differently politically than they do in a football context, for the most part anyway. In principle it's much more holistic, given that it doesn't matter where you came from. There are a handful of regional caveats within that and it is conditional on quality, so while it's not ethically perfect, the opportunities remain in place.

The privilege of resources extends far beyond any reach. It's not simply the ability to go out, diagnose and treat weaknesses both on a large and a small scale. Adding players into a squad has often been likened to a gamble. Manchester City with their setup under Pep Guardiola have since 2016 been playing with loaded dice. Spending is a side issue in this sense; it's a numbers game of a different kind. Having put together an initial side that then evolves through coaching as it grows together gifts them the one thing money can't buy: time.

The conveyor belt may be an old, almost certainly outdated metaphor. Still, as ever the mechanism moves forward. At this level it doesn't have the pressure of producing a whole team or making sure that there are people constantly coming through because more senior players are being pinched by bigger clubs.

All they have to do is find one player, someone capable of supplementing the squad. In most cases this is the easy part. Identification is important but it's hardly an exact science. All over the country there are first XIs and beyond filled to the brim with observable ability. It's what happens next that is the crucial part.

Talent makes up the corners of the jigsaw puzzle that is football. Filling in that middle picture is what matters. Most managers and fans cannot wait for everything to come together. Inner turmoil at club level can lead to a spiralling set of circumstances, all designed to sail closer to stability without ever really knowing which way the wind is blowing. Manchester City have had more than a fair share of chaos over the course of their history, let alone within the confines of the Premier League. Through a succession of owners and managers, what was variable became invariable. Teams don't have to win everything to be assured of their place. The ones who are in full control of their own lives who know that the only thing that can befall them is expectation, they're the ones built for the beyond. Primed to conquer today and tomorrow. By the time everyone else realises it, it's already too late.

Everyone knew he was coming. Guardiola's arrival in England had been foretold in so much as he'd signed a pre-contract agreement in February of 2016. Following him in that summer were signings of significance and inadequacy, which is not how Ilkay Gündogan and Nolito choose to be collectively known. They were both signed for meaningful amounts of money, a sign of the times no doubt. Yet it wouldn't be long before Oleksandr Zinchenko followed for the paltry – albeit unconfirmed – sum of £1.75m.

After the acquisition comes the waiting; the professional limbo that for most players leads only to an even deeper oblivion. An unspectacular loan spell at PSV may have been the start of a familiar pattern. Failing to make the grade at a team like Manchester City is only a mark of how difficult a test it is, given how few actually get to the point of taking it in the first place. Chelsea didn't invent the idea of having so many spinning plates on the go in terms of who they had out on loan at any given time but it's a process that's worked for them in the past; certainly for allowing academy talent to find their way. City – or more specifically Guardiola – found a different way, one that would work for them all the same.

With an ever-growing trophy cabinet behind him and the 2022 World Cup ahead of him, Phil Foden has the world at his feet. Before he had even staked a first-team place at the Etihad, there were a thousand different conversations broadcast about what was best for his future development. Unlike Zinchenko, Foden's ascendance to the top of the English game was foretold. The two had very different paths to the top but both were products of the same vision. The fashion in which they were woven into the structure of one of the strongest teams in the world relied little on so-called experience. If you were good enough and could learn, Guardiola would teach you his way.

What starts out as nothing can very quickly be something. By the time Zinchenko made his Premier League bow, City were halfway through what was already an incredible 2017/18 season. On course for a routine 4-0 win over Swansea at the Liberty Stadium and having dropped just two points in the 16 games prior, there came an opportunity. Injury had already led to a peculiar switch in Fabian Delph performing left-back duties and so it was like for like in that sense. Zinchenko's cameo yielded little drama: played one, won one. This was to become a running theme.

The games got harder and the minutes got longer; still the result remained the same. By the time Chelsea, Arsenal and Leicester were all brushed aside in quick succession, the only question that remained was the limits to which this team could reach. The Arsenal 'Invincibles' planted an idea, one which the compulsion towards comparative criticism drove to a questionable conclusion. Using the amount of times Arsène Wenger's team had drawn that season, somehow going unbeaten wasn't enough. There was a new pinnacle in sight as far as Manchester City were concerned. It would take a kind of ruthlessness that hadn't been seen before. Not in Premier League history, in English top-flight history. That May, having overcome Southampton 1-0 at St Mary's, the 'Centurions' were christened.

Hidden among the numerous accolades that tumbled that year was Zinchenko. City's march to the title was as smooth and seamless as his transition into the team for that second half of the season. At the end of a season that saw him not only get his hands on the trophy but also spectacularly drop it during the celebrations, he had maintained a perfect record. Eight games in the Premier League, victory in every single one of them. It's a number that might not have ever increased had he made the move to Wolverhampton Wanderers that summer. Once again faced with a crossroads, having had to once train on the streets of Moscow just to keep himself fit, Zinchenko bet on himself.

Not that there are that many of them – and perhaps for this very reason – the utility player often becomes cursed by their own usefulness. Every summer players are brought in with the sole aim of performing a singular role or bolstering a particular position to the degree that no such emergency measures are ever needed. Being cut off before getting a chance isn't ideal but it's very much a part of football; it's sitting there with the knowledge that a contribution can be made that rankles. Yet there were no signs of disruption or disharmony. From day one Zinchenko was a team player both on and off the pitch. His attitude and social media presence over the years has helped harness a very special place within the setup at the Etihad. Possessing this kind of personality on top of that kind of talent has also helped at international level.

At club level there was a ceiling to break through in terms of playing at the very top; for Ukraine the sky has always been the limit. The fifth-youngest to play for the national side as well as their youngest ever goalscorer and captain. Playing in a more familiar role in the middle of the park as opposed to that which he performs in a Manchester City shirt, he was able to enjoy a productive European Championship run in 2021 as well as starring along the way. With the mileage in their extra-time victory over Sweden taking an ultimate toll in the quarter-final with England, it is still a young team that has yet to discover its true potential.

Gunning for the title – even one which generates a record-breaking points total – with no direct rival there to fend off, there was something missing. This wasn't Manchester City's fault or even concern, it's just that they were on a level nobody else could match up to. What would happen then, when someone did?

The Premier League title race in 2018/19 should go down as one of the greatest in any league from around the world from a consistency standpoint. There were no great twists and turns the likes of which enthral audiences regardless of their allegiance, but that's what made it so spectacular. Down to the wire, Manchester City and Liverpool went punch for punch, delivering knockout blows to everyone else in the league. Injuries hampered Zinchenko's participation in those early exchanges but when it really mattered, down that key stretch of games towards the end, he was able to stand up. With no room for any slip-ups of any kind, City were able to keep their hands on the title. Zinchenko: played 21, won 21.

Two games into the following season and the streak was to be broken, but not without controversy. There's more than a certain amount of contention regarding VAR. The subjective nature of football makes it impossible in some cases, not least of all having to decide which frame to take a decision from. But in this case, with Tottenham holding on to a point after Gabriel Jesus's late winner was ruled out, regardless of the context and correctness of the decision it still feels quite hollow to be denied in such a way. This was one of the first major decisions that technology swung the result of, and in the couple of years since the application has improved slightly but is still at the mercy of those using it.

Zinchenko created his own destiny, making his way through every challenge that has stood before him and ensuring his place among a Manchester City team for the ages. A side that wants to challenge at the very top needs players who are not just skilful enough to adapt to different circumstances but willing and able too. Players of this era are all but bred to feel uncomfortable in their own skin. If it's not social media poking and prodding at physical deficiencies, there are behind-the-scenes factors at every turn wanting to inflate or deflate an ego depending on which way the wind is turning, especially when what lies in the balance here is a career on the edge. Could Zinchenko go and have a perfectly good career elsewhere? Certainly. But the effort that's been put in around him – that may even at first have been incidental – has eventually led him to this point. It's not a bad position to be in.

When Guardiola eventually leaves, a question will be asked. What happens now? There's every chance he could go into his original midfield position and have a remarkable second act or continue doing what he does best in the role he has carved out for himself. As someone that's not one of the leading lights in the team there may be talk of him needing to prove something. To a new manager, to everyone. As it is, he won't need to.

7

Dion Dublin

THE PAST shines a light, hindsight knows where to look. Pouring what we know retroactively into events gone by often creates a heady concoction of sentiment, wisdom and intrigue. Empires are built upon an aggregation of results, all without the need for retrospection. Some of them are more extravagant than others, some are put together with a much more solid foundation. Looking back at how things are constructed shows just how much work has gone in. As such, the very first building block of Manchester United's Premier League dominance comes from the most unlikely of sources.

For United and in the 1990s, the word 'first' conjures up very specific imagery. When it comes to goals specifically, among all the accolades is a quirk of fate that offers a glimpse into a very different reality. Monday, 24 August 1992. The Premier League is but four games young. The eventual champions have acquired an underwhelming one point from the previous three matches. This fact alone stands out as something of an outlier to the times as they are universally remembered. On this day Manchester United do in fact get started on their path to a first English title in over a quarter of a century, with a 1-0 victory over Southampton at The Dell. In another reality Dion Dublin would be among those closely associated with the success that was to come. Without knowing it, a decade of dominance had been put into motion. For every domino that falls another will tumble right behind it, as the man himself would soon find out.

Whatever comfortable reality settles down in between the possible and the probable fails to sense the rug underneath it. Things can change very quickly, even if the path that events are set on seems both fitting and fixed. Dion Dublin arrived at Old Trafford late in the summer of 1992 after Alan Shearer opted to go to Blackburn Rovers over Manchester United; this decision alone creates several ripples throughout the immediate and intermediate future of English football. Truth is, this outcome is already the result of other actions. Go back just a few months to find Blackburn and Dublin's former club Cambridge United both in the then Second Division play-offs. One went up and participated in the first Premier League season, the other had to face a much more arduous journey.

Strikers thrive off taking advantage of a situation; being put into a position whereby they can reap the rewards of either all the good work done elsewhere or something that wasn't meant to happen but they were in the right place to capitalise. It didn't matter how it had manifested itself, Dublin was primed and ready to be the man who would fire the Red Devils to Premier League glory. But just when everything seemed set, destiny took another turn. A broken leg in early September left Dublin on the sidelines and United in the transfer market once more. Six months down the line and they had filled his vacancy rather aptly. Eric Cantona walked through the doors at Old Trafford and never looked back. Having kick-started their campaign to win the title, Dublin would now have to move on to do the same with his own career.

When the Premier League formed, like every big bang it took a while for things to settle down. Those early years were the most unpredictable. Teams had no settled starting point and even those who could be pigeonholed defied the odds in both directions. Through either repetition, saturation or sheer mismanagement there were more clubs that had less certainty around them. One year would be a cause for optimism, followed by a disappointing dip down towards the relegation zone. Perhaps the first case of inevitability was Coventry City and their run of avoiding the drop at all costs.

Though there might be a multitude of external reasons, in terms of on-the-field play teams usually find themselves down at the bottom end of the table for two simple reasons. Either they don't score enough or can't keep a clean sheet. For £2m in September 1994, Coventry had solved one problem. Unfortunately, even in locating the right player to lead the line and get the required goals, it would still take time for Dublin to become the player he would eventually be. By the time he was consistently scoring the goals that would eventually keep the Sky Blues safe, they would be letting them in at an equally frequent rate that saw them dragged down into danger in the first place.

The transition from Ron Atkinson to Gordon Strachan looked to be ending in ruin before it had even gotten the chance to get going. The autumn of 1996 saw a run of form so disastrous that it might have been beyond all hope. One win from the first 16 games led to Atkinson moving up to work at boardroom level, while the former eeds and Scotland midfielder took over the mantle as a player-manager. Results upturned to the point where Strachan was named Manager of the Month for December but all that initial hard work was undone almost immediately as Coventry's form plummeted once more. Another three months consisting of just one win left Coventry with it all to do.

Trips to Liverpool and Spurs underpinned a treacherous end-of-season run. It was in the very last minute of the game against Liverpool that Coventry's luck began to turn. David James came flying off his line to claim a corner he was never going to get, leaving Dublin to prod home a winner. The light at the end of the tunnel only got brighter with a victory over Chelsea three days later. Draws against Southampton and

Arsenal before defeat to Derby County meant Coventry had to win away at Tottenham and hope results went their way on the final day.

Once again when he was needed the most, Dublin opened the scoring in a 2-1 victory. Sunderland's defeat at Wimbledon and Middlesbrough's draw at Leeds meant that once again Coventry somehow managed to land safe. There was one more reason why they were able to avoid relegation that season. Their points tally of 41 was enough as things stood but only because Middlesbrough had been docked three points themselves for being unable to put out a team in January. In order to ensure it never got that close again, Strachan would have to build around Dublin, who was now at the very heart of this Sky Blues team. Adding talent around him would soon have to take a back seat to simply keeping him around.

The 1997/98 season started off with a bang and neither Coventry nor Dublin looked back. An opening-day hat-trick in a come-from-behind victory over Chelsea kick-started a campaign that – on the back of an imposing home record – propelled them into the comfortable heights of mid-table. Were it not for a remarkably large number of drawn games, 16 in total, European football would have been very much on the cards. Dublin accelerated his goal pace throughout the season, claiming 18 in the Premier League and a further five in the cup competitions. His tally saw him at the very top of the Premier League scoring charts that season, alongside Chris Sutton and Michael Owen. With a World Cup on the horizon, competition was fierce. Ultimately, England manager Glenn Hoddle decided to go with the experience of Les Ferdinand and the explosive pace of Owen, leaving Dublin out in the cold. If there was controversy surrounding his exclusion, it wouldn't be the only dispute he would be involved in as the summer rolled on.

One of the bigger grievances of modern football is this idea that footballers hold too much power. They can break fans' hearts in an instant and there are no consequences for it, deciding to opt out of a contract at a moment's notice. No one would ever put in the same kind of loyalty to an everyday job nor would anyone ever think it necessary. At a point where many clubs were looking to take from Highfield Road and add to their own, Dublin played his hand. During negotiations with Blackburn Rovers, a fixture against Luton for Coventry in the League Cup turned a straightforward transfer into a saga. Dublin – having had permission from chairman Bryan Richardson – ruled himself out of the game due to a combination of talks going on until hours before kick-off and also the risk of injury. For his actions Dublin was fined two weeks' wages, a figure he successfully recouped later that year in court. Getting back the money was one thing. In among all this was a fanbase that felt like their star striker had turned his back on them. Hope of repairing that rift might have been on the cards in rejecting Blackburn's eventual offer, only for local rivals Aston Villa to come along and put down the right number to secure his services.

His move from Highfield Road to Villa Park was one of those transfers that hurt in the moment. Instrumental in everything for so long, there was no denying his absence would be felt. On and off the field there was much more to Coventry's demise than just the hole left behind by Dublin. In the blink of an eye Robbie Keane came in, did what he could to be that figure and then left for Serie A. Twelve months later the Sky Blues would tumble down into the second tier. The promise to move away from Highfield Road proved to be even more complicated than anyone could have ever predicted. More turmoil, financial disarray and being uprooted to Northampton made for a grim few years for Coventry fans. After all that, with some real villains involved and a club very nearly torn apart, Dublin's decision-making and subsequent transfer – as much as it left a sour taste in the moment – doesn't quite hit as hard.

Joining Aston Villa in November of 1998 before there were transfer windows was something of a quirk of the era that would eventually be ironed out of the game as it moved on. Villa were already flying by the time Dublin signed and his impact was instantaneous. Seven goals in his first three games laughed at the idea of needing a bedding-in period. Unfortunately for John Gregory's team they were unable to sustain such a level of results. Ending the 1998/99 season in sixth wouldn't have been disappointing from the outset; being in the top two up until February then falling below was thoroughly unsatisfying. Coming in and already being a key part of the team in such a short space of time, Dublin's absence the following season would be keenly felt by all, not least because of the significance of it.

An injury earlier on in his career changed the course of it completely. Against Sheffield Wednesday in December 1999, his entire life could have been affected. So serious was the head trauma that the ambulance transporting Dublin to the hospital that day was advised not to travel over 30mph so as to not take any unnecessary bumps in the road, which could have paralysed him. The idea of playing football again had to take a back seat to simply walking. Surgery to remove part of his pelvis and use it to replace the crushed vertebrae was successful and so began the recovery process. Something as traumatic as this in theory would take many months, maybe even a year to return from. Dublin was back playing by March.

Things line up in such a way sometimes to appear as though they are meant to be. While Dublin had been out, Villa made their way through the early rounds of the FA Cup, reaching the semi-finals and a tie against Bolton Wanderers. Despite his rapid recovery, Dublin wasn't quite ready to start such a game but came on for the last 20 minutes. Extra time meant even more time on the pitch but it was never a question of fitness, it was more down to fate. With the full complement of time allotted unable to separate the two sides, it came down to penalties. After six spot kicks, Dublin walked up knowing a successful strike would send Villa through. It was never in doubt. Chelsea winning 1-0 in the final spoiled what would no doubt have been the ultimate return. Such is football. Being able to still play at all, let alone so soon after such an injury, was a victory in itself.

In the years that followed, Dublin once again solidified himself as a fan favourite at Villa Park. When he was on the pitch he was always able to contribute. As ever with age there came a gradual decrease in minutes. Even in a loan down to the First Division with Millwall he was still able to find the net. His goal in the first leg of their 2001 play-off semi-final with Birmingham wasn't enough to see them through but he would be seeing the Blues again. One of only three red cards picked up during his Premier League career stemmed from a clash of heads with Birmingham's Robbie Savage. It served only to highlight how out of character it was.

Dion Dublin. The name alone evokes if not epitomises English football in the 1990s. His association with the game spans both before and after, not least for the younger generation of fans that have to square the circle of a television presenter who deals in the stairs leading up to the bedroom as much as he does the players coming out of the dressing room. For those that watched this evolution in real time, it's still quite jarring.

8

Gunnar Halle

CONSIDER HOW much can happen within 90 minutes. How a single game can spin a thread that can last for years upon years. Imagine then the result of a generation or two of those cumulative actions, of those compounded effects. Distance matters when it comes to separation. Propulsion can be perpetual, the things that ultimately resonate are the space between two distinct points.

Lived and experienced change is so much different to how it plays out after the fact. Certain things that altered in the moment and in turn began to resonate into other areas until the reasons why things are the way they are become clear. This may be interpreted as part of some grand evolution but ultimately every point along that path is independent. Progress happens every day; innovation occurs over time. Rarely does one specific thing counteract everything else that has come before. It's a series of events that add up to an inevitable conclusion. What turns the dial doesn't stop until it's gone all the way.

The Premier League didn't set out to become one of the multicultural hives of modern football. There was no way it could have been. English football throughout the years has resisted outside influence as a point of principle. Coaching, systems and playing styles; all seen through rose-tinted glasses. From infancy into its teenage years and beyond, the scope of which continued to expand. What began as a handful grew into a contingent.

Gunnar Halle was among that original few. He had arrived before the newly christened Premier League. The difference at the beginning was non-existent, serving nothing more than branding purposes. There was no huge demand to look elsewhere for some large expansion in terms of playing staff for clubs because this was the First Division as they had known it under a different guise. What eventually became this behemoth of hype and wealth began as just another season for Halle and Oldham Athletic.

Precedents exist as an illustration of a moment in time. Everything that has ever been taken for granted was at one point unique. In a sporting sense, evolution is how the phenomenal becomes the nominal. Drawing a line between these two points creates a very specific picture. Both in terms of the growth of foreign talent in the top flight of English football and indeed Oldham playing a game within it, Halle becomes the ultimate cross section.

There is no bigger sign of how things have changed over the years than the story of Oldham in the Premier League and what happened thereafter. Relegation from the football league in 2022 is in stark contrast to the fact that not only were they among the list of teams to contest that inaugural season but also the remarkable end to a campaign that saw the very first great escape. With other places all but assigned, it came down to Oldham and Crystal Palace to seal the first Premier League relegation spots. It doesn't get more backs-to-the-wall than needing perfection at the end of an arduous season. Even worse, they needed more than just nine points from nine. On top of the demands on the Latics' shoulders, it would all be for naught if Palace got more than a point in their final game. Even before getting to the finish line, they would have to run the gauntlet.

Aston Villa were first up, in a game which fulfilled the cliche of having an effect at both ends of the table perfectly. The

Villans needed a win to keep their hopes alive of an unlikely title push while Oldham simply needed to keep hope alive. Nick Henry's first-half strike simultaneously allowed for a stay of execution while once and for all killing the chances of the Premier League trophy heading to Villa Park. Liverpool came to Boundary Park just three days later and even though they weren't the footballing superpower they had been in years past, they still had the ability to hurt anyone. With the Latics 3-1 up at the break, Ian Rush closed the deficit on the hour to give them a testing last 30 minutes with absolutely no margin for error. Two victories out of two meant that their fate would be decided on the final day.

There's something in the air about a last-day relegation battle; a tension that those at the top will never feel, to their detriment. The nervousness of winning doesn't compare to the knowledge of what this kind of failure means. Missing out on a medal may be deeply dejecting but the scars of getting this close to escaping relegation only to be pushed face down into failure last a lifetime. Southampton stood in between Oldham and safety while at the same time Arsenal would have to provide safe passage and defeat Crystal Palace. Ten goals over 90 minutes across the country to decide the fates of two teams. The very essence of football.

Early nerves within the Oldham ranks were eased as Ian Wright obliged early to put Arsenal in front against his former side within the first ten minutes. So long as that result stood, for the first time in this week-long run it was finally in their hands. All the same the task hadn't changed. No matter what, only a win would do. In these circumstances everything helps. The infamous Boundary Park pitch had drawn its fair share of criticism in years prior and wasn't necessarily conducive to a free-flowing passing game but the days of it being a plastic nightmare had long gone. Sometimes all you need to help is a particular gust of wind, as was the case when Neil Pointon opened the scoring directly from a corner. Matt Le Tissier equalised five minutes later. If anyone was going to spoil the party, it would be him.

Save for a magnificent international hat-trick against the might of San Marino, Gunnar Halle wasn't really known for scoring goals. Having accomplished this particular individual feat at the start of that season while on international duty for Norway, however, there must have been some attacking juice still left in his system. Playing in a more advanced role than he would for the majority of his career, Halle was a threat to Southampton throughout. It would be generous to call it hold-up play but the ball stuck to him to create the scramble that led to Ian Olney putting Oldham in front. Ten minutes into the second half, Halle took the ball down the right-hand side and crossed for Andy Ritchie to score a third. The roles were reversed a few minutes later with Ritchie putting Halle through on goal. His finish wasn't particularly clean, striking Tim Flowers in the middle of the goal, but the ball trickled into the net nonetheless; 4-1 to the Latics and the hope would have been that the home crowd in theory could relax. But Southampton's number seven once more loomed over proceedings.

A bobbled free kick almost immediately after Halle had scored cut the deficit before Jeff Kenna's persistence somehow found Le Tissier perfectly to head home and leave Boundary Park thinking the unthinkable. A nervous, precarious, excruciating few minutes would have to play out. As the pressure inside the stadium grew and grew, all eyes were on the referee. Blowing the full-time whistle brought with it elation on a momentous scale. The weight of an entire season condensed into three games, eventually lifted in the most spectacular of afternoons. Oldham were, however, relegated the following season.

Divergent paths at different times call for often unusual solutions. Trying to recover from a serious injury and also make his way into the Norway squad for the 1994 World Cup meant Halle being loaned out back to Lillestrøm in an attempt to gain match fitness. Meanwhile, Joe Royle and the rest of his team were embarking on yet another memorable campaign. Getting to the FA Cup semi-final and being pegged back by a last-minute Mark Hughes goal for Manchester United led to a hammering in the replay. Oldham were never quite the same and three points and no wins from their last eight games would see them down. Halle went to the USA to play for Norway in that summer's World Cup and then returned to Boundary Park in spite of their demotion to do what he had always done and get on with the job.

Part of the narrative that would be peddled for years to come was this idea that players brought in from foreign shores simply wouldn't care enough. Halle stayed long after the Latics' relegation to the First Division and is still spoken about in glowing terms some 30 years later. Standing the test of time is easier for some than for others. Those who stand out often become a footnote as time moves forward and those feats fade into the background. Forebears should never diminish in significance but they do often find themselves buried under the weight of the history that is to come. It is for that reason that they should stand out for longer.

Halle remains to date the most-capped international player in Oldham's history. This record will likely remain intact for some time. When it eventually is broken, the achievement will not erase all that has gone before. What has happened since serves as a reminder that every legacy should be preserved, not just those at the very top. Tearing away at the fabric of English football is a stab into the heart of every fan. Every tale is special because together they add to the full story. When the past is erased, the future loses even more. The Oldham fans have been left in the dark from the latter 2010s onward and even in spite of how bad things have gotten, hopefully their struggles are near to an end.

As part of what Halle had done in establishing his own credibility during those early years in the Premier League, he was sure to be offered a return. As English football began testing the waters much further abroad, Scandinavia offered hard work and talent at a discount rate compared to mainland Europe. Leeds United paid £600,000 in 1996 to reinforce the team and that's how it played out. Not every signing is meant to be the be all and end all of a process that ultimately ends in glory. Patience might have been on longer supply during this period but squad players who play their part have always been useful. Especially when there is a change in management and whatever plans that may have existed get thrown out the window. When George Graham replaced Howard Wilkinson and demanded more solidity, the Norwegian was more than capable. Over the course of three seasons and a team that crept from dogged defence to outright attack, Halle never let Leeds down.

Given his credentials, in the summer of 1999 newly promoted Bradford took the opportunity to add someone reliable to their squad. With seemingly very little hope of staying in the Premier League, they would need all the help they could get. Paul Jewell's team fought valiantly against expectation all season but still could not put enough of a run together to reach safety. It would all come down to the very last day of the season. As Oldham had shown before, sometimes that's all that is needed. Especially for Halle, who was once again in the thick of things.

Unintended consequences make for the most tantalising of connections. As Liverpool went to Valley Parade, they too had something to play for. With a Champions League place up for grabs between them and Leeds, it would be David Wetherall and Halle who would seize the moment for their former employers. The goal forever lives on in Bradford history; the Norwegian delivering a free kick right on to the head of Wetherall who made no mistake in putting it beyond Sander Westerveld. Unlike what happened with Oldham all those years ago, there was to be no more chaos and carnage, only some 80 minutes of resistance. By the end it was impossible to contain both the stress and the Bantams fans from spilling out on to the pitch. The final whistle could not stop them. They were staying up.

Once again, an incredible escape preceded a very unambiguous demise. What was left after going down with Bradford a year later was for Halle to play out the remainder of his career in England in the First Division before returning once more to Lillestrøm. The Premier League was a very different place after that first decade and Halle had been there through it all, from just 13 foreign players on that opening day to every club looking aboard to complement their squad. Far from the flamboyant foreign players who would later arrive, his determination and consistency was enough to widen the scope of what was out there in the wider world.

9

Glenn Murray

TRADITION, SUPERSTITION and repetition. Mix them together and you have the recipe for most things in English culture. Honouring what came before, trepidation as to what comes next and silently agreeing that things will forever continue as thus. From a footballing perspective, heritage exists well beyond the 92. It's more than just the existence and propping up of old practices, however. It is acknowledging and celebrating what connects every team, both historically and structurally. As such, the Football League pyramid is the foundation upon which everything rests. The top doesn't exist – certainly in this current guise – without the bottom, regardless of what some might think.

Structure and history work in tandem. A larger cache of the latter enriches the former. An abundance of rivalries and stories make up the rich tapestry of English football and because of that, the present day incarnations of teams have deep connections to everyone around them. Each season is a further accumulation of all these stories. Chapter upon chapter being added to, compiling for the record who will be the main characters at any given time. Without the context for all of it, the prize itself diminishes. When looking at the full picture, every brushstroke matters. If every different step along the journey means nothing, then the destination is pointless. Who cares about conquering a league system whereby nothing means anything?

It's partly why the reaction to the European Super League was so visceral. It had to be. It was one thing for the fans of the clubs involved to take umbrage with that which was being presented to them, entirely another for everyone else to react in such a way to something that would kill the structure as it exists stone dead. It would have shattered one of the principal foundations this entire system is built upon. The idea that anyone can rise up.

Competitive sport is designed to separate, to elevate and dismiss, and ultimately to rank. On any given day, who – or whom – was better. At this point there is an important cultural divergence that is as vast as the oceans that divide us. Among many of the differences between North American sports and their European counterparts is the issue of parity. The idea that a level playing field should exist is indeed a noble one. But whereas the collegiate and draft setups over in the US attempt to redress a balance, the alternative – in principle anyway – is to reward the winner.

Even before 1992, football was weighted towards the big clubs. At this point the definition of which was more about the size of fan bases and attendances as opposed to their cheque books. It was a delicate balancing act that could lead to rapid change within a short space of time and yet the historically great teams were able to maintain their time at the top. Unexpected challengers would emerge, contend and either take their place or fall back down. Within that, there was still room for a period of dominance that would be defined by a single club. To the victor go the spoils.

Up until relatively recently, the idea of it all being a meritocracy still held some hope, if not weight. During the 1990s, Manchester United held the financial clout above all others – give or take a notable exception – but they had earned that right with their superiority on the pitch. Over time it becomes a chicken and egg-type scenario. Winning absolves everything. Everything. Does a team have the resources because of their success or is it as a result of the money spent? Eventually that line becomes so blurred it is commonplace. It happened with Chelsea and with Manchester City. In time it will likely happen with Newcastle too.

It's not quite that the game is rigged but certainly the deck is stacked. A system that feeds the top first only ever leads to greater disparity lower down. That's not to say that there aren't exceptions, more so that they stand out more as the odds are so against them. That's why we celebrate those who break through. Why it matters even more that the playing field is recognisably uneven and yet a path is still made. In the short term it's a pacifier, an unacknowledged fantasy that the underdog can still truly have its day. The reason why we care is not because it is a reality, it is the remaining existence of it as a concept. When this notion is finally cut off once and for all, that's when English football is dead.

Glenn Murray rose on that basis. He fought his way through from the sixth tier to the top. It was only then that the real battle for him began. As far as dates go, February 2014 was the official start, having gained promotion with Crystal Palace the previous season. His last appearance was a crucial one, at Selhurst Park some nine months earlier. Despite it being a goalless draw, Murray's season was over. A cruciate ligament injury meant that while Brighton succumbed to a two-goal defeat in the return leg, there would be no celebrations.

Before obtaining their place in the promised land, Palace would have to play the play-off final without their 30-goal striker. Murray would have to watch as the club he had fired to this position held his fate in their hands. Any idea that they would have needed him was evident by the fact that the final went to extra time. Kevin Phillips put the game to bed from the penalty spot, however, just before half-time in extra time. Promotion assured, Premier League delivered. Having reached the top, now the real battle began.

Some players are destined to have the career they have; others have to fight for it. A struggle all the way to the top – given all the cliched connotations – should be a bit more appreciated. Still, there is something of a stigma in regard to having had to make the climb in the first instance. Ascension frightens as much as it inspires. Coming up in the first instance demonstrates the depths, so for those who stare into the relegation abyss, they know full well what it means. In that regard clubs get scared. Success leads to succession in the sense that whichever group has executed must – in a way – be executed. Progression is duplicitous, in that what it gives it also takes away.

Murray had three seasons in the top flight for Palace, the first of which was all but ruined through that previous injury. In between there was a loan down to Reading in the Championship and a brief but pivotal spell for Bournemouth after their own elevation to the top table. Just because someone isn't a perfect fit doesn't mean they can't contribute, especially to a side that needed anything and everything from everyone in their first Premier League season. The Cherries had no room to stand on ceremonies and played out a first half of a campaign that had all the hallmarks of a one-hit wonder.

Two wins before December placed them in the bottom three. Thoughts turned towards January and being able to bring players in during the transfer window to alleviate the situation. In between those two dire – and slightly higher – situations, Bournemouth went on a run. Three wins in a row during the critical Christmas period took a certain amount of pressure off and allowed them to buy in the forthcoming transfer period without being dead and buried. The set of victories began with Murray coming off the bench to score an unlikely winner against Chelsea. Benik Afobe came in a few weeks later and did enough to fully soften Bournemouth's landing; still it was after what happened at Stamford Bridge that propelled them.

Half a year virtually out of the picture at Dean Court was never going to prove anything, regardless of how the dots could be joined up. Back Murray went to Brighton; a team and a fanbase who knew him all too well. Even before putting them to the sword for Crystal Palace some years before, he had been one of them. Back in 2011 he had swapped Seagull for Eagle wings and this was very much flying in a full circle. The flight path towards the Premier League was one of clear skies as Brighton finished on an incredible 93 Championship points in 2016/17. Were it not for a handful of defeats once promotion was confirmed, Murray and his 23 goals would have contributed to a title-winning campaign. Even with Newcastle taking advantage right at the very end, all that mattered was that Chris Hughton's men had their ticket to the big time.

Every challenge has its hurdles. Starting their first season in the top division for over three decades up against eventual champions and centurions Manchester City, followed by going away to former champions Leicester, represented two large ones right away for Brighton. Top-flight scraps mean getting points on the board as early and often as possible. In every game they were underdogs, but without any tangible victories there really is no room to breathe down the bottom end. As such it was Murray to the fore again, putting West Ham and Swansea to the sword after wins over West Brom and Newcastle had set the table. With a consistent, proficient goalscorer to lead the way, there was never any sense that the Premier League trapdoor would open underneath them. A point proven, among the 40 earned. Murray had been there before, now he had done it.

If familiarity breeds contempt then there is nothing more contemptuous than a former striker returning to an old patch. Form and ability go by the wayside – both individually and collectively – as it always feels like something else is at work to ensure the same source of joy is now a source of pain. Everyone knows that when someone that used to play for them turns up, all hell is about to break loose. It's not even necessarily an irrational fear as there is potentially some knowledge in the familiarity they have within the surroundings. Trying to put a striker off their game revolves around making them feel uncomfortable. In these games they can be at their most comfortable.

Hostilities in football rarely emerge from nothing. Some have deeper, more intense roots than others, but the vast majority of them are years in the making. The other thing to bear in mind when it comes to footballing rivalries is that it can only take a handful of matches to light them up. Constant make already combustible encounters even more volatile. It wasn't the career of Murray – going between them as he did – that started the feud between Crystal Palace and Brighton, but he certainly came to exemplify it. From the 1970s and a series of matches between Alan Mullery and Terry Venables all the way down and back through to the Championship and beyond, with victory seemingly enabled by one man, regardless of which colours he was wearing at the time.

In the six times Murray played against Brighton for Palace, the Eagles were only ever defeated once. Another half dozen games on the other side of that coin saw just two more defeats in all competitions. During the course of all of those matches he managed to get on the scoresheet in seven. This record gained even more emphasis during Brighton's second season in the Premier League. Victories home and away over Crystal Palace, the latter of which in March with nine games to go was not only their last win of the season but also by virtue of two points the result with which they stayed up, were both finished off by the boot of Murray.

One player cannot define a club. They can go on to represent a period, for good or for ill. The ex-striker returning to haunt once more, reminding fans how the club got to that point or the striker who had been under-appreciated elsewhere but his value means more than a price tag ever could. What's more, his journey is a shining example of how a system that undervalues and at times even neglects all that comes below the top tier can be infinitely richer for the work that goes on underneath.

10

Cesc Fàbregas

IN A game pinned down by numbers, it is the romance that cuts through. Value is assigned to so many different things throughout the course of a match, a season or even a career. What matters more than anything in the moment might only ever depreciate over time. Common sense says that the scoreline is the only thing that counts and that alone can overrule sentiment. Results will always dictate destiny, but matters of the heart are never that straightforward.

There has never been an equilibrium between ability and achievement. The former derives many more opportunities for the latter but one of the great levellers of football is that this alone is not a guarantee. Ability is but the claim to a key that unlocks something special. Picking the lock in a footballing sense may very well be the most succinct way to describe one of the most technical processes that exists in any industry.

Being plucked from Spain at such an early age – even before a ball of note had been kicked – represents both a specific place in time and also a very precise mandate. Hoovering up young players, regardless of age or location has since been a concern for UEFA in regard to the imbalance of both persistence and finance being used to tempt talent to the Premier League. In Cesc Fàbregas's case it was not so much the road ahead of him that convinced him as the lack of obstacles in the way. Spain's loss became England's gain. Arsenal took what Barcelona were preparing and added their own flavour to it. Fàbregas would have emerged as a world-class footballer regardless of upbringing.

Substituting culture is more than a case of speaking the language. Football is a dialect unto itself, continually connecting those that otherwise share no common bonds. Being on the same page is about having a common method of communication. On the pitch, Arsène Wenger made sure his players all spoke fluently. Yet, at the centre of it all was still a teenager. Simply stepping on to the pitch made him a record-breaker; a 1-1 draw with Rotherham in the League Cup saw him become the youngest first-team player in Arsenal's history. Against Wolves in the following round he went one further in becoming their youngest ever goalscorer. In the winter of 2003, the future looked incredibly bright. This would apply to the short term as well as anything else.

Gaining the proper footballing education is very similar to any other walk of life in that the right circumstances will allow anyone to thrive. Putting aside even the talent available at the club at the time, there are some experiences even training alongside Patrick Vieira cannot replicate. In terms of harnessing Fàbregas's true potential, there won't have been many better learning experiences than the Highbury setup during a season in which they won the league in such a way. Without a single league appearance during the 'Invincible' 2003/04 campaign there was to be no token medal at the end of it for Fàbregas. Both in terms of earning a place in a truly remarkable side and then the rewards that would come with it, there was a fight on his hands. The first part of that became remarkably straightforward; the second part less so.

Not only did a young Fàbregas survive the early onslaught that Premier League football threw at him, he thrived. As ever, games with Manchester United punctuated his early forays into first-team football. Cardiff and the 2004 Community Shield put down a marker. It might not be the most regarded of fixtures in the calendar but it was still a clash between two heated rivals during which he was able to showcase himself. Fàbregas's second contribution that season left a mark on Alex Ferguson in the form of an airborne slice of margherita pizza, as tensions boiled over in the aftermath of Arsenal's defeat at Old Trafford. A cameo in another disappointing return at Highbury had potential to sour what had become a burgeoning career at the top level. Back at the Millennium Stadium he was able to pick up what was to be a first major honour in the FA Cup. Seventeen days after his 18th birthday, it seemed as though this would be one of many. But in football things are rarely as they seem.

Flair both frightens and excites the English in equal measure. Almost as if without the steel and resolve at the forefront, everything else is seen with a tinge of suspicion. The game was played with very different rules in mind and that someone like that would never be anything more than a luxury. Lining up against some giants of the game on a regular basis and wanting to emulate them has nothing to do with size. Technical ability is not the absence of tenacity.

Racking up the stats at an unprecedented level does so much to draw the eyes, after which the true test begins. The beauty of Fàbregas was that in addition to the adulation he was receiving from the Arsenal fans, he appealed to a wider selection of the football-watching public. If there is to be a greater compliment than the hatred of a rival, it's the respect of a neutral. Throughout the early years of his career he enthralled more than just his own supporters. The full spectrum of fandom is to adore those who play for us, hate those who don't and be for the most part indifferent to everyone in between. For Fàbregas to break through that hold spoke volumes about his ability. While this kind of appreciation does carry some weight, it was nothing in comparison to the growing pressure of holding up an Arsenal side that had begun to fall away from the very top.

Within leagues all around the world, pockets of quality dictate so much and very little at the same time. The growing frustration with Arsène Wenger as the 2000s wore on was not that Arsenal were a bad team, far from it. Following on from a disappointing but perfectly reasonable defeat in the 2006 Champions League Final – a game in which Fàbregas left the field with the Gunners still a goal to the good – getting over the line became harder and harder. Arsenal were still getting those opportunities however, all the while maintaining enough of a league presence to be involved in the title race even if they were a few yards back. Every cup knockout or lacklustre Premier League finish would have been lapped up by so many other clubs up and down the country. This is what high standards do.

Moving from Highbury to the Emirates Stadium in 2006, Wenger looked to bridge the gap between generations and Fàbregas's shoulders bore the brunt. Captain of the side by 2008, he would have to relinquish all responsibilities for four months having suffered a knee injury. By the time he came back, any hopes of pushing further up the league had vanished. Rescuing a season by finishing fourth and securing Champions League football once more was not the theme it later became; still he came back and helped ensure it. It was in that very competition that a particular body blow had deeper consequences: a familiar foe in Manchester United, embarrassing them on their own patch. If the 3-1 victory that saw Cristiano Ronaldo run wild and secure their place in the final wasn't damaging enough, the 8-2 defeat at Old Trafford that followed a few years later put the final nail in that particular coffin. By that time Fàbregas was long gone. In between those two points, everything came down around him. In spite of the incredible numbers and all that effort, it wasn't good enough. Here was a mercurial player, carrying a club on his back almost alone. Such is the fickleness of football that somehow there crept in a sense that the hype had gone too far.

From the outside there may have been a sense of contempt; a misguided patriotism that there was no way someone so young could take to the English game with so much aplomb, no matter how talented. Similarly, there was a 'golden generation' within English football – individually beyond all that had ever been seen – and yet here was a postcard from tomorrow. A herald of what was to come, both in terms of Spain's chokehold over international football and more of a general indication of where the game was going as a whole. Technically they were all on a level below. All the while, their trophy count grew. The numbers that loved him so were ultimately working against him.

Ring culture – as it's known in the NBA – is the idea that all that matters is championships. The conversation around team sports grew more immature as it passed. At this point everyone can name one or two players who have won a league title to throw up insincerely against someone who hasn't. They make sense of petty issues between clubs and nothing more. Just because Fàbregas hadn't won the Premier League didn't make him a poorer player. This wasn't the case as so often happens that someone doesn't quite reach the highs that were predicted. If anything, he broke all expectations and then some.

In 2009/10 Arsenal finished third and barely made a dent in any of the major competitions. Meanwhile, Fàbregas was putting in work as their top scorer in both the league and all competitions, all the while laying on even more goals in the form of assists. He ended the season with 39 goal contributions in 37 games. It should go down as one of the great individual campaigns of all time, yet partly because it was a given that he was that good and Arsenal themselves did very little, it is lost.

There's more to Fàbregas departing for the Camp Nou than just what was going on at the Emirates. He had given so much to the club, had grown up both as a player and a person, and there could be no begrudging the idea that his trophy cabinet shouldn't have been as bare as it was. At the same time, Barcelona was where he had started the journey all those years ago. To some degree there was almost a sense of relief among the Arsenal fans in that someone they treasured would finally get his due. To that end, at the very least Fàbregas was able to get his hands on some silverware a much more consistent basis.

Pep Guardiola had built a force of nature at Barcelona. Coming off a season in which they were the best team in the world, to then bring in a player who had the potential to unlock another dimension, it was almost unfair. A record-breaking 100 points from Real Madrid prevented them from retaining La Liga and Chelsea coerced Gary Neville into making noises never heard before by human ears as they pipped them to the Champions League Final. All this fed the narrative, one that had switched just as Fàbregas had gone back home. It didn't matter what he won, with so many good players around him.

Tiki-taka took over the world. In between what Barcelona were doing domestically and what Spain did on the international stage, a particular dominance had been on display for four years, so much so that by 2012 it had exhausted everyone. With a specific set of highly intelligent and technical players, football looked to have been completed. Having Fàbregas within that particular orbit flew in the face of his Emirates endeavours. Of course he could tally up his medals in and among that team. It was impossible not to. Even with nothing left to prove, there was still time to underline his ability. The only problem with this particular unfinished business was that it involved a certain amount of heartbreak.

As one team fell, another rose. Chelsea were not directly responsible for what happened to Arsenal, their fates independently linked by virtue of the games that were played out in the mid-2000s. All of the good faith from a certain part of London that arose upon his move to Barcelona was rendered somewhat hollow. What made it worse was his role in bringing new life to a Chelsea side that were not guaranteed another run at the title. The second coming of José Mourinho electrified English football once more, with Diego Costa and Fàbregas at the very heart of their efforts. Finally he had his hands on the Premier League title some ten years after it seemed inevitable.

Nobody could ever have imagined that it would be wearing Chelsea blue.

Fàbregas continued to bloat his trophy haul through the additional three and a half years he spent at Stamford Bridge. Another Premier League title, the FA Cup and a League Cup added to the collection in quick succession. Perhaps the most galling aspect of them all was a painfully easy Europa League triumph over Arsenal in 2019 for which he got another medal for despite leaving Chelsea some six months before. From a dynamic, innovative teenager, Fàbregas enriched the Premier League. At once unable to hold up a falling superpower, at another a cog in an all-encompassing winning machine. Cherished for his talent when he wasn't winning, neglected when he was.

Nobody watching football ever falls in love with an honours list. Important players should always want but never need that kind of decoration. The pursuit of success relates to many different factors. None compare to that warmth of feeling, that aesthetic beauty that makes football worth watching. The numbers matter, but they should never be everything.

11

Wilfried Bony

MOST OF the noises heard within a crowd on matchday aren't premeditated. The tension builds within the stadium as the play builds. Some of it gets released long before the ball. Screams of frustration and encouragement all the same. Vocalised gridlock. Then the ball breaks.

Collectively, thousands of people take a breath. What comes next – joy, relief, irritation or anger – are all reliant on a matter of centimetres.

When success or failure is defined within such finite and minuscule terms, quality becomes a coin flip. It's a binary existence whereby the other option is to be on the bench. For the player in question, it doesn't often matter how many of them they take or don't take; what does matter is that taking one can change everything. It's just that nobody will ever know when that moment will arrive.

The same applies to teams as it does to players. Circumstance makes a mockery of both ability and intent. Pretty much every club up and down the land has a story involving a previous incarnation that should have gotten over the line but didn't. Cruel as it may seem, it's not enough to simply do. Finding the right window of opportunity is just as important as climbing through it.

In Premier League terms, Swansea City were an overnight success, which is to say that anyone to whom that term can be applied has long put the work in. From League One and Roberto Martínez onward, plans were put in place that were to carry them right through the divisions. They wouldn't be restricted to the departure of certain players or managers.

Everything that goes on in regard to player recruitment is a lot more structured and precise than the results bear out. Because the sum of all these efforts can result in very little there might on the face of it appear to be much less of a science to it. However, the clubs that have everything in order are able to consistently find, attract and land the right players for their requirements. Conversely, clubs with greater pulling power can skip most of that process and try to reap the rewards all the same. With varying degrees of success.

By the time Wilfried Bony turned up at the Liberty Stadium, there had been a long list of players who had come – and gone – who had performed with distinction. From Lee Trundle through to Michu, Roberto Martínez as a player and then a coach and Leon Britton just being Leon Britton, their climb through the divisions relied on an incredible consistency, both of those players they already had and a remarkable record in the transfer market. Practically everything they touched turned to gold.

Swansea's first year in the top flight turned heads. The application of their resources, the results they were getting and the style in which it was all achieved put some of the teams around them to shame. As ever when a plan above and beyond simply getting a group of good footballers together comes along, there was a degree of scepticism in regard to whether they would be able to cope. There was nothing new or revolutionary about the way Brendan Rodgers and his team were playing, but it flew in the face of conventional wisdom. Being so open was going to catch up with them. There's no way they would be able to keep the ball as well as they had done in the Championship.

It wasn't easy and it wasn't instant but Swansea stuck to their guns and outside of an acclimatising first month were never in any danger of going down. With all the plaudits and congratulations for a job well done came an offer. Rodgers was off to Anfield, tasked with breathing new life into Liverpool. After a whirlwind decade that had seen them rise from League Two – while it was still called the Third Division – to the Premier League, this was seen as the point at which it would stop. There was no more room for improvement, surely? No more dreams to dream. As ever in football, where hope is alive, there is always room for more.

A new manager, a new badge and celebrating 100 years as a club. There was a lot to savour for Swansea fans in the summer of 2012 before a ball had been kicked. Stepping into the hot seat was a household name. Michael Laudrup's appointment was as much about the raised profile of the team as it in turn had a similar effect on the eyebrows of those watching on. In conjunction with the turnaround in the dugout, the revolving door of personnel saw an influx of soon-to-be cult heroes join the club. In addition to those that remained who had already established their legacies, this new-look team was about to deliver Swansea's first major trophy.

Domestic cup competitions have taken something of a battering in the 21st century. From Manchester United not taking part in the 2000 FA Cup through to questionable team selections, the gloss that had previously been on them had dulled a little. Even within that, the 2012/13 League Cup provided more than enough stardust to inject some life into predictable proceedings. The story for the majority of it belonged to Bradford City. Languishing in League Two, their victories over Arsenal in the quarter-final and then Aston Villa over two legs in the semi-final set them as history makers for being the first team from the fourth tier to even get to an English final. That being said, Swansea themselves had somehow quietly gone on a run that saw them emerge victorious at Liverpool as well as overcome

Chelsea in the semi-final. Cup romance aside, the occasion itself was inevitably one-sided with Swansea powering over Bradford to win 5-0. When it comes to a game like this, the method is irrelevant. All that meant for anything in terms of the record books was that Swansea's name was on the cup.

Arriving at a club at the top of their game makes integration into the squad a whole lot smoother. All that jubilation is infectious. Immersing into a new environment as their most expensive signing comes with a certain responsibility. That pressure can in turn make some players lose a little something. Along with stability came credibility. For other clubs going through a particular period of uncertainty, spending so much money to take a player from the Eredivisie may have been a bigger gamble. Thirty goals in his last season for Vitesse notwithstanding, there have been many players who have made similar moves in the past which haven't worked out well for anyone. In Bony and Swansea's case, everything fell into place pretty quickly.

Winning a cup is its own reward, from the anticipation hours before to recalling those memories years later. In the immediate aftermath, however, it unlocks certain doors which may have been closed for years before and may not open again for some time. Bony made his competitive debut in Swansea's first game in Europe for more than two decades. It was to be their first win on the continental stage for over 30 years. Malmo went down 4-0 that night and lost the tie by the same scoreline before Bony scored in another emphatic first-leg victory over Romania's Petrolul Ploiești. The dream had been for silverware and it had long been turned into a reality, so attention now turned to the chance – nay the possibility – to get one over on one of the household names across the continent.

Valencia have both grown and diminished through the distant observation within English shores over the last 20 years. The late 1990s and the beginning of the 21st century saw the breakthrough of more and more teams from countries in Europe as the Champions League was moving further away from its knockout format into the collection of superclubs it would later become. Héctor Cúper led a team that didn't carry the same name value as the likes of Real Madrid or Barcelona to consecutive Champions League finals. That side would then be handed over to Rafael Benítez, who guided them to two La Liga titles in three years. While everything that's happened since 2004 can hardly be called a complete disaster, their automatic role behind the two traditional Spanish giants in among the rise of Diego Simeone's Atlético Madrid has seen their star fade.

Swansea capturing the League Cup was from a consequential standpoint the much bigger victory. But going to the Mestalla Stadium and winning 3-0 so comprehensively may very well stand as the greatest moment in Swansea's history. Bony opened the scoring that night as the European adventure began with a bang. Though the rest of that group stage never quite reached those levels ever again, their defiant performance away to Napoli as they were eventually knocked out fulfilled that bittersweet cliche of doing the fans proud. Bony continued to add to his total in 2013/14, Swansea's leading scorer in all competitions both collectively and individually. Picking up where he left off, nine goals in the first half of 2014/15 underlined his status as one of the leading strikers in the Premier League. It was at this point that those from above had heard enough.

The upper echelons of the Premier League have very selective hearing. When it comes to talk of reform and doing things differently, they're nowhere to be found. What's more, they're ambivalent even in regard to the conversation of appropriating credit further down the table. Whenever someone is doing well, it seems like a huge inconvenience for those further up that they won't just take their medicine and come back around again next year for another dose. The only thing that makes the right amount of noise for their ears to prick up is when someone makes a racket in the goalscoring charts. Only then are they more than willing to talk. Unfortunately when those kinds of conversations are had, it's incredibly hard for the player in question to say no.

Bony's move to Manchester City was very much in line with what teams of that calibre do so often. They are in a position to pilfer those who are doing exceedingly well below them in full knowledge that if it doesn't work out then there will be another transfer further down the line that will do the job just fine. In between signing and playing at the Etihad, Bony capped his growing list of achievements by winning the 2015 African Cup of Nations with Ivory Coast. What followed was a torrid time of missed opportunities, both on and off the pitch. So much goes into the surrounding contributions of forward players and if anything those around him at City limited what he was able to do rather than encouraged it. Injuries played their part, as often they do in this kind of situation. Different clubs have vastly different circumstances and aims, as well as pecking orders that were much more out of his favour in spite of his previous goalscoring record.

Everything changed at City once Pep Guardiola walked through the door. The days of simply grabbing a striker in a rich vein of form from someone lower down the league were gone; everything had to fit within a very specific plan both in the short and the long term. As such, Bony was inevitably shifted towards the exit door. Stoke wasn't so much a way out as it was a road to nowhere. Only ten games were played in an entire season with two goals registered, both somewhat cruelly against Swansea in the same fixture. It was clear whatever magic had been there previously had all but gone. There was only one place to try and rekindle it.

Moving on doesn't necessarily mean to better things. Bony was one of those shooting stars that the Premier League happens to have within its orbit every so often. Those heady days at the Liberty Stadium came and went and by the time he returned there in 2017 it was a club on the way down, albeit from a truly great height. The weight on teams like Swansea to unearth these gems, ensuring they get everything right, only for it to be taken away is part of the contemptuous cycle of football. Form doesn't last, players don't stay. That's why it's so important to make those memories that do.

12

Nick Barmby

TO MAKE a long-lasting impression is to grab at immortality. The stories of heroes and villains, passed down from generation to generation, never occur within a vacuum. Being a part of something momentous should by definition come with its own set place in history. And yet smaller roles don't seem to matter as much, regardless of how integral they may have been to the bigger picture. Players who have such an infamous catalogue of indelible moments fall down the cracks. It is in one of these collective memory holes that we find Nick Barmby.

Achievements are measured one moment and forgotten the next, which is to say that simply being around certain events isn't enough to guarantee being remembered. This in turn is open to some interpretation for there is a world of difference between winning medals and creating history. The trophy cabinet can take second billing if a particular achievement matters enough. Footballers have very different motivations to those who support them. Most of the time.

Barmby ticked all the boxes. There are a plethora of incidents across the arc of a footballer, whose final act alone reads like a Hollywood cliche. Any athlete facing the twilight years of their career has to face a choice. Primarily whether it will be they who get the decision to call it a day or whether it will be made for them. A startling sense of athletic mortality creeps in, forcing players to choose between hanging up their boots while they're still able to perform or simply savour every moment until the very last.

For Barmby it wasn't even as if the writing was on the wall. He was just 30 years old when he made the decision to sign for Hull in the summer of 2004. Not everything had been plain sailing for him leading up to this but he was still dropping down to the third tier at an age where he would definitely have had some suitors higher up. In essence, that was the whole point. The desire to play for his hometown club had been there for some time and there was no point in making that leap for the sake of it. Barmby still had something left in the tank, Hull had just moved into a brand new stadium and together they were going to see where it would lead.

Folklore begins at the end. A destination or a culmination that enhances the events prior. To say that the Premier League was never in sight for Hull is only to emphasise the mileage of the journey laid out in front of them. Four seasons it took to rise from the third to the top tier of English football. What Peter Taylor started in 2004, Phil Brown was able to see through, with Barmby the common denominator. His goals against Watford in the 2008 Championship play-off semi-final were enough to take the Tigers to the edge of glory, after which Dean Windass spectacularly obliged.

Having a larger connection to a club and a community and being able to put it on the centre stage meant more than just simply playing at the top level again. A by-product of this success was that kids who had grown up just as he had done would be able to see Hull on the same footing as the Manchester Uniteds and Liverpools of the world. Football teams always need an injection of life and success drives those doses. Children who may have not necessarily gravitated towards this particular team or even those that may have only had a passing interest in the game had their eyes opened to what could be possible.

In terms of actual playing time, by this stage he was having more and more of a cameo role; only completing the full game on two occasions across the two seasons that made up Hull's opening spell in the top flight. The sight of Brown crooning to the crowd at the KC Stadium at the end of the 2008/09 season following on from the 1-0 defeat to Manchester United that saw them survive certainly goes down as one of the more surreal Premier League visuals of all time. It wasn't so easy the following season whereby there was no escape. Having achieved so much in the six years since Barmby had arrived, the same applied then as it always did. When Hull needed help, he was there.

Making the move from playing into coaching was maybe not the easiest transition for someone who wanted to keep on playing. Back in the Championship he was still being used off the bench but was still playing in more games than before and showing his ability hadn't completely disappeared with five goals scattered throughout the season. It was the following year that threw the curveball and set the stage for the final chapter of his career. With manager Nigel Pearson lured back to Leicester, Hull needed someone to steady the ship.

New managers can take time to get to grips with a club, but Barmby needed no such bedding-in period. With the crowd behind him and all the will in the world, as caretaker he kept them in and around the play-off picture. Consistently inconsistent at first with an even split of wins and losses among his first ten games, he finally announced his retirement from playing with the intention of concentrating solely on managing the team and was announced as their permanent head coach just a few days later. Finishing the 2011/12 season and trying to get back into the top six seemed like a fair enough challenge; though he guided them to eighth and narrowly missed out was disappointing enough, but to be sacked before then seemed unthinkable.

Apathy can be dangerous because people do nothing. Caring means doing things. Actions are interpreted in very different ways. Barmby remarking to the media about the club's ability to buy players in January, and the need for further signings in order to get back up to the Premier League isn't necessarily unheard of from a manager's point of view. These things happen all the time. But not on Ehab Allam's watch. Barmby was swiftly removed from his position for his comments 'unjustifiably cast public doubt on the honesty and integrity of the board and its members'. Appealing the decision resulted in it being ratified by Assem Allam. If distrust in the ownership began here, it only festered after they attempted to change the name of the club officially to Hull City Tigers. Somehow, among all this, Barmby's replacement Steve Bruce managed to get the team promoted for a second time to the Premier League. Where it left Barmby though was formally retired, following a job he was reluctant to take but felt he had to. This is not a tragic story though. Far from it; there was so much more he managed to pack in.

Way back in 1990, a highly rated teenager from Hull signed for Tottenham Hotspur. By the time he was ready to make his debut, already so much had changed. The inaugural season of the Premier League wasn't a bad year to burst on to the scene but doing so under joint head coaches in Doug Livermore and Ray Clemence preceded even more turnaround when they left the following year and in came Ossie Ardiles. Along with Teddy Sheringham and Darren Anderton and soon to be joined by Jürgen Klinsmann and Ilie Dumitrescu, it was full throttle both on and off the field.

However, there was an investigation into the financial affairs at the club dating back to the 1980s. A mooted points deduction as well as being banned from the FA Cup on top of a heavy fine was what prompted a move for those players who were to become part of an exciting attacking unit for Spurs. Though Ardiles didn't get to use the full extent of them in 1994, Klinsmann, Sheringham and Barmby in particular all plundered their fair share of goals. Having just signed a new contract not long after new manager Gerry Francis came in and then won an England cap in March of 1995, it looked like the future was headed in one direction. Things change fast in football.

Homesickness can be a powerful motivator, one that can only be ignored for so long. Signing for Middlesbrough the summer following his contract extension at White Hart Lane came as a shock to say the least. Boro, meanwhile, were keen to put something of a showpiece together not just for returning to the top flight but also to show off the new Riverside Stadium. Following Barmby's acquisition, a diminutive Brazilian by the name of Juninho burst on to the scene and into the hearts of all those who loved watching attacking football. Remarkably, this team only managed to score some 35 goals this season, yet the addition of Fabrizio Ravanelli swung things entirely the other way. A total of 51 in 1996/97 proved they certainly had more firepower; unfortunately it came with finishing 18th and being relegated. During the latter half of that second ill-fated season, Barmby fell out with manager Bryan Robson. Another move followed, this time to Everton, and later a particularly galling trip across the Mersey.

Things at Goodison Park were as they ever were during the 1990s: problematic. Everton were in the mire of being very good on their day but having nowhere near enough of them. Reputation-wise both were suffering. Barmby's three and a half years at Everton were all about trying to move forward and live up to that initial billing of promise. Having previously been seen as someone for the future in regard to national team prospects, that future had arrived and there were plenty of people passing him. Year upon year his stature grew as the Toffees tried to build, only to find their feet cut from underneath them. On the flip side, when it mattered most Barmby fluffed his lines. Coventry at home, needing to win to guarantee survival. A penalty miss that went unpunished. In spite of other protestations Bolton may have made about how the end of that 1997/98 season transpired, the bottom line is that it was goal difference that would ultimately separate the Toffees and the Trotters. Everton had their foot near the trapdoor several times; never had it been closer than this.

From Howard Kendall's precarious third spell to the green shoots of recovery. In 1998/99 Everton finished 14th, on paper a world away from the razor-thin escapes of recent years. But with six games to go they had been in the relegation zone. Four wins in that time launched them to the lofty heights of the lower mid-table area. Walter Smith would finally be able to lay down a solid enough foundation for David Moyes to punch much higher than they had been able to previously. Just as that process was starting, Barmby did the unthinkable.

Defections never end well. It had happened before over the years but this was the first time in about half a century that a player had moved from Everton to Liverpool. There are many cross-city clashes up and down the leagues; this had for so long been set apart. Rivalries cut deep. Still there were once images of families and friends sitting together regardless of their allegiance and where the game was being played. It may not be the friendly derby that it once was, but Liverpool is a city that has been pushed together in very different circumstances. To that end, what it means to be united and divided hits differently.

Objectively, it was a sensible move as far as the Reds were concerned. Saying goodbye to the likes of Stig Inge Bjørnebye, Phil Babb and Steve Staunton as well as shedding more recent cult figures like Rigobert Song and Titi Camara, Gérard Houllier was putting together some finishing touches. Winning a cup is a game of starting 11s, whereas the league is a testament to the squad. Both involve a little something from the manager. For the trophy haul that was about to transpire, it would take all of them.

Liverpool's 2000/01 season was about a unique feat as much as it was the multiple additions to the trophy cabinet. Winning the League Cup, FA Cup and UEFA Cup didn't necessarily put them back on their perch, but at the very least it showed significant strides in the right direction. Playing in every single game available in every cup competition is what happens when taking 'one game at a time' is extended to the nth degree. Twenty-five matches in total were added on to their 38-game Premier League season in which they were still actively looking for Champions League qualification. Barmby's goals in key moments in the cup competitions were more frequent than in the league, save for the inevitable strike at Anfield against Everton in October. What made the difference in that first season became his downfall just a year later.

The term 'squad player' is most definitely damning with faint praise. Good, but not good enough. For all of the quiet contributions Barmby had made to a treble-winning season, that success unlocked a door, one which he wouldn't be allowed through. A familiar face reached out and offered another chance. Terry Venables had given Barmby both his league and international debut, so there was very little in the way of hesitancy in terms of a reunion. Neither party at the time had any idea of the challenge to come.

Joining Leeds in August 2002, Barmby would be their only purchase for two years. The financial escapades of the previous few seasons were on the verge of spiralling out completely. Gambling the future of the club on Champions League football sounds like a bad idea in the first instance, let alone when that prophecy is fulfilled. All of these decisions and choices were made well above, yet Barmby served as a proxy for what was going on around the club as a whole. Injury curtailed his effectiveness. Were it not for the call to come home, this is where it would have ended. Even then, as far as Barmby's place in history is concerned, there is more to consider.

Time can be tortuous, bending understanding to an uncomfortable place. Barmby not only played in the Euro 96 semi-final but was down to take the next kick in the fateful semi-final shoot-out after Gareth Southgate. It's hard to foresee a future in which Barmby becomes the England manager in quite the same way. Maybe he would have scored. Football percolates these opportunities in both directions. The imagined scenario gets dwarfed in the face of an incomplete reality.

On 1 September 2001, England went to Germany and won 5-1. It was Germany's first qualification defeat on home soil. Regardless of whether or not Barmby was one of the main characters, to be a part of this performance and result should be enough to ensure a legacy. For a particular age group of England fan this was as good as it ever could get. One of these teams would go on to the World Cup Final, the other would bow out soon after the group stage. This is Barmby's fate. A 20-year career consisting of memorable moments left abandoned. It was only after all this that he went and did something unforgettable.

13

Chris Sutton

HIGHS AND lows tell a version of the story, rather than complete chapter and verse. Assembled with fragments and fused together with assumption. While certain situations are always going to stand out, neither one is a complete picture. From the outside looking in, it is all about those headlines. An entire career whittled down to a shortlist of successes or failures. It's possible to digest the grand total of a sporting life in soundbites but the summation of all that industry is a little harder to chew on. For those actually writing the story, it's a life taken out of context.

If football transcends language then goals punctuate it. They are at once the questions that need answering and a – very extreme – point of exclamation. A finish, both figuratively and literally. As such, the power of potency will always be able to craft the reality around it. Being blessed with the golden touch doesn't mean that everything will turn to gold, however.

For Chris Sutton, what was meant to be was scrapped almost from the very beginning. He came through the ranks at Carrow Road as a defender before being converted into a striker in the process of breaking through into the first team. Unintentionally using those two years prior to the formation of the Premier League, by the time Norwich were ready to go ahead of that debut season, there was no idea of quite the rollercoaster that they were about to embark on.

Norwich are a club that has more of a close association with the bottom half of the Premier League followed by a barnstorming promotion the following year. But there was a time – by dint of circumstance – when everything could have changed for them. Having had a torrid end to the season in 1991/92 and avoided relegation by just three points, talk of following it up with a title challenge would have seen even the most ardent Norwich fan raise an eyebrow or two. Such is football.

That first game of the new season at Highbury set the tone. There's something to be said for the opening match of any campaign. Everyone starts on the same points, which isn't to say that everyone starts on the same resources, but it's hope. This is gonna be the year, at least for that one afternoon. Norwich had already gone into the season on something of a downer having sold leading scorer Robert Fleck at the start of that season, so any optimism may have been tempered with the feeling that it may all go wrong so quickly.

Two goals down at half-time, it would have been very easy for all that belief to disappear completely. Sutton's place in this particular comeback was to be as the man brought off for Mark Robins to ignite a comeback for the ages. Four Norwich goals in the final 20 minutes were enough to stun those inside Highbury regardless of which end they were in. New season and a new league; the dream was alive even if only for a day. It lasted a bit longer than that.

Some title races are that by name alone. Others have included competitors who aren't ever really in the running. That first Premier League season, however, was a real scramble to the finish. Everything that happened as a result of it made the eventual victor poised to rule over English football for some years to come. At the time though it was a three-way tussle between teams who had little in the way of immediate pedigree at the very top. Between Manchester United, Aston Villa and Norwich it would be the Villains who were the most recent champions; even that was more than a decade in the past by this point. As is always the case in these kinds of scenarios, by the time April came along Norwich would host Villa before Manchester United would arrive just a few days later. John Polston's solitary strike some ten minutes before time set up what was to be arguably the most important match to have been played at Carrow Road.

Big games can be over in the blink of an eye. Before the contest really gets going, it's effectively decided. Ryan Giggs, Andrei Kanchelskis and Eric Cantona put Manchester United three goals up within the first 20 minutes. Unlike what happened on the opening day at Highbury, this time there would be no spirited comeback. Here was the final stop in what had been one hell of a ride.

Just five days later the chance of a reprieve for Norwich came in the form of Sheffield Wednesday's visit to Old Trafford. They were leading courtesy of a John Sheridan penalty but once again the pendulum swung. Cue Steve Bruce's unlikely late two-goal heroics. The sight of Alex Ferguson bouncing for joy on the touchline at Old Trafford as that stoppage-time header bulleted into the net became a seminal Manchester United moment. This was the moment they pulled away, cemented their place at the top of the league and a dynasty began.

The 1993/94 season was at once the fruits of an unforeseen labour and also the harsh realities of a moment past. For all their remarkable efforts the previous season, Norwich were not unrewarded. A UEFA Cup place allowed the Canaries to spread their wings somewhat, having previously been restricted to more domestic affairs under the guise of continental competition. Dispatching Vitesse Arnhem in the opening round would lead to the red carpet being rolled out. European royalty in the form of Bayern Munich were coming to town.

To encapsulate all that Norwich had done in their Premier League efforts the year prior and how surprised everyone was, going to the Olympic Stadium and emerging victorious was somehow an even more extreme version of this. The first English team to ever beat Bayern at home, in the face of an expected demolition. Jeremy Goss and Mark Bowen etched their names into the history books with their first-half goals before Christian Nerlinger pulled one back. Bryan Gunn was the hero of the day, saving everything that came at him during a second-half bombardment. Even then, there was a second leg to come. Bayern took the lead early in the first half but Norwich stood firm.

When it comes to real torment, football favours the favourites. Time after time, dreams get crushed with an almost heartless remorse. That's why fans of all clubs get swept away by not just the actual giant-killing but the whole process of it. Had Norwich lost to Bayern during that second half, they would still have been revered. But seeing it through is what makes the stuff of legends. Mark Bowen's cross headed into the path of Jeremy Goss by Chris Sutton, delirium for Norwich. European nights have something special in the air and it was definitely there that night at Carrow Road. That they couldn't go any further didn't matter, they had made an everlasting mark in European football. This tie and those nights will always shine brightly in the hearts and minds of those who were there and stand as something to be proud of for those that came after.

Domestically, Norwich were on a comedown, playing and winning for the first half of the season before falling away somewhat during the second. The difference between the two came primarily in the dugout. After the exploits at Carrow Road over the preceding 18 months, Mike Walker was offered the chance to take over at Everton. John Deehan foresaw the spring slump that saw Norwich fall from seventh in January to finishing 12th. As the team's stock was falling, Sutton's continued to rise. Not only did he finish the season as top scorer with 25 goals, he was also about to become the most expensive player in English football.

Three years after it had begun, the Premier League in 1994/95 was set for a proper heavyweight clash. Blackburn had arrived in the top division with a real sense of ambition and purpose. Led by Kenny Dalglish, with Alan Shearer at the forefront of their attack, they had been close to challenging Manchester United's dominance the year previously, but needed a little something extra in order to get them over the line. The addition of Sutton up front proved to be pivotal, with Rovers' hopes of the top prize in English football relying on a strike partnership for the ages. The SAS – as they would come to be known – were unstoppable, with an incredible 49 goals between them. Even a late-season scare couldn't prevent the title heading to Ewood Park, including quite possibly the most remarkable last-day defeat which everyone could enjoy.

King Kenny strolling around Anfield with the Premier League trophy in tow. Save for actually winning it at home, fate could not have picked a better location for the climax to Blackburn's triumphant campaign. The intrigue as to whether Liverpool would simply forgo any semblance of a competitive edge in order to prevent Manchester United from winning the championship in the end counted for nothing. Jamie Redknapp's last-minute free kick to win the game on another day might have ruined the mood; on this day there was just enough going on elsewhere for it not to matter. The team that took Blackburn to the championship became legends, while the duo who fired them there became iconic.

Considering its legacy, their partnership didn't last very long. At first it was Sutton himself who disappeared, going down the following season with injuries; in 1996/97 he was back but Shearer had moved on to St James' Park and Newcastle, his home club. Blackburn had become a very different team in the interim. Not that it was going to be easy to replace Shearer but they hadn't yet figured out how to replace Kenny Dalglish. By the time Roy Hodgson came in, all of that momentum that led to the title-winning run had completely gone. Sutton found form again in 1997/98, with 18 goals not quite enough to arrest a run of horrible form from February onwards. Then came the call to come and play for England. Or rather, England B.

The idea of international reserve teams even in 1998 seemed a little obsolete, certainly as far as Sutton was concerned; having been one of three joint top English strikers it was something of an insult to ask him ahead of the World Cup in France. His objection became an outright refusal and as a result he never played for England again at any level. Things went from bad to worse back at Ewood Park; not only did constant setbacks prevent Sutton from being more of a presence for Blackburn over the course of 1998/99 but also showed how desperately they needed him. Just a few short years after Blackburn had been at the very top they were relegated to the First Division again.

Chelsea's decision to spend £10m on Sutton seemed like a fairly reasonable one at the time, but his spell at Stamford Bridge very quickly became a nightmare. Trying to justify his price tag became a fruitless endeavour and that his only goal during his solitary season there was against Manchester United in a 5-0 rout only adds to the sense of bewilderment around this time in his career. Sutton himself has been very upfront and honest throughout his time in the media, saying that he regrets everything about what happened with the national side and that the blame for his Chelsea performances rests with him alone. In spite of the sometimes confrontational image that was put forth while broadcasting in the days since retiring, Sutton is very forthright with everything he says, especially in regard to his time in Scotland.

With all due respect to the standout set of circumstances that saw him move from Aston Villa to Birmingham City at the very end of his Premier League years, Sutton's time at Celtic was the last meaningful spell of his career. It was significant for the trophies that he won and again for the partnership that was formed. Henrik Larsson is a very different type of player to Alan Shearer but the two were on an equal footing when it came to making the difference at the top end of the pitch. These kinds of attacking connections fell out of fashion for a long time, only to emerge once more in a very different sense during the mid-to-late 2010s in the form of a front three. Because of Sutton's association with more high-profile names, there is a tendency to overlook the contribution he made throughout his career and instead focus on the fall in between his time at Blackburn and Chelsea. In between the high and the low, there is the detail. The full story.

14

Bukayo Saka

EMOTIONAL STAKES take a toll. Misery stockpiles whether it's one defeat or 100. At some point enthusiasm becomes apathy and that's where the real danger lies. For something that is meant to be enjoyed, for the outsider looking in that can be hard to see at times. That much maligned phrase 'it's only a game' encapsulates the divide from those who cannot fathom a life that can be devoted to – and a weekend can be ruined by – the outcome of a single match, let alone a whole lifetime's worth.

With experience comes bitterness. Having seen it all and believing that what remains can only ever be bleak. The energy of thinking there's nothing new to see is commonplace. That any particular decline will last forever, specifically because it's all that's ever been known. This kind of heartache can be cured. All that's required is to counteract the lethargy that comes with expectation.

Supporting a club for long enough allows enough time to believe that there is nothing left to see. Whatever mixture of good or bad that exists on the pitch, it's important for those in the stands not to fall into indifference. Glory days can pass by in the blink of an eye for those not prepared to cherish them, regardless of how long they take to arrive. Setbacks outweigh success and the heft of history leads even those clubs who once pushed forward to slow down.

Momentum means a lot once it's there and getting it in the first instance can be incredibly difficult. Trying to pick it back up after everything has ground to a halt is even harder. Reference points of prosperity from days and years past exist to inspire but inevitably achieve the opposite. When football moves on, clubs have a hard time shaking off these measuring sticks of old. Knowing they once meant something is no guarantee of anything in the present day. The past is dead. If there is to be any progress in the future, then that's where it has to come from.

Arsenal didn't invent the concept of entertaining football, but their role in elevating the Premier League experience came with a price. Ticketing has been an issue for quite some time, for all clubs. Charging exorbitant amounts to support a team lends itself to the issue of tourism against fanaticism. In the latter stages of their stay at Highbury and those early days at the Emirates, the Gunners were absolutely value for money. Football has come a long way from the days of rickety old grounds, three-quarters of which don't have a roof, and from being played on swamps of pitches upon which nothing good can happen. In changing all that, crowds were able to be enthralled by what could be possible. Unfortunately, along with it, came a sense of entitlement.

Paying for a seat entitles the ticket holder, especially when a large sum of money has been exchanged. That transaction – at that level – fundamentally alters the game. Teams give back to those who support them in the form of collective memories, not some kind of presumptive performance as though it's just another TV show. Losing is a part of it, as are all the frustrations that come with a side lacking in either one or multiple areas. It hurts even more when things used to be so different. When everything clicked and that enjoyment came in the form of winning in a manner and a style that captivated everyone. The problem with expecting that which isn't there – even if the price point suggests it should be – is the damage it could do to the next generation even before they've had a chance to change anything.

Failure is not what holds back, it's the fear which is much more poisonous. As such the worst thing that can happen to either a group or a single player isn't doing something wrong, it's being persuaded by outside factors not to try. Players of all abilities make their first forays on to a football pitch free of anything holding them down. Bold and brash, with nothing but good intentions. This can either be embraced or worn away. Hope derives from the prospect of someone trying to make a difference as much as those with the ability to do so. Having no one to come to the rescue is as painful a prospect as defeat itself. In these troubling times, when there is no other recourse, teams and managers must turn to the youth. The inexperienced are uniquely capable of dealing with even the most ridiculous of pressures because they have no experience of that kind of futility.

Good things happen when risks are taken. Those really special achievements are always just out of reach, something will have to be done to get to them. Fortune does indeed favour the brave but nowhere near as readily as is made out. Standing still in football is an assured failure, so movement of some kind is always required. At some point every step feels perilous. The stress of repeating the same mistakes again leads to a stalemate. In these moments, inexperience can find a way through. Not having the heavy baggage of disappointment allows them to lead to a place of not just safety but potential prosperity. For Arsenal, Bukayo Saka can take them anywhere.

Regardless of prestige, the Europa League is hardly the most cherished competition in England. Going from the UEFA Cup, this particular rebrand feels to have had an opposite effect to that of the Champions League/European Cup but then again one was always much more prestigious. What was once a tournament to cut your teeth against the up and comers on the continent, those who are on the verge of challenging for top prizes, has become something of an inconvenience for clubs with eyes on bigger glories. From a playing perspective, however, it's an opportunity. While everyone else is too busy lamenting the fact that these fixtures don't matter too much, for Saka it was a dream come true.

Arsène Wenger's departure from the Emirates was always going to have consequences. It's not even that they were that far removed from tangible success; so many clubs would have built statues for the three FA Cups in four years during the mid-2010s. Even when winning, Arsenal were losers. That was the trouble with the latter part of Wenger's tenure; the noise around the club at the time was so loud and divisive that moving on would involve muting all that agitation more than it would anything else. Winning hearts and minds as much as trophies. When Unai Emery was then unable to do either of those things, the reset button needed to be pressed once more.

At first, the rebuild required some old heads. First Freddie Ljungberg returned to Arsenal in November 2019 to try and lift the spirits and then a month later Mikel Arteta came along to do the same but with more of a long-term plan in place. With work to be done, an opportunity presented itself in the first team for Saka, albeit as a left-back rather than in a more attacking role. Any signs of fragility or being out of place in the moment soon gave way to a capability and the freedom that comes with being something of an unknown quantity. In those early months as foundations were being laid, Saka's directness and ability on the ball were able to put the smiles on Arsenal faces just as much as the results were towards the end of that season. There was just the small matter of a pandemic looming on the horizon.

To single out an authority that was slow to react to Covid-19 would be like shooting into an empty net. That the Premier League acted quicker than even the English government is some state of affairs, yet it took a particular case for that to occur. On 13 March 2020 it was announced that ahead of Arsenal's match with Brighton at the Emirates, manager Arteta had tested positive for Covid-19. This led to that weekend's fixtures being shut down entirely and with the Liverpool v Atlético Madrid Champions League tie just a few days earlier being linked to so many cases in the area, no doubt the decision stopped the spread being even worse than it would turn out to be.

As a summer of football ensued, the sun shone on Arsenal. The restart allowed Arteta and his team to gather some momentum, not least of all in the FA Cup. Beating Manchester City and Chelsea – along with Liverpool in the Premier League – as ever had the potential for being over-exaggerated. The Gunners have been on the verge of greatness and also rotten to the core often within the same week. Brevity should not outrank optimism, but those who get lost in a fantasy land are the first to hit out when their expectation doesn't meet reality. With a trophy in the bag and confidence ready to take off, Saka was about to fly.

Among the many difficulties in disappointment are the little things that point in the right direction. The 2020/21 season was hardly vintage for Arsenal, who had their early momentum clipped very quickly. Among the wreckage of those first six months were some very good results. Beating a previously all-conquering Liverpool side for the second time in a few months furthered belief that they were on the right path. So too did a win at Old Trafford and victory over Chelsea. What tripped the Gunners up were not the games against better opposition as had been the case for so long; it was in giving points away in the games where they were the favourites. Burnley, Aston Villa, Wolves and Leicester all came to the Emirates in quick succession and left with three points in the bag. But in finding their form again, the dynamic of the team changed completely.

Handing the team over to the younger players coming through does not mean to completely abandon everything else. Older established players can reach a plateau that if nothing else, the crowd expects. It became apparent quite quickly that Saka and Emile Smith Rowe would be where that extra impetus would come from. Being able to share the burden as such helped both of them. Alone they may have been bogged down by expectation. It also opened the door for others in the academy to join them. Not only were they showing the way for the first team but also paving the way for those yet to blossom. Saka's form that year might not have been enough to drag Arsenal back into European football but it had caught the eye of Gareth Southgate, and the European Championship beckoned.

If Arsenal's fanbase required a dose of enjoyment, the England faithful were in need of a full prescription. Veering from controversy to irrelevance, the Three Lions had all but been sedated when it came to the international stage. Waking them up involved a similar kind of shift in mentality, primarily moving away from the kind of panic and anxiety that had gripped them for so long. What's more, the divisions in the squad that had curtailed a previous generation had long since dissipated. Following on from their efforts in getting to the semi-final of the World Cup in Russia in 2018, this was – for the first time in a very long time – a proper team. In terms of a representation of a country, this group of thoughtful, caring, talented young men were about as good as it could get. Of course there was an element who resented that.

The state of English politics in the 21st century has been intentionally divisive and hostile for the majority. From 2016 onwards it managed to find another gear entirely. Football was seen as off limits from its reach, both in terms of those who think the two should be completely separate and that there was never really a conscious desire for those who kick a ball around to want to get involved on such a scale. Times change. Except for some people they don't. Taking the knee was meant to be the very minimum. Peaceful protest at its most composed and straightforward. Not good enough for the ignorant or the decidedly disruptive. The power that this simple, beautiful game has is in its ability to connect. To rise above all barriers whatever they may be. Even those in the Houses of Parliament bet against the wrong team in the summer of 2021, despite what they tried to claim afterwards.

Saka ended up taking one of the most important kicks in English football history at the tender age of 20. Getting to the European Championship Final and being there to step up in the first place was already more of an achievement than most of those who came before. One of the preserving images of that tournament, however, will be that of Saka being pulled back by Giorgio Chiellini as he tried to run free from the veteran Italian centre-back in the final. The epitome of youth and experience, of being so close and yet so far. Of what it takes. Yet it will likely not come to define him. So too will his name be as far removed from the darkness that surrounded it following that painful penalty shoot-out. He is too talented and there will be more than enough opportunities to write his own headline. Proof of what joy can be brought, when it comes to embracing hope and abandoning fear.

15

David Unsworth

THERE ARE too many coincidences in football. All too often it appears as though those quirks of fate are something more. Ghosts of the game cannot exist and yet at the same time, it feels haunted. Results, actions and protagonists are all not only remembered but brought back to prominence by a force that cannot possibly be that knowing.

Destiny doesn't mean that every single event is controlled. Even the perception of a predetermined outcome doesn't mean something that was always meant to happen. The game itself is played out as a chess board, with the idea that when certain pieces are put together within a certain set of circumstances, it can only ever play out one way. Football has a reputation for having a cruel sense of humour, and that is well-founded. The ever-complicated ways in which the future picks up on seemingly innocuous things from the past and casts them into the spotlight. Triumph and tragedy, its fickleness makes a mockery of anyone who either dared to doubt or dared to dream.

The last game David Unsworth played in the top flight was on the final day of the 2006/07 season. It's a match that the neutrals will struggle to remember. Conversely, those that weren't may never forget it. As the curtain fell down on that campaign, Sheffield United – more specifically Neil Warnock –

felt particularly aggrieved. Events elsewhere seemingly conspired on the day and in the weeks prior which meant that as far as the Blades' manager was concerned, both Liverpool and Manchester United were guilty of sending out reserve sides. These were games that didn't register with the teams higher up in the table but would mean everything to how another side was able to retain its Premier League status.

'The integrity of the league' is a phrase that has become increasingly thrown around in the last few years. As squads up and down the Premier League have bloated, the respective management of them has come under increasing focus. Ultimately it is every team's – and manager's – right to pick their respective line-ups and approaches as they see fit. Management is literally the name of the game. This will mean that certain teams are disproportionately affected and the cold, hard reality is that some will play harder games than others. This is the game. Win your own battles and this doesn't become an issue.

For Warnock, it mattered that other points were up for grabs for sides who wouldn't normally have been able to reach them. Liverpool were preparing for the Champions League Final and Manchester United had already wrapped up the Premier League, so it was their prerogative to rest whomever they liked. When it was all said and done Sheffield United needed to beat Wigan Athletic at home on the final day to retain their Premier League status. What transpired – in spite of everything else that was going on around them – was very much a disaster of their own making.

One game with the whole season on the line. The complexities and nuances of a 38-match campaign all resting on the outcome of a solitary 90 minutes. Sheffield United's Premier League existence has been a rather cruel one. Fast forward to their only other appearance and the last game at Bramall Lane before Covid-19 shut everything down with them flying high in seventh. A surprise package defying all expectations and dreaming of a brighter future, only for the next time there would be a crowd there it was to be the last day of the following season and they were already relegated and bottom of the league. Even with all that, their fate in 2007 was especially merciless. Though the Latics weren't in their relegation-defying pomp, this was still going to be some task. Step forward David Unsworth.

Twelve yards is both an insignificance and the most significant. Adding the chance of a goal while removing everything else. Reducing everyone else on the pitch by 20, leaving a team game in the hands of just two. It's a kick in isolation that can either emphasise or defy all that which has gone before. An exercise in certainty, given that even the most proficient of penalty-saving goalkeepers are still not given a chance. So much of the language that surrounds either the game or the players themselves emphasises and underlines the importance of a certain kind of mental strength. The decisions that make up not what happens but why – and how a lot of results and even campaigns are forged around a particular buzzword; character.

Sheffield United's Paddy Kenny got close to the effort. This unfortunately played out like a metaphor for their entire season. There was much more time left to play after Unsworth dispatched his spot kick in the 46th minute, so in a sense outcomes were not definitively decided right there and then. What was rendered at the final whistle was so much more than three points, not just in terms of either team and their final destination but also the link between the two and his now central role in how everything played out. Unsworth kept one team up and consigned the other to the Championship. Why this one stung for them even more was that as recently as five months earlier, he was playing for Sheffield United.

Everything that pulls from the past takes with it a certain amount of sharpness. Consequences of immediate actions are only half the story, especially in regard to the dissection of a season that ended so infamously. They are the moments that might have been. Being in position to score against his former employers was enough of a wrinkle in time, yet there was even room for more. The Blades were relegated by virtue of goal difference. In a brutal addition to the spot kick that sent them down, during his limited time at Bramall Lane that season Unsworth missed one for the Blades. Drawing the line between both penalties doesn't quite paint a full picture; still, on such fine margins are fortunes decided.

Aside from a season rife with ramifications, Unsworth has played out much more of a supportive role. Supporters up and down the land clamour for players as committed to their particular cause. In among the glitz and the glamour of those more illustrious names, there is something to be said for those who commit themselves to the cause in a much more auspicious way. Solid and dependable, the dichotomy between aptitude and application draws a particular admiration in the sense that the fans in the stands will always fall into one of those categories with a particularly uneven split. One of the great domestic traits of the British Isles, desire alone does not produce, no matter how hard anyone tries nor how meaningful it would be if that were the case. There does come a point where the dividing lines are so thin, those who want it more can reach across a particular talent disparity.

Unsworth made the difference by perseverance. Like most players of his ilk, what he achieved was usually found within the margins. Regardless of how it played out in the end with Sheffield United, he was still a part of the team that brought them to the Premier League in the first place. Even just before that – during a short, otherwise uneventful spell – with Portsmouth in 2004, he opened the scoring from the penalty spot to earn them a memorable victory over Manchester United. A win like that against a team of that standing had traces of another famous conquest. One from the early part of his career, and the club that he gave everything for.

Beating Manchester United to a trophy during the 1990s meant something. A few years before, the same was true for Everton. The 1995 FA Cup Final was a heavyweight clash of differing history no doubt, both in terms of the wider context as well as events not long past. The Toffees had just escaped relegation while their opponents had been denied the Premier League title on the final day. Relative success and failure were put into perspective and unleashed over 90 minutes. Paul Rideout's goal compounded United's misery and gave the Toffees hope to hold on to. Its significance becomes increasingly bittersweet as the years roll on.

Trophies aren't always a sign of further success. Sometimes that one day when everything came together is just that. Incredible though it was, trying to infuse consistency into Everton's overall aims became a increasingly difficult task. Their success in the cup underlined a need to move up the table and get away from the relegation spots that loomed ominously over them. In 1995/96 there was a real step in the right direction with a sixth-place finish and – after a poor start – looking much more like the team that the Goodison faithful wanted to see. Andrei Kanchelskis moving over from Manchester United in particular was such a revelation it looked like a real corner had been turned. Selling him to Fiorentina six months into the following season saw Everton right back where they started.

Being in the right place at the wrong time makes a person look around. After years of service, Unsworth made the decision to move away and left Goodison Park in the summer of 1997, only to find himself back on the very first day of the following season. Lining up against his former team-mates for his West Ham debut was another one of those chance outcomes that football is so fond of. His time at Upton Park is only really notable for the circumstances surrounding a departure that never was. Leaving the Hammers after a year to start anew once more at Aston Villa, Unsworth played exactly no games and lasted a month before reaching out over a move back to Everton because he had miscalculated how close the West Midlands was in regard to his home in Merseyside. Of all the notable signings up and down the league over the years, this one remains one of the more absurd. At the very least Villa made their money back and Unsworth went back to where he was most comfortable. Whether or not it was the wrong time, for him it was the right place.

As the 1990s came to a close, Everton were in dire need of revitalisation after decade of disappointment, with every escape from relegation vowed to be their last. Though they weren't quite in the doldrums that they had been previously under Walter Smith, still there was a sense that more could be had. In 2001, the decision was made to appoint someone new and to take a punt on a promising lower-league manager who the club could get behind and really build something from scratch with. Given everything that was to come, this is both completely understandable and also somewhat head-scratching but David Moyes was at the time the fresh new face of the Premier League.

With nine games to go of the 2001/02 season there was still some work to be done. Everton were out of the relegation zone on goal difference when they took to the field against Fulham on 16 March 2002. The first goal of what was a key game was scored with less than 30 seconds on the clock. A long throw was controlled by Tomasz Radzinski and laid back to none other than David Unsworth. His powerful strike beyond Edwin van der Sar kicked off the Moyes era.

The mid-to-late 2000s saw the light at the end of the tunnel as far as Everton were concerned, competing at a much higher level than all but those with the most money and resources, although 2003/04 could have spoiled all that even before it began. Finishing on 39 points and yet still managing to avoid the drop by six was a feat of sorts. As the swansong for Unsworth's playing career at Goodison it might not have been the most glamorous end but fitting in the sense that he did what he'd always done; give everything for the shirt. He even came back as a coach later on down the line and helped them off the pitch, looking after the youth team from 2014 onwards. A six-month spell as the actual caretaker manager had all the goodwill in the world behind it, but wasn't meant to be. In the end he remains part of Everton, just as they are part of him. Sixth in the list of most appearances in the Premier League, 24th in terms of all time. A huge commitment, to a grand old team.

16

Jimmy Floyd Hasselbaink

PHYSICAL JOURNEYS have specific destinations with clear-cut pathways. Not only is the passage of time much more symbolic but its course is much less defined. Ending up at the same place doesn't matter as much as the route taken and underneath that, the question of how that path opened up still remains. Jimmy Floyd Hasselbaink played in the English top flight on either side of the millennium. If the distinction between what was the First Division and the Premier League was becoming increasingly more distinct, what happened next would shape it for the foreseeable future.

Perception fills in the blanks even when there aren't any. The truth stretches further than many are prepared to reach and it's much easier to latch on to a much more convenient misconception. Rarely is it ever positive but for the most part it comes from a place of innocence rather than maliciousness, a result of falsely connecting the dots. Rather than having to try and paint the full picture, it's much quicker to tar with a single brush. Whether it's players or clubs, their abilities or achievements become twisted. Sometimes a little, more often to the point of either outright ignorance or complete misrepresentation.

As the Premier League grew out of its infancy, so too did the scope for the superstars it was beginning to both attract and create.

In between the likes of Alan Shearer and Andy Cole leading the way in the mid-1990s and before we were treated to Thierry Henry and Ruud van Nistelrooy at the start of the 2000s, there was Hasselbaink. Part of what made transfers so intriguing in this era was that they really did come with no expectation. There was no deceiving YouTube highlight reel, nor any newspaper articles claiming to know exactly how anyone would fit in at any given time. In order to judge, you simply had to watch.

George Graham's Leeds were not the great entertainers. Perhaps as a cultural inverse to Kevin Keegan's Newcastle, somehow they went about their business in 1996/97 by finishing 11th in the table having scored only 28 goals in a season. More firepower was needed and so after having scored over 70 per cent of Leeds' league total for Boavista that year, Hasselbaink was brought over to England with no real expectation or sense of what was to come.

The goals didn't flow right away. During his two years at Elland Road, Hasselbaink scored 34 in the Premier League, but by the halfway point in his first season he had only netted five times. It wasn't the speed with which he adapted or the effervescence with which he played that captivated, however. He was a showman. Some people either shirk from the spotlight or outright try and escape it. Not Hasselbaink. His trademark celebration of a somersault followed by a deliberately slow pumping fist meant that there was never any ambiguity that all eyes should be on him. With such nifty close control and a ferocious finish, he imbued Leeds and the Premier League with the kind of star power that would become the norm over the next few years. As quickly as he rose to the top, his exit was even more sudden. Just as Leeds were on the cusp of breaking through to the next level, he left.

Football insults come in all shapes and sizes. Rarely do they dip into the New Testament, however. Exits don't even have to be particularly bitter for them to become biblical in the eyes of the fans. The act of contemplating a move away can sometimes be enough. When it comes to wage demands, the view is rarely a sympathetic one. In trying to sort out a new deal, Leeds were prepared to double his salary and make Hasselbaink their highest-paid player. In spite of this, an agreement couldn't be made. None of these decisions are ever made with finality; there's usually room for players to be brought back into the fold, unless the fans make that decision for them. Being selected in a friendly at Birmingham was an attempt to carry on as normal but the writing was on the wall. More specifically, a banner held up from the Leeds end that read 'Jimmy – Greedy, Selfish, Judas'. In the eyes of those supporters, there was no coming back.

What goes on behind the scenes at a football club usually stays in house, but every now and then it spills over into the public domain. The manager and chairman at the time, David O'Leary and Peter Ridsdale, were both incredibly forthcoming when it came to offering their opinion in regard to the protracted contract negotiations that were to end with the striker being sold to Atlético Madrid. Hasselbaink's stay in Spain wasn't particularly protracted; just the solitary year for a player who was really starting to come into his own. What a season it was too – the second-highest scorer in the division with 24 goals in a struggling Atlético side that ended up relegated, while the surprises continued at the other end of the table with Deportivo La Coruña winning the La Liga title. Having amassed the goals at the rate he had been, there was no realistic chance of him spending a season in the Segunda. Twelve months after leaving England in controversy, he was coming back.

Chelsea were on the up and not shy of putting down the cash. A fee of £15m doesn't sound like a great deal by more modern standards but in 2000 it was equal to the highest paid by a British club. When Alan Shearer broke the world record to move to Newcastle, he had gone there as both a hometown hero with a Premier League title to his name. Hasselbaink was not at all weighed down by the price tag or those comparisons; if anything his performances and ambitions were unmatched by

Chelsea. A poor start to the season not only washed away any hopes of finishing higher up the league but also saw Gianluca Vialli depart as manager. Who walked through the door to replace him was at once someone Hasselbaink had previous with but also went on to criticise – it was also the point at which so-called modern Chelsea was born.

Claudio Ranieri is one of the biggest characters in Premier League history. Though he didn't win anything at Stamford Bridge, he very much influenced what was to come. The period between his appointment and departure as Chelsea manager saw a revolution that went under the noses of so many but was noticed by so few. At the forefront of all of it was an irresistible attacking force led by Hasselbaink, Eidur Gudjohnsen and the majestic Gianfranco Zola. So well was the mercurial Italian able to capture the hearts and minds of both the Stamford Bridge faithful and neutrals alike that the combination of fire and ice around him somehow faded into the background.

Even though they had an ever-growing cast of gifted players and some momentum, it wasn't easy for Chelsea when Ranieri first came in. A string of trophies across the late 1990s and early 2000s meant their reputation as a club had shifted. Still they didn't get the respect that those exploits should have earned. Not even yet having established superiority within London let alone the Premier League, as high as the levels were, there was still a leap to be made. What hindered progress even more was an increasing threat from behind the scenes. The club was drifting ever closer to financial insecurity. What they desperately needed off the pitch was a change in fortune. On it, Champions League football became a must. Those two factors combined to set in motion a transfer of power that would change everything.

Going into the 2002/03 season, there were already gears in motion that served to prop up the next phase of English football. With four places up for grabs in the Champions League – two of which would have to go through the qualification process – suddenly there was much more scope for those underneath the title race to find themselves mixing with Europe's elite. For Chelsea it was a golden ticket. Hasselbaink and Gudjohnsen played their part, while Zola led the way. Along with a breakout season for Frank Lampard who had been brought over from West Ham, the Blues were all set for a tilt at the top and all the riches that came with it. The team who stood in their way would become something of a frequent foe. Once again the fixture list played its part. Liverpool headed to Stamford Bridge on the final day of the season; in terms of finishing in the top four, it was winner take all.

There might have been more decisive games within the Premier League era but not too many quite as important. Before or since, there have been few 90 minutes of football that caused such a wide-ranging ripple effect as the one that took place on 11 May 2003. Coming from behind to beat Gérard Houllier's Reds allowed Chelsea to finish fourth. In grasping on to a Champions League qualification place, it also prompted Roman Abramovich to acquire the club. Almost overnight the complexion of English football had shifted. Over £100m was spent on players during the following season alone as Chelsea went through the gears of competing at the very top. Glen Johnson, Wayne Bridge, Damien Duff, Joe Cole and Claude Makélélé all arrived in the summer alone, to complement an already stellar squad. Chelsea were mounting an assault on all fronts but it still took a change in the dugout to become the machine they would develop into.

The difference between José Mourinho and Claudio Ranieri at the time was one of personality as well as tactics. One of the men was seen on the forefront of European football and having guided Porto to win the Champions League it was hard to argue otherwise. The other, meanwhile, got just one game tactically wrong and set Chelsea down the next part of their path. Of all the possible scenarios that could have unfolded in this moment in time, the two meeting up in the 2004 Champions League Final could have again spun English football off in a very different direction. As it was, Ranieri's decision to chase the game in the first leg of their semi-final with Monaco led to the French side advancing. Hasselbaink could have been a Champions League winner with Chelsea before Mourinho even walked through the door. Would he have even still made the move?

Having spent a season fighting for his place ahead of Hernán Crespo and Adrian Mutu and still coming out on top, staying at Stamford Bridge might have been on the cards for Hasselbaink. Didier Drogba's arrival shortly after the 'Special One' meant a new destination would be required. Middlesbrough wasn't necessarily seen as the most glamorous of footballing havens but what Steve McClaren was building there at the time was very much about to pay off. That first season proved – if there were any doubts – that Hasselbaink still had it and though it wasn't exactly a repetition of what had come before at Chelsea, in Mark Viduka he found himself a more than willing partner to run it back one more time.

Repeat the conditions, change the details and circumstances. The science of football will never be exact, which is to say that every 90-minute experiment is not necessarily guaranteed to have a different result – in terms of winning and losing – but the scorelines will change. As mid-table teams go, Boro were quite formidable. Certain elements are more volatile than others. This applies as much to clubs themselves as it does players. For a period of time, Middlesbrough did not mix well with members of the upper echelons of the league and certainly they were able to find the formula in terms of building a squad. It all came together spectacularly in 2005/06, whereby the Riverside hosted a series of incredible nights the likes of which had never been seen before.

The kinds of games seen that season leave fans breathless; where emotions swing from one side to the other and the energy they bring with them. Middlesbrough's run to the UEFA Cup Final was so unique in the sense that for most of it they were clinging on by their fingertips. Supposedly nobody cares about how victory is crafted, yet there are varieties of them that are better than others. Football is never better than when a game becomes so frenetic it takes on a life of its own. It's one thing to be brought to the edge of your seat by a moment of individual brilliance, even those that come out of nowhere. But nothing holds on to the spirit like the comeback. What's more, there's a moment when everyone senses it and it feels tangible. And it doesn't matter whether it happens or not, all you need to do is believe it's a possibility. Nothing gives a team that belief quite like doing it and Middlesbrough did it time and time again.

After beating Roma, overcoming Basel in the quarter-final and Steaua Bucharest in the semi doesn't on paper appear quite as intense. Very much the opposite; Boro needed four goals to win with little more than an hour to do so in both games. Massimo Maccarone's time in England was otherwise fairly nondescript. In these ties he came to life. Such was the run towards that final in Eindhoven, there was a sense that Boro could come back from anything. Sevilla certainly put that to the test and their 4-0 victory, with three of the goals coming in the last 15, made the scoreline seem much more conclusive than the game itself. It was also the last match Hasselbaink would play for the club, bowing out with a bang but not in the way anyone would have hoped.

After relegation with Charlton in 2007 and FA Cup Final misery with Cardiff the following year, the last two chapters of his playing career fell flat, a complete reversal of how he had arrived in England. The Premier League is all about superstars, flair, showmanship and skill. And, most importantly, goals. Jimmy Floyd Hasselbaink was there right at the forefront of a new wave of striking talent as football moved into the 21st century. Having been in the eye of the storm as Chelsea moved to a position from where they could take over, he was still able to help Middlesbrough along in one of the most exciting stretches in their history. Nobody knows what lies on the road ahead. The best players can pave the way.

17

Jason Puncheon

FOOTBALL WORKS its magic from an early age. In most cases it has very little to do with anything you would care to associate with the game itself. Strip away the 90 minutes, remove every childhood hero and yet there is something left. Everything about it captivates, not least of all for the collective sensory bombardment. Being a fan is part of an unwritten language and these are the first words. So much of what follows is how much of the language we want to pick up.

Childhood roots burrow deep, forming entire personality traits. That yearning for belonging always stays there but what we see in those early years, those connections, those bonds are for life. They influence our decisions and our hopes for the future. If only we could make a difference when the time comes.

When you get close enough to touch it, what happens if the dream ends? If the events that led up to what promised to be the pinnacle of ambition leads to the rug being pulled from underneath? Does it make the anticipation any less sweet? Does it make you stop believing altogether?

Jason Puncheon's Premier League career ended not with a bang but with a whimper. The prospect of making a difference and yearning for a better finale both for him and the club in question are all but dashed immediately. It's the fault of neither but rather events that were already well on their way. Going to Huddersfield in 2019 was as fresh of a start as a player could have at that time, in terms of both their late-stage career and the team itself still being desperate to establish a firm footing.

Huddersfield's arrival in the Premier League in 2017 was part of a wave of unexpected teams rising up from the Championship and of the model of how to get things right at a lower level; the result of what happens when everyone gets on board and pulls in the same direction. Given nothing, not even hope in their first season, the Terriers defied the odds and retained their top-flight status. A dream became reality.

As the Premier League lurched closer to its third decade, it had become at once so segmented and damaged that the lower half of it was filled with teams who all fit the criteria – and sometimes performance – of those who should be at a lower level. Every year, every survival should on principle strengthen those that remain. In theory they're better than the replacements that come up. This kind of malaise has been shaken up. In 2017/18, Brighton and Huddersfield took advantage of more established teams who eventually got relegated below them. An injection of new blood like this keeps everyone on their toes. Unfortunately these gaps open up so frequently that when Wolves and their assembled team of Portuguese professionals arrived for 2018/19, somebody would have to take the fall. As such, Huddersfield fell hard.

By the time Puncheon arrived the Terriers were in trouble, terminally so in regard to injuries. On top of that, the man who had orchestrated all of the previous success, David Wagner, left the club almost immediately. It's harsh to imagine being punished for success but this was the result of having over-performed. As such everyone was getting their body blows in. The hype of the Premier League with all the might of its financial inequalities leaves nothing up for maybes. As a system, it is ruthless beyond belief.

Having to queue up to get beaten down by a handful of superteams assembled by billions and then be behind those who can spend millions beyond any other reach leaves everyone sore. After that what you're left with are the teams that desperately need to win. Both the top and the middle act like they're somehow superior and that's just what happens in the away end. What was a ritual becomes an experience.

Look around at a crowd that has swollen and it's hard to shake the sense that some of those who have only recently begun to populate the stands will both abandon their post very quickly, while in the intermediate future detract from the momentum that had been cultivated in years prior. They say the worst thing in the world is not getting what you want and the second worst is getting it. Whoever 'they' are must not have heard of Wimbledon.

Way back when, a lifetime before Jason Puncheon debuted in the top flight, he was being relegated from the First Division. To make your first foray into first team football in these circumstances is a very specific kind of sporting pandemonium. Eight games played in the latter half of spring 2004 for Wimbledon FC make for a deceptively notorious beginning. They were a club infamous for a variety of reasons, but it wasn't unheard of at the time that former Premier League teams would find themselves in trouble at the bottom end of the tier below. It's not any of his appearances that would court controversy, nor even a particularly dreadful campaign. What mattered – then as it does now – was what happened off the field, and a summer the likes of which has never been seen before or since.

Puncheon didn't play in the final game of the 2003/04 season as Wimbledon overcame Derby 1-0, registering only their eighth win of the campaign as they were relegated at the bottom of the second tier. Over the summer that followed, he wasn't sold to any other club nor released, yet the side he was now playing for was irreversibly different. The birth of Milton Keynes Dons was then and remains one of the more contentious affairs in the entirety of the English game.

In a world filled with considerable expletives, franchise may very well be the dirtiest word of them all. Those at boardroom level are known to have committed many different acts in regard to their running of a particular club, but there can be none so heinous as pulling it from its roots. More than a decade of mismanagement as development of their home ground at Plough Lane became such a mess, the owner at the time, Sam Hammam, even suggested moving the team to Dublin. That the eventual relocation was much closer than across the Irish Sea doesn't give this story a happy ending. Trophies, players, managers and owners all pale into insignificance when compared to the identity of the club itself.

From Stadium MK and back again after being released and making his way back through the divisions, Puncheon's career truly began at Southampton.

Finding the Saints in League One, they were a club in need of bringing back to life. Having evaded relegation from the Premier League for so long, going down in 2005 and then again in 2009 meant that they were a long way from where they wanted to be. Their predicament was made even more difficult with many Football League clubs still reeling from the 2002 collapse of ITV Digital, a media platform that had invested money into the competition only to go bust and leave many in dire financial straits. Alongside Southampton in the third tier were several teams who had fallen from the top including Leeds, Norwich and Charlton. This, combined with being shot at by all the other clubs in the division looking for a scalp, made the process even more difficult. Trying to turn everything around at the time was Alan Pardew, someone who saw something in Puncheon and who would go on to be a key figure in his career. When Pardew was shown the door a year later and replaced by Nigel Adkins, coupled with the emergence of Alex Oxlade-Chamberlain, the open opportunity that he walked into the club with slammed shut.

Going from League One to the Premier League may have been the dream for Southampton but it was Puncheon who got there first. After he had gone on loan to Millwall the previous year and shown what he could do in the Championship with five goals in seven games, Blackpool were in desperate need of bringing in some firepower to shore up their slide in the second half of the 2010/11 Premier League season. After having done so well in the first half, they just needed a little something extra to get over the line. Though Puncheon did manage to set up a last-day showdown at Old Trafford with a goal in the penultimate win over Bolton, overall it wasn't enough to keep the Tangerines afloat.

By the time he returned to Southampton, they had managed to find that momentum that rockets a team through the leagues. Back into the Championship by virtue of Adkins guiding them to second place, they were on course for a successive bounce, one that would lead back into the big time.

Chances again may have been limited and another loan up to the Premier League, this time with Queens Park Rangers, resulted in even less playing time. For many players this would be the end of the line: limited chances in the first team and a manager that has moved on with a team appearing to be firing on all cylinders about to return to the top flight. Yet the tide turned. Having been ready to leave at one time, Puncheon worked his way back into the squad and played a bit-part role over the spring of 2012 as Southampton battled their way to promotion.

Upon their return to the Premier League his playing time expanded even further. The manager, the player and the club had all met their goals and then some. Enter Mauricio Pochettino. The Argentinian's arrival on English shores surprised many, for Southampton didn't appear to be in the kind of peril that would see Adkins sacked. Once again, as the 2012/13 season drew to a close, Puncheon found himself on the fringes. In order to find first-team football he would have to go back to where it all began.

Puncheon grew up a Crystal Palace fan. From watching in the stands to putting on the shirt, this is the childhood dream made reality. Joining initially on loan from Southampton in August 2013, his performances in what was a tricky first half of a season for Palace saw his move made permanent after scoring three goals in four games that helped them out of the Premier League's relegation zone. Puncheon went on to ensure their survival with a run of form in April that saw him contribute to three successive victories. If this wasn't enough to captivate the Palace faithful, there was more to come.

For about two minutes, Puncheon had written his name into history. The ink wasn't even dry before Juan Mata and Manchester United tore that particular page out. Conjuring images of the 2016 FA Cup Final may only ever produce that bizarre dance by Alan Pardew on the touchline but to so many of the Eagles fans at Wembley and watching on elsewhere, when Puncheon scored in the 78th minute they were within touching distance of something truly incredible.

Delight in the moment made way for anger at the bench. Puncheon had been in good enough form in the run-up to the final and not being in the starting 11 was a source of great frustration, one that he took out on the Manchester United defence. From sitting in the Holmesdale Stand at Selhurst Park to scoring what could have been the winner in a major final – these are the fairy tales that are dotted throughout the game, what makes it great. Unfortunately for Puncheon and Palace, it wasn't meant to be. His career at Selhurst Park as a player lasted for another few years before being shuffled out of the team and on to Huddersfield. For Southampton it was to get back to where they once were, for Crystal Palace it was that brief moment where cup glory seemed possible and for Huddersfield it was the chance to stay alive in the top flight. What happens if the dream ends when you get close enough to touch it? You go again.

18

Edwin van der Sar

GREATNESS STANDS out in any era, free from the shackles of time, existing within a broader definition. A select few are capable of slotting into any generation and are capable of thriving but their qualities shine through all the same. Possessing of a persistent consistency that adapts as the game itself continues to evolve, they are at once talent and application at its apex.

It's almost a certainty that for them the game moves at a different speed. Certainly anyone who has ever sat behind the goal and felt the simultaneous embarrassment and wonder at a shot that appeared to be floating wide only for it to dart into the top corner at the last second knows how easy it is to get caught up in whatever vortex occurs from the moment the ball leaves a travelling foot. To that end, it's simultaneously to their credit and detracting from the excitement of the moment those who make it look easy.

A really good save reaches out from the darkness. Both in terms of the grudging acceptance and the physical act, a solitary arm is all that can be needed to pull everyone to safety. Every reaction in the stands comes from that moment of pre-emption, however. The more assured a goalkeeper the less likely anyone is to be concerned should they be called upon. As such, rather than acceptance it becomes disbelief when they're finally beaten. Such standards are so high, it's almost impossible to appreciate.

During the late 20th century, impatience became a way of life. The pursuit of grandeur led to an ever-shortening fuse. To confuse matters even further there was more of it, in a certain sense. Football had been a global game for a century at that point but only now were the eyes of the world trained upon all that could be consumed. A perfect lesson in geography, from Scandinavia to Liberia; everyone was now able to be present and accounted for. Teams attracted the most exotic talent from around the globe and everything sped up. There was no time to build a team; it had to be ready to go from day one. As a result of this, the influence and dominance that a club like Ajax had during the early 1990s was quickly able to be dismantled and scattered across the continent. Money really did make the world go round and the Premier League had it by the bucketload. By the early 2000s, all of these things came crashing together to reshape the football landscape completely.

Think of all the incredible teams of days gone by, when a single side ruled English football. From Herbert Chapman's Arsenal through Don Revie's Leeds all the way to Liverpool during the 1970s and '80s as well as what Manchester United had done during the first decade of the Premier League. Winning trophies will always be the sign of a good team, but the very best hoard them. It just became so much harder. Periods of potential supremacy have been pulled down long before they could be considered to be truly great. With Chelsea in 2005 and Manchester City in the mid-2010s, just as it looks like they've fully grabbed that mantle, competition comes along to match it. Pep Guardiola may be able to change this during the remainder of his days at the Etihad but ultimately it's become a struggle to find the balance between recency bias and those incredible teams of the past is that now there's more likely to be a fly in the ointment.

Edwin van der Sar arrived in England on the back of a pivotal point in Italian football history. He was only just into his 30s – it's widely accepted that goalkeepers are perfectly capable of performing at a high level for a few years still – yet Juventus made the decision that they were going to look to the future. Even with a goalkeeper of such immense quality, it's hard to say they made the wrong choice in paying Parma £32m for the services of Gianluigi Buffon in 2001. No doubt with a fair amount of suitors – including Sir Alex Ferguson – van der Sar would have his pick of places to come and ply his trade next. Which was why when he signed for newly promoted Fulham, it sent shockwaves all around the country if not the continent.

Teams make their way through the divisions with regularity. Reaching the Premier League after a climb up the lower levels is one of the more fantastical and heart-warming aspects of the football pyramid. More often than not, it isn't quite the Cinderella story that everyone had been promised and instead the work of some fairly high-profile people working with larger than usual resources. Bought by Mohamed Al-Fayed in 1997, it wasn't long before Fulham had Kevin Keegan in the dugout and were able to pay Chris Coleman £2m to play in the third tier. With a remit of getting to the top flight within the next five years, the Cottagers set down a marker and continued to flash the cash as though they were a Premier League team in all but name. This continued with their actual arrival, adding Steed Malbranque, Sylvain Legwinski and Steve Marlet to a team that already contained Louis Saha, John Collins and Luís Boa Morte. Behind them all now was one of the most accomplished goalkeepers in European football.

Hollow though it may seem, for some clubs talking the talk matters. Fans often speak about the marquee signings that at times reach even beyond their wildest dreams and though it's no guarantee of success, what it does is send a message. If Fulham had previously given off the impression that they were nothing more than the toy of a rich businessman, this was exactly the kind of signing that forced everyone to take them seriously.

Merely acting like a Premier League team, however, will only get you so far. Results on the pitch go hand in hand and with van der Sar in goal they were almost inevitably going to be safe. This came into stark contrast in the season after his arrival when an injury sustained in an unusually unsteady game against Newcastle would eventually lead to him being out for the rest of the campaign. Though Maik Taylor was a more than capable understudy, results would not go well for the next couple of months, to the point where the man who had taken Fulham to the Premier League in the first place, Jean Tigana, was sacked.

The Premier League has never seen the likes of Tigana, not before nor since. In taking Fulham to the top tier and also proving capable of keeping them there, his dismissal in April 2003 came somewhat out of the blue. Coleman took over the reins and in spite of his inexperience carried on where his predecessor had left off. Over the course of those next couple of seasons, Fulham made themselves at home in and around mid-table. Good enough for the occasional upset, all the while never in any serious danger of being in any real peril themselves. If van der Sar's signing in the first instance had been seen as something of an oddity from the outside looking in, it didn't matter. He had fulfilled his duty and now it was time for another tilt at the top.

Manchester United had an issue. From the moment Peter Schmeichel left the club in 1999 there were big gloves that needed filling. All those who had auditioned for the role in the following years had varying degrees of success and failure. Massimo Taibi's inexplicable error against Southampton that following season was seen as such a big deal because the Red Devils finally had a weak spot. Even someone like Fabien Barthez – who played more than any other – didn't quite have the same kind of influence. The shift in power at the top of the Premier League meant that Sir Alex needed more than just good enough and he brought in van der Sar for an undisclosed fee believed to be around the £2m mark in 2005; value for money doesn't quite cut it.

The first title wasn't a formality. Chelsea and José Mourinho had done such a good job in obtaining an iron grip over the Premier League in the few years previously that for once United were underdogs. All eyes were on a meeting between the two in the penultimate game of the 2006/07 season but it was a week before when everything was decided. The Manchester derby and Chelsea taking on Arsenal made for a mouthwatering double bill. Cristiano Ronaldo's goal and van der Sar's penalty save meant victory for the Red Devils while Arsenal held Mourinho and the Blues to a 1-1 draw, which meant the trophy would be returning to Old Trafford. For van der Sar, it meant his first English championship. He was not done collecting.

The following season saw another battle down to the wire with the side from Kings Road. This time it went down to the very last game before United clinched the title. There was more than just domestic superiority at stake between the two this year, however. Moscow played host to the 2008 Champions League Final, the first time two English sides would compete for the grandest club prize in world football. When it came down to a penalty shoot-out, the signs suggested that maybe Chelsea had the advantage. After all, van der Sar had been eliminated from three successive international tournaments with the Netherlands via shoot-outs. Despite this unfavourable record, he managed to stop Nicolas Anelka's effort in sudden death and make Manchester United kings of Europe once more.

The following season presented a very different challenge. Chasing down an 18th league title, it was Liverpool who suddenly posed the threat. Back-to-back defeats as Liverpool won at Old Trafford and a week later at Fulham meant that what at one stage looked like a stroll became an actual race. What United were able to do, both before and after the wobble in March, was clamp down on everyone. Rio Ferdinand, Nemanja Vidić and van der Sar along with the rest of that back four formed an impervious line of defence. Along the way they went a record-breaking 21 hours and 51 minutes without conceding.

Clean sheets are the ultimate comfort among the chaos, like laying in a freshly made bed while a thunderstorm rages outside. There comes a point in every match whereby once the main objectives are achieved, trying to tag on extra incentives becomes competitive. Not least because those teams that get into the habit of conceding late do sometimes come unstuck in other situations. Forming good habits is such a part of winning and keeping clean sheets is a key component to that. You'll exhaust the opponent. Make them think there's no hope.

What became the final challenge for van der Sar and Manchester United was not Premier League matters, however. Pep Guardiola's Barcelona stood in the way of a dynasty as they looked to build one for themselves. At the 2009 Champions League Final in Rome, before Cristiano Ronaldo versus Lionel Messi was even a thing, it would be the Argentine who would leap above the competition. His heading ability was supposed to be one of the weaker parts of his game but it didn't look that way as he clinched the game and the Champions League with Barcelona's second goal of the night. This was only the appetiser; the two sides would meet in another final two years later.

Wembley wasn't quite Old Trafford but there was a semblance of home territory in 2011. Despite that, Barcelona arrived in a conquering mood. Though there were moments after Wayne Rooney's equaliser while the game was finely balanced, what Manchester United were on the receiving end of that night is one of the greatest team performances at that stage of any competition. It was football perfection from the Catalans. What's more, it was to be van der Sar's last game for United. Bowing out on the losing end may be bittersweet, but after a game like that and the career he'd had there was nothing at all to feel bad about.

Whenever talk in the media turns to comparing eras or putting together whichever team is hot in the moment against those from the past, there are always those who get left behind. From record-breaking defensive stretches to the trophies that they enabled, van der Sar and the late-2000s Manchester United are often inexplicably left out. That heralded side of 1999 no doubt gets the credit from a single-season perspective but in terms of three Champions League finals in four years and only being prevented from more by one of the best sides of all time, does more for their legacy, not less.

Edwin van der Sar moved to England on the back of an already legendary career not to make a name for himself but for the club that signed him, then went to one of the biggest teams in the world and made them better. In terms of leaving a lasting mark throughout the eras, he is up there with anyone.

19

Nicolas Anelka

REGARDLESS OF how intricate and satisfactory the answer may be, venturing towards the uncharted tantalises in a way that familiar comforts cannot. The known has limitations; knowledge has set parameters. A ceiling can be placed upon that which is expected whereas the unknown cannot be capped.

As a generation of talent set the tone for the Premier League, they were also the first to be discarded. What emerged in those early years may have established itself as familiar furniture but their sheen had begun to wear away. The arrival of other talent helped inject some new blood but no individual burned so brightly, no player did so much in such a short period of time as Nicolas Anelka.

Arsène Wenger all but invented a power struggle. Without his influence the first decade and beyond would have belonged to Alex Ferguson. That being said, it wasn't a single step that overtook them. There was no great flux between Manchester United's 1999 all-conquering treble and the 2004 Arsenal 'Invincibles', they simply traded blows and shared silverware. The millennium provided no unequivocal dividing line as both teams had their say in regard to supremacy. One of the oft-forgotten seasons is the 1998/99 title run-in and how close and how hard Arsenal pushed the eventual winners. Before they were able to knock out the champ, this was the ability to establish they could land a body blow. Anelka was at the forefront of the force that made them seem mortal.

Anelka was a supernova of a player who arrived without much fuss and brought the heat with him in such a way as to redefine the league itself. All of this was encapsulated within that first spell in England when, from 1997 to 1999, he went from relative unknown to ultimate prominence. There aren't many who could take the place of Ian Wright, let alone do it in such a way as to remove the doubts surrounding his absence. Replacing a legend like that in any instance can be difficult. There was no way to know it at the time but he was to be sandwiched in between two; following on from Wright and playing backup to Thierry Henry. Anelka was so much more than an understudy.

Bringing the Premier League trophy to Highbury in 1998 gets lost for a multitude of reasons, both of the prominent rationales being what they and their rivals that year would go on to accomplish. Wenger's new-look Gunners were brimming with strength, stability and surprise. The perfect package to not just win the title but with 12 wins out of 15 from February onwards, do so in a manner that laughed in the face of Manchester United's ability to chase down come the end of the season. That year Anelka was but an exciting part of the run. Players can have adequate campaigns and take home all the glory or alternatively grab all of the headlines but be left with no medals. However, 1999 was a dominant year that wouldn't count. Taking a treble-winning team to the wire doesn't matter if they are to reign supreme. Someone was paying attention, however. For Real Madrid, the way in which Anelka had become the perfect fit for a team that was hungry for attention.

The Galácticos era did two things simultaneously. Firstly there was a modern blueprint set, of a continental superteam that others have since been weary of or leaned into. It also kicked off a perpetual growth and then harvesting of talent from England to

Spain. Foreign leagues wanted nothing to do with the previous generation, those plying their trade within the British Isles, at best dabbling in a free transfer or two. This marked both a change in attention and product that would never be the same again. It also led to what would be the cross Anelka would have to bear for the remainder of his career.

Fans can be temperamental sometimes, and fickle with their affections. It's the way things are and there's very rarely any consequence for that. But if the man himself is to be believed, it was losing an Arsenal club poll to Wright that was the catalyst for Anelka wanting to move away. Though it may have been petty and a complete overreaction, such is the sensitive nature of certain individuals. Wanting – needing even – the warmth of the crowd, at that age, in that position and during those circumstances, rightly or wrongly Anelka felt he had been slighted.

For all its ills, social media has been able to – however thinly – bridge some of the gap that has opened up between supporters and players. Of course soulless social media managers exist but it has allowed for a more immediate connection in an age where increasingly nothing else existed. There are a lot more contentious suggestions online than simply putting the man who at that stage was Arsenal's all-time top scorer at the front of a poll. If this really was the motivation, Twitter would have been far too much fuel to the fire. Anelka already had enough enemies in the media as it was.

To play the way he was playing, there were always going to be plaudits. It's just that for the first major one, Anelka didn't turn up. Tony Adams collected the Young Player of the Year award in 1999 on his behalf, and a reputation was born. 'Le Sulk' was the nickname that stuck and this image of a petulant, spoiled child was cultivated among the press. The Premier League was filled with homegrown, salt-of-the-earth type talent and seasoned with a touch of charismatic, affectionate foreigners. This wasn't Anelka's game and for as much as he paid the price for his petulance, casting him out into the cold was a shame for a player who had lit up the league so brightly.

Getting away from the British media was all well and good; the years that followed were not. A solitary season at Real Madrid ended with a Champions League and still managed to feel unsatisfactory. Returning to his first professional club, Paris Saint-Germain, may have briefly provided some respite but again dressing room spats and issues with coaches gave the sense of a bright young career destined to be dragged down in controversy. With that the unthinkable happened. In order to start again and see if some of that initial magic could be recaptured he would have to go back to England.

Six months at Liverpool towards the tail-end of the 2001/02 season was only significant for what happened next. Liverpool opting for El Hadji Diouf over him set back the groundwork that had been laid there significantly. It's not necessarily the most pivotal of sliding doors moments for Liverpool but it probably is for Gérard Houllier, whose transfer record was never the same again. Manchester City came next, Kevin Keegan putting all his chips in the middle after their promotion to the top flight with a record signing during a time when City's wildest dreams were very different to where they are today. Much like this period of their history in general, all of this is remembered more as part of a quiz question. There were moments to savour, however. Scoring the opener in a 3-1 victory over Manchester United in the final derby held at Maine Road is certainly one way to endear yourself to a fanbase. Having helped settle the club in the Premier League and re-establish themselves ahead of what was to come for Manchester City, it wouldn't be long before he would be travelling himself again.

A year in Turkey did nothing to help the feeling that Anelka's star was fading. This had less to do with the destination than it did the fact that he had become something of a footballing nomad (this is even before getting into all of his national team bust-ups throughout the years). It seemed as though his search for somewhere to call home was destined to be an ongoing one. No one could have guessed that the road to recovery went through Bolton.

Sam Allardyce was many things but among his skills there was a knack of being able to rediscover long-lost treasure. For all the infamy attached to his name regarding a specific playing style, at Bolton he had a great knack of mixing the discarded goods with the solid workhorses. Their whole ethos was around being underestimated and undervalued and in the one year the Trotters had Anelka they were firmly in the top half. A more than respectable seventh-place finish belies the fact they could arguably have gone even higher. As ever with Anelka, there was a parting of the ways but he wasn't going anywhere just yet. After Allardyce stepped away and the side began to struggle, it felt like only a matter of time given the form he was in before he too would be leaving through the exit door.

In 2005 Chelsea were at the forefront of English football and appeared to be set for years to come. In the space of two years, their assumed dominance was already in question. Just as Anelka himself had a hand in bringing down an empire in Manchester United, here he was on the other side helping pick up the pieces following José Mourinho's departure from Stamford Bridge. Surreal though it seemed at the time, even stranger was the choice to replace him with director of football Avram Grant only to sack the Israeli at the end of the season too. For a player who had lived life in the fast lane, perhaps this was finally more his speed.

Anelka had arrived late, joining in January to reinforce an attack that contained Andriy Shevchenko and Didier Drogba. With summer signing Claudio Pizarro misfiring, this added dimension allowed Chelsea to go on a run that saw them only drop points in five games between his arrival and the end of the season. For the first time in Anelka's career since that breakthrough season in England, there was no real pressure. He was able to be used in specific roles for particular games. This was not only fine but a real asset for Grant in always having a card to play down the stretch. Even with all of the chaos off the pitch, on it they were superb, finishing in second place after settling into a rhythm and ultimately just two points off top spot. A respectable league campaign still had the promise for more; that which had eluded Mourinho and was but a twinkle in Roman Abramovich's eye: the Champions League. Their opponents? The team who had just pipped them to the league title.

Being on the wrong end of a decisive action that delivers a Champions League can only ever feel misrepresentative. Denied by the outstretched arms of the Manchester United goalkeeper Edwin van der Sar, Moscow must have felt that much colder during that night in May 2008 for Anelka. Bringing players in off the bench for the sole purpose of taking penalties remains a decision that will only ever be judged in a very specific way. To say that Grant lost the game by bringing Anelka on so late may be a stretch but leaving him on the bench for that long is also conclusively questionable. So many misses of this kind come to define an entire career; such was the complication of this working life, it failed to make a dent in a very specific reputation. As it was, both player and team would go on together to more success.

Perhaps the biggest strength of the Abramovich-era Blues is that of being able to deal with setbacks in such a way that doesn't ever spiral for too long. The appointment of Luiz Felipe Scolari and everything that followed would set other clubs back for an inordinate amount of time. Chelsea, the autonomous unrelenting machine that they were at the time, followed up with a Guus Hiddink and Carlo Ancelotti double which in 18 months both healed their wounds and made them Premier League champions once again. For a club that relied on volatile changes, this was a period of relative stability.

Didier Drogba's dominance is very much associated with a very specific – Mourinho-influenced – period of time. Scoring nearly 30 goals in the 2009/10 season paints a very different picture. Following on from their advances in the earlier part of the decade, it would have been so simple to fall away. Anelka was never the focal point during this period in the same way he had been so incendiary earlier on in his career.

André Villas-Boas joined the club in the summer of 2011, charged with the task of refreshing Chelsea in such a way that would facilitate a new generation. This is a season that would end in the very same European Cup glory that had eluded them for so long, although under the leadership of Roberto Di Matteo after Villas-Boas's spring exit. In the meantime, during an attempted clearout, Anelka departed for China. So much money was pumped into that particular part of the world it seemed as though it would become a much bigger deal than the reality that transpired. Moving to Juventus a year later could easily have been written off as the last big surprise. Nobody foresaw a return to England, however. Even those who could would never have predicted the location.

After everything else, Anelka was ending his career in English football at West Bromwich Albion. He also ended it in disgrace. A goal celebration in the form of an anti-Semitic gesture carries very little nuance, especially in regard to the source; a so-called comedian who has a litany of deplorable stances. Explanations both at the time and documentaries since have attempted to offer a degree of understanding to what happened, all of which can at the very best of interpretations be defined as naivety. Anelka arrived on English shores as an unknown quantity, someone who burned brightly and yet still – through a series of synthetic rehabilitations – found a way back to the top. In an era of stars who became superstars, Anelka may have flown too close to the sun.

20

Robbie Savage

NOT EVERY game can be a masterpiece. In reality, very few are. An orchestra of 22, conducted by chaos. The placid rhythm with which some are content to play the game is at odds with those whose existence is played to a higher tempo. In spite of all the action that can and does go on, there are times when nothing happens. Where proceedings need a little bit of life brought to them, whether on the pitch or elsewhere. Crescendos can only be crafted by a certain few.

Who needs actions when you've got words? An entire industry has not just grown up around football as a whole but very specifically the way in which it is spoken about. In the wrestling world there is this idea that being booed or cheered matters above all else, even if that's not what's supposed to happen. Any reaction is better than none. During those early years of the Premier League, as coverage began to expand, the voices became quieter. Conscious of the ever-narrowing parameters of what not to say, being a character in the first instance drew attention.

When it comes to the news cycle, the worst kind of conclusions to arrive at are the reasonable ones. They are the sideways pass of mass consumption. Continuing the conversation in a way that simultaneously halts any sudden movement. Football will never be short of over-reactions. The media harvests it very well. Opinions became a form of currency. In that regard there are few richer than Robbie Savage. As far as entertainment is concerned, insight takes a back seat to indignation. Polarising fans fuels a debate that doesn't need to take place. In the business of provoking a backlash of emotion, football does the job automatically. It needs no guiding hand to descend into madness. Those who are prepared to give it a push, however, have a certain spotlight that surrounds them wherever they go.

More careers start with a setback than never have them at all. There's enough motivation in football when it comes to a simple love for the game, or even more cynically the fame and fortune behind it. But the desire to prove someone wrong shoots to the top of the list when it comes to what drives those who make it to the very top. Robbie Savage being released from Manchester United flipped a certain switch. It wasn't a case of if he would make it, it was a question of where and how.

Playing in the third tier of English football for three years, there wasn't really any spectacular rising through the ranks that completed Savage's story. If anything it only really began once he had made it back. After helping Crewe Alexandra to promotion via the Second Division play-offs in 1997, Martin O'Neill and Leicester came calling. Redemption in a sense, yet there was still nothing quite like the reputation that Savage would come to build during his time in the Premier League.

Strategy has no integrity. Whatever is necessary to get the job done will always triumph over anything that fails. As such, while breaking the rules is very much off limits, bending them is nothing more than a feeling-out process. Pushing people refers to an act that works on both sides. Competing at the top level is very much that and ambition needs to be seen for it to be believed. Whether it then goes on to encourage team-mates or discourage opponents, having the will to make things happen doesn't necessarily always mean to do anything other than be there in that moment. Tactically, there's something to be said for simply hanging around.

The art of being the last man standing is one of dedication. In principle, holding off the enemy for such a length of time is to draw them closer to the inevitable mistake they will make. It's not about winning, it's about fighting long enough so that the opponent is unable to think ahead. It's not about glory, it's about making them so frustrated with being on the battlefield in the first instance they would rather shoot themselves in the foot than engage with you any longer. And in that moment, victory appears.

Savage was a better footballer than his reputation suggests. But it's also one he played into. If you pick a lot of battles you've got to be prepared to fight a few wars. With Savage it was never about his ferocity, it was always about the insistence of his antagonism. In terms of consistency this was the most dependable aspect of his ability. Mind games get mentioned a lot in various different contexts but when it comes to the mental aspects of football, avoiding this kind of battle was as important as winning anything physical. He gave relief to those around him in terms of clearing the way to allow them to contribute in a much more constructive manner, all the while not giving the opponent a solitary second of peace. Loved or hated depending on the shirt he was wearing, those who supported or abhorred him both did so for the exact same things.

The Premier League's pantomime villain made his first real appearance in the League Cup. Making a show of himself at the conclusion of the 1999 final set the tone for needlessly upsetting an opposition fanbase. Following an errant, reactionary swing of the arm from Justin Edinburgh, Savage's theatrical collapse to the floor in order to get him sent off was at once on the milder end of misconduct and simultaneously a histrionic line that shouldn't be crossed. Returning to Wembley a year later under much more straightforward circumstances, Savage put on a different kind of performance in order to claim his sole piece of silverware. By this point, Leicester had become a reliable mid-table team and this was right at the point where they would have been looking to kick on ever further. Their manager Martin O'Neill did move on, leaving the Foxes behind for Celtic.

The negative impact of a prominent manager leaving is something that many clubs have felt over the years. So much time is spent waiting and hoping that someone can come along and bring prosperity with them and all too often they've gone in an instant and it's all over far too quickly. What happened to Leicester in the immediate aftermath of O'Neill heading north of the border was a series of one wild swing in form. As soon as the winds changed at the end of 2000, things were never the same again. A full year and a half of struggle followed, split over two seasons. The players brought in to halt the slide in the summer of 2001 fell flat – Ian Walker aside – and it was left to the older guard within that Leicester team. The likes of Frank Sinclair, Matt Elliott and Muzzy Izzet as well as fans' player of the year Savage were powerless to rescue them from finishing bottom. Perhaps the only bright spot came in the form of winning their final game against Spurs, the last to be played at Filbert Street. This then goes on to explain what came next and why Savage wouldn't be part of it.

Barely two weeks after the end of that horrendous 2001/02 season, Savage put pen to paper on a move to Birmingham City. The progress that had been made before and during his time at Leicester had come back to bite them. Needing to move on from the traditional – albeit outdated – home of the club meant financial implications, ones that were made even worse due to their relegation to the First Division. As a key piece within that midfield withstanding even the comprehensive failure of the year previously, Savage was the first to be sold off; slotting in at St Andrew's and becoming an equally integral figure within Steve Bruce's team.

Returning to the top flight after a sustained absence gives a whole new generation of fans the chance to savour certain encounters. Coming up against the leading lights in English football not only represents a challenge to be relished. There was only one fixture that Birmingham had in their sight upon the fixture list being released. An opponent they'd been kept apart from for far too long, having spent years in the lower leagues. Aston Villa travelled to St Andrew's for the first time in nearly a decade; the teams had not met in a league match for 15 years. The anticipation was palpable. An howler for the ages from Peter Enckelman in conceding direct from a Villa throw straight to him – his light touch on the ball before it crossed the line meant the goal stood – underlined a momentous 3-0 victory for the Blues. When it came time for the reverse fixture at Villa Park in March, all the ingredients were there.

In a game that was almost inevitably going to catch fire, Savage had no qualms in pouring fuel. Derby matches are intense affairs at the best of times and cool heads are needed to prevail. Of all the people to become embroiled in a physical altercation, Dion Dublin was possibly the least likely but something snapped. It wasn't the most aggressive headbutt of all time, granted, but it was still more than enough for Savage to get the referee's attention and be worthy of the subsequent red card. Birmingham went on to win that game 2-0 and with it the bragging rights that they had so longed for.

Fans let themselves fall for certain teams and players within those setups all too often. Unlike everywhere else in the country, everyone at St Andrew's adored Savage. He was at the very core of a workmanlike, tenacious squad that very much reflected the crowd that cheered them on. It takes so long to build a team that is held up in the eyes of the support in such a way that also does its job on the pitch. The unfortunate dilemma for every manager then becomes wanting to change it and move away from that. Steve Bruce was adding dashes of quality to his team on a regular basis with the likes of Christophe Dugarry, Matthew Upson, David Dunn, Emile Heskey and Jermaine Pennant. Each year moved ever so slightly further away from the side they had become. Not all of them worked; see Mario Melchiot, Jesper Grønkjær and Luciano Figueroa. The flops didn't matter so much. So long as Savage was the anchor in the middle, they would never lose what made them work so well.

Between personally and professionally, desires can clash. Wanting to change an employment situation seems harmless enough. When it came time to engineer a transfer to Blackburn Rovers, there were better ways of handling it. Firstly Savage claimed that the move was to get closer to family, which turned out not to be the case. Then there were even more subversive tactics like turning up to training when the rest of the team had the day off and telling the press that he was being forced to train alone. On the occasions he did train with the team, Savage was disruptive, all of which came to a head when he scribbled a transfer request down on a piece of paper and handed it to Bruce. All the while, he was still their best player. In the end he got his wish.

Some history you can blink and miss. Or rather, the points between the start and end get blurred. Blackburn's high point and their fall into League One are the exit and entry points which will eventually be used to retell the story once they do make it back to the Premier League. What this overlooks is a period after being initially relegated and coming back to establish themselves. Graeme Souness had brought them back to the Premier League and after a few years things looked to be on the wane again. In came Mark Hughes, closely followed by Savage in January 2005.

As far as forgotten one-off campaigns go, Rovers' 2005/06 season ranks highly among them. Finishing sixth and missing out on the Champions League places by just four points, Blackburn put together an incredible run of form that just wasn't quite good enough to be truly remembered. This was a team packed with quality from Morten Gamst Pedersen and Tugay to Benni McCarthy and Craig Bellamy. Brad Friedel, Lucas Neill and Steven Reid were all still putting in shifts at the back and with Savage at the epicentre of it all, Ewood Park became an incredibly difficult place to visit once again. Building on that feeling of positivity proved difficult for Blackburn. Players were sold off just as quickly as they began to find their form and Savage himself suffered a long-term injury in January 2007 that would eventually see him not be able to fully reclaim a place in the side. There was still one final chapter to play out for Savage, but it just so happened to be one of the most infamous seasons in Premier League history.

Of all the things Savage has done, he is known for a specific few. Similarly Derby County had spent six straight seasons in the Premier League in the late 1990s and early 2000s but it's their 2007/08 campaign that they're forever going to be known for. For a player who doesn't turn up there until it's pretty much all over, Savage's association with that season is still pretty strong. He signed for Derby on 9 January 2008, by which point they had already accumulated seven of the 11 points they would get for that season. Of the four they obtained after his arrival Savage was absent for the home 0-0 draw with Sunderland, so three points from 16 games is perhaps the biggest standout number from Savage's Derby career. People want accolades, just not like that.

Some things in football can be explained, and rationalised even to some degree. But Derby getting 11 points will not only never make sense, it will never be beaten. Every season more or less there's a side that does horrendously and this record always comes up. Without fail every time they're miles away from it. To beat this record requires averaging a quarter of a point per game. One win completely knocks it off course. In spite of being intertwined with such a historic low point and looking very much like his career at Pride Park was over, Savage stayed there for three more years to salvage what remained of a career spent in the spotlight.

Savage thrived on the drama. He cannot exist in the silence, cannot tolerate inertia within the game itself. Football is a sport that lives and breathes within these moments. There are certain players and certain positions with whom it's easier if everything passes by. When nothing happens, they're successful. Not so with Savage. He'll bring the noise where necessary, as well as those times it isn't. In a world devoid of character, the ones who show any signs of it become exaggerated by default. With every story you need an antagonist, even if they're simply playing the part.

21

Kieran Trippier

WATCHING A team at an important juncture can be exhausting. The most draining experience that involves very little in the way of physical activity. There's one very simple reason – how overwhelming the strength and depth of feelings can be both in their size and also their proclivity for rapid change. Momentary joy can give way to grave anxiety at the thought of victory being taken away. Conversely, going behind isn't always rectifiable and that frustration inevitably gives way to a foreboding acceptance. These feelings don't go away either. Long after the game has finished, those initial bursts of emotion stay with us. They grow to define the matches more so than the results, because of the context they put those results in.

No matter how much it ever feels like it, nothing is set in stone. Things often seem that way after the fact, whereby the dizzying heights and awful lows still remain yet hindsight only underlines what happened, not that it was inevitable. No matter how happy or sad you felt at the time, the knowledge of what's to come will always colour a particular lens. Unfortunately because football is so cold-blooded, just because a moment felt good in the moment and turned bad doesn't mean that the reverse is true.

Take two moments; isolated events that don't define outcomes but instead encapsulate what becomes imprinted on a fanbase. The first took place in Madrid. A minute is a long time in football, especially when it ends in the concession of a penalty. As rudimentary tactics go, everything that happened in those opening few exchanges was all about playing in Sadio Mané behind Kieran Trippier to kick off the 2019 Champions League Final. Though it wasn't his appendage Mané struck the ball against, it will forever be a defining moment in Tottenham's history.

A year earlier, swap out dejection for delight. A free kick which meant for over an hour Trippier scored the goal that would propel England into the World Cup Final. Either one of these instances would be enough to define an individual career. Things that go underneath the headlines and yet will be forever remembered, for good or for ill above the scorelines themselves. That both of them ultimately end in heartbreak is all but conclusive proof of how cruel football can be.

If the story ended there, it would be understandable. Particularly from the perspective of England fans who seem to engorge themselves on a solid nostalgia diet. In the last 30 years there have been but a handful of strong showings on the international stage for the Three Lions. Going again in Euro 2020 wasn't a given, if for nothing else that the tournament was put on hold for a year and any momentum gained in that time had all but disappeared. Croatia themselves were a very different side by the time Trippier would next line up against them in the summer of 2021, the game representing more business to be attended to rather than a full-on exorcism of demons. Even Germany in the round of 16 held less in the way of drama. That would be saved for much later on in the tournament.

As Trippier played that looped ball in for Luke Shaw to volley home for England in the second minute of the European Championship Final, it would have been almost poetic for it to be that moment to set them on the way. Again it wasn't to be as Trippier was the player sacrificed after Italy had equalised in the second half and the need to add more in attack emerged.

In the end, all that was passed along was the baton for another landmark memory to be filed away in that big drawer marked 'What if?'

While there was to be no international redemption for Trippier, 2021 was still an incredible year. Winning the La Liga title with Atlético Madrid may not have seemed plausible from the outset and yet they were able to capitalise where others faltered, holding firm in the home stretch, with key points against both Real Madrid and Barcelona as the former threatened to spoil the party. Winning those last few games of the season meant more in the way of relief over anything else, in the sense that it had all been far more straightforward earlier on in the season.

Being on the pitch during that run-in mattered more due to an imposed absence in February. Trippier had been banned for ten games due to infringing upon betting rules, divulging information of his imminent transfer to Atlético at the time to a group of friends who then placed money on it happening. Gambling and football have something of a shady relationship in that there is a paper-thin pretence of responsibility that gives way to an omnipresent bombardment with adverts, sponsorships and offers of incentives to appeal to a very specific kind of fan. Foolish and unjust though it may have been for him to do this in the first place, the existence of these betting markets alone is a much bigger problem.

Arriving back on English shores always seemed likely. Over the space of his two-year stay in Spain, persistent rumours of a move to Manchester United gave more than a hint that there would be another chapter to play out within Trippier's career. In terms of twists, heading off to St James' Park to play out wasn't in anyone's crystal ball at the start of the 2021/22 season. It's a new beginning in many ways, not least of all because the Newcastle project needed immediate attention before anything could be built in the longer term. The difference his goals made in terms of helping Newcastle to relative safety cannot be understated in terms of how much relegation would have set back the project at St James' Park. As far as foundations go, Trippier's inclusion in the team and the goals – from an unlikely position – that he can bring will be equally invaluable.

Before Newcastle and Madrid, before any of those moments in Europe and in major tournaments for England, it began in Burnley. Technically it began inside the Manchester City academy and then Barnsley, but it was the Clarets' Sean Dyche who put Trippier on the path to the Premier League. Tales of players not necessarily looking after themselves properly from a diet and a physical perspective at a young age aren't hard to come by. There often needs to be a guiding hand, one that can steer someone with the right amount of potential away from wasting it.

It's safe to say that Dyche has moulded many in a Burnley shirt. With Trippier arriving in 2011 at a club that already had a stint in the Premier League – as brief as it was surprising – Burnley needed a pick-up. In addition to their inability to return immediately to the top flight, there may have been a potential sense of being left behind with successive mid-table Championship finishes and both Owen Coyle and Eddie Howe jumping ship three seasons apart. It wouldn't take long for the direction of travel to change, with Trippier very much at the heart of the forward motion.

Being a star player for a side that eventually succumbs to relegation has a certain amount of credibility, even without the gloss of survival. Burnley scrambled for position in 2014/15 to ultimately be cast aside. Plucked of the two prominent feathers of that season in regard to Trippier and Danny Ings, it would have been all too easy for the Clarets to not return to the top flight. Too many teams – especially those less fancied – have their moment in the sun only to never be seen again. Turf Moor can't be forgotten that easily. Dyche transformed whatever money was available and spun it into obtaining and then retaining their status as a Premier League side, right up until the point he could no longer.

Ambitions further up the table don't require a different set of skills but they do open a door to a more distinctive playing criteria. Moving from clubs that have different targets has no effect on ability and yet the transformation is assumed to be instantaneous. Trippier's four seasons at Tottenham were among a period of gradual improvement that ultimately led to the biggest one-off game in club football. Mauricio Pochettino moulded his Spurs players into arguably one of the best English sides to never win a major trophy. This comes as absolutely no comfort.

To suggest that Spurs finished third in 2015/16 having been in a two-horse race is to select either wilful ignorance or something a little more venomous as far as the London club are concerned. Leicester won the league that year independently of those falling down around them; it just so happened that the noise surrounding a single game at Stamford Bridge spoke louder than anything else. Arsenal sliding into second on the final day of the season poured salt into an open wound. No shot at an always unlikely glory only to fall foul of an almost equally implausible embarrassment. As far as that part of London was concerned, another year of red rule and another laugh at the expense of their rivals. However, even if the writing wasn't in the record books that year, it was most certainly on the wall.

Bedding in takes time. Whether this is due to avoiding the scrutiny of a merciless media or something as simple as a manager giving a player the chance to learn the setup fully before throwing them in, a lot of signings take longer to be given the reins. Eighteen games across all two seasons was but a taste of the responsibilities that first-team football at the top level entailed before the opportunity presented itself. Manchester City's pursuit and acquisition of Kyle Walker left a hole at right-back behind him.

Over the course of Tripper's time as understudy to a first-team role, Spurs had taken centre stage and were shaking off one London rival to battle with another; Chelsea again the source of their pain during 2016/17. Yet these successive setbacks did nothing to deter the progress under Pochettino. By the following year they were among one of the most technically proficient, tactically astute teams in the division, fronted by a generational talisman in Harry Kane. By contrast Trippier wouldn't have had quite the same amount of headlines surrounding him; a goal in all of his Champions League starts during that campaign may have been a precursor of what was to follow.

How it all ended in the Wanda Metropolitano changes nothing in terms of how remarkable the run to the Champions League Final in 2019 was for Spurs. They were up against it in being paired with Inter Milan and Barcelona during the group stage to begin with, even more so after losing to both of them. A goal down to PSV Eindhoven away from home and it was a journey that could have been over before it even got going. The first step back was from the boot of Lucas Moura, whose own adventure would come full circle in the semi-final. Both he and Tottenham finally got off and running courtesy of a cross from Trippier. Missing the final two games in the group after winning at the fourth time of asking in the return match against PSV with injury, Trippier would have watched on in hope rather than expectation. Victory over Inter Milan was followed by an incredible late Moura equaliser at the Camp Nou. Pochettino labelled it 'mission impossible' following the final group game. They had clawed things back in the most unlikely of circumstances. Well, almost.

Borussia Dortmund were beaten without any of the precariousness of their group stage progression, only for all of that drama to return tenfold in the two ties that followed. After a fairly tame first leg with Manchester City in the quarter-final, all hell broke loose in the second. Trippier's contribution to one of the most pulsating Champions League games ever witnessed was – as far as the scoreboard is concerned – among the most vital. It was his corner that was put in by Fernando Llorente to give Spurs the goal that would see them through on away goals. With 14 minutes to go, that would have been enough in a game that had already seen numerous twists and turns. As ever, the cruellest moments in football are saved until the very last.

Raheem Sterling's disallowed stoppage-time goal exists in an emotional vacuum. The initial wild celebrations were to be ruined; even with an open roof such elation being ripped from the fans in the stadium had an audible astonishment to it. It was soon to be replaced by two distinct roars of amazement, one for what it meant and the other for the final whistle. One more opponent stood before Tottenham and the final. At the very least, there was no way things could possibly get any more intense, surely?

Aside from those in attendance and a scattering of fans of other clubs across London, that last half an hour in the Johan Cruyff Arena on 8 May 2019 is a representation to everyone why the game is so revered around the world. Three goals down at half-time is one thing, but there is nothing more dramatic than the last-minute winner. Moura will haunt the dreams of Ajax fans for years to come, much in the same way that Tottenham can look back to this particular high with a sense of poignancy. Sport has a unique power to drive such complex and overwhelming feelings to the fore and those post-match celebrations, specifically the interviews given by Pochettino himself, that mitigates all that comes after. Only ever celebrating the end result ignores the happiness that can be felt along the way.

Wayne Rooney's wonder strike against Arsenal at Goodison Park in October 2002 catapulted him to the epicentre of English football.

Charlie Adam celebrates his equalising goal in Blackpool's 2010 Championship play-off final victory.

Oleksandr Zinchenko bursts forward for Manchester City against Brighton at the Etihad in September 2019.

Gunnar Halle is chased down by Francis Benali during Oldham's incredible 4-3 victory over Southampton that kept them up in 1992/93.

Glenn Murray shapes to shoot as Brighton take all three points in their encounter with Bournemouth in December 2019.

Cesc Fabregas and Arsene Wenger celebrate Arsenal's equaliser against Manchester United at the Emirates in November 2007.

Nick Barmby and Dean Windass celebrate a goal in Hull's 2008 Championship play-off semi-final victory over Watford.

Chris Sutton goes wild after Jeremy Goss scores a famous goal to help Norwich eliminate Bayern Munich in the 1993 UEFA Cup.

Bukayo Saka driving Arsenal forward in their 4-2 Premier League victory over Leeds United in February 2021.

Jason Puncheon scores the opening goal of the 2016 FA Cup Final against Manchester United.

Robbie Savage hands a coin thrown toward him to an official as he prepares to take a corner at Villa Park in 2004.

Darren Bent is congratulated by his Sunderland team-mates after scoring against former club Spurs in April 2010.

Jermain Defoe celebrates a winning goal at Upton Park in January 2003.

Matt Holland patrolling the middle of the park in Charlton's game with Southampton at The Valley in May 2004.

Sol Campbell in the honorary redcurrant kit to mark the last season at Highbury in 2005/06.

Jan Åge Fjørtoft delivers his trademark aeroplane celebration after scoring against West Ham for Swindon in March 1994.

Alisson Becker points to the heavens following his dramatic last-minute goal against West Brom in 2021.

James Beattie is congratulated by Southampton team-mate Rory Delap after scoring against Wolves in 2004.

Patrick Vieira walking up to take the decisive penalty and his last kick as an Arsenal player against Manchester United in the 2005 FA Cup Final.

Robert Huth scores against Manchester City and brings Leicester one step closer to the Premier League title in 2016.

22

Paul Ince

SPORTING CONTESTS draw the most extreme and yet natural of comparisons. Single match-ups, be they club-specific or opposing players, become gladiatorial clashes for the ages. The hyperbole that is then leant into – by all forms of media – is nothing new. At most there has been a rise in the visibility and insistence on certain clashes as the news cycle has become increasingly dependent on fuelling those fires.

Football is inherently tribal. The what and the when dissolve in the face of the who. Victory takes on a very different context. Suddenly it's not about the scoreline and more about the incidental things that add up to victory. Winning battles becomes literal more than figurative. There's a silent understanding that the process of defeat has to be forceful. Regardless of not just the gaps that may exist in regard to ability but the size of them too; nothing will be given. This idea not only entertains the notion of violence as a pacifier, it courts it directly. A lack of ability can always be forgiven; the absence of fight is inexcusable.

What the game demands is attention. It takes hold and doesn't ever let go. Maybe that's why we're drawn to players who do similar things. Among the more elusive metaphors that everyone can definitely describe in no uncertain terms, grabbing the game by the scruff of the neck is definitely one of them. The flow of a football match is a rodeo that few can ever really lay hands on. So often it threatens to get out of control and so few are able to corral it in such a way. To assert themselves in the very epicentre of the game and allow everyone else around them to do their job.

The game doesn't have to be a conflict on a physical scale but there will come a point. Some teams will ensure that all of it is a struggle, a 90-minute slog in which even a second of relenting gives them the game. Others have neither the players nor the desire to get bogged down in such a way. For the very best there will come a time where both are called for. At the start of the Premier League and as it grew, more sides wanted to scrap than had the capability of playing, which is why Paul Ince was the perfect product of the era. Even so, long before he came along and well after he retired, the necessity of winning that midfield battle never goes away.

Images of victory that are anything but. The picture of a bloodied Ince after a goalless draw with Italy to send England to the 1998 World Cup is one that resonates deeply with those of a specific age; defiant and resolute, encompassing all that is supposed to be reflected within the English game, and doing what is necessary but also in such a way that feeds the national psyche. It's unlikely that the game would be remembered quite as fondly had England won comfortably. The issue with such a theoretical triumph is that their importance over time without substantial success will all be for naught.

Ince contested the midfield long before the Premier League was even born. His war wounds were front and centre well before 1992 and all that would come after. What he represented – before and after the First Division was eventually rebranded – was very much at the forefront of a new generation. As part of the tactical merry-go-round at the time, there were no defensive or attacking midfielders. The position required comprehensive coverage. An Ilford boy making his way through the ranks, if anyone was going to take West Ham forward into the 1990s and beyond it would be Ince. Except they didn't go forward, and in 1989 they were relegated. No doubt there would be clubs looking to take advantage of such a situation, such was his quality. This alone was perfectly understandable. It was the leak of a photo of Ince in a Manchester United shirt from the *Daily Express* while no formal transfer had been announced that angered the east Londoners. Ince had gone on holiday and expected everything to be sorted by the time he returned to England, to an incessant West Ham faithful. Hammers manager Lou Macari even left him out of the team, such was the strength of feeling. To no one's surprise, even after an initially failed medical, the move was officially announced not long afterward.

'The Class of '92' is one of the most iconic phrases in Premier League history. Manchester United's crop of youngsters, who it was thought you couldn't possibly win anything with, did go on to prove one pundit in particular spectacularly wrong, but it was not the team who had to end a 26-year-long title drought. Instead 1992 was indeed a pivotal year for those at Old Trafford as well as English football as a whole. Rather than the likes of David Beckham, Paul Scholes and Gary Neville this was all about Mark Hughes, Peter Schmeichel and Paul Ince. The sheer wave of talent that was about to break through would still have had some form of impact in shaping English football throughout the 1990s. Without that initial grounding, however, and with the weight of history pulling down on them, it would have been so much harder.

From having broken a barren spell to being desperate to have it all. Were it not for Aston Villa winning the League Cup in 1993/94, United would have captured the English domestic treble. The addition of Roy Keane into that midfield gave them a combative edge they didn't even need. It was the footballing equivalent of giving the Terminator an endless supply of bullets. Maybe that was part of the issue. They were so good and very clearly ahead of everyone else in those first two years of the Premier League that they needed to be taught a lesson.

For nearly three years, Manchester United had been untouchable. The one-two punch of Blackburn and Everton at the end of the 1994/95 season forced a reaction from Alex Ferguson. Had they managed to get over the line in either the Premier League or the FA Cup, it could have been chalked off as a blip. As far as the immaculate standards of what Ince himself had helped set at Old Trafford, failing to win them both in quick succession was a step too far. Blackburn had taken the Premier League by storm that year and with five games to go led by six points. West Ham looked to have done United a favour by beating Rovers, which allowed the title race to go to the last day. Upton Park again played host, only this time they had no intention of doing right by Ince.

United had to win as far as the mathematics were concerned. On an afternoon of assumptions, regardless of what was taken for granted elsewhere, they still had to go out there and get the job done at Upton Park. Whatever history Ince had with West Ham was nothing compared to that in the process of being made. The Hammers had a front-row seat for a humbling. Blackburn may have been beaten at Liverpool but Manchester United were blunted. With the league title heading to Ewood Park, the FA Cup Final offered an immediate reprieve. Rather than allowing United a helping hand, Everton kicked them when they were down. Though nobody could have seen it coming at the time, these defeats encouraged Ferguson to press on with integrating Nicky Butt and some of the other youth players coming into the team and move on from the names of the past. Ince had played his last game for Ferguson and would be moved on immediately.

Two seasons in Milan with Inter was an eye-opening experience, to which those with lesser talent would have fallen. Moving to Italy at this particular time was a combination of Ince taking his combative abilities and underlining a technical ability that was often overlooked. At a time when English players rarely moved abroad, making the switch to Serie A came as quite the surprise. When the move was announced United's fans were absolutely blindsided. If his departure from the country was unexpected, the return two years later would be even more shocking.

Footballing metaphors are often found lacking. The last piece of an actual jigsaw is at once something that completes the picture but is also the least important. When referred to in terms of putting together a team capable of winning, that emphasis is switched. There were a multitude of opinions when it came to Ince coming back to the Premier League, not least because of the shirt he would now be wearing. Roy Evans made the decision that he would be the player who could help bridge the gap between an extravagant attack and a lacklustre defence, and much to the surprise of everyone around the Premier League the former Manchester United midfielder was to be on patrol for Liverpool.

Even with Inter Milan in the middle, there was still a particular heat to a transfer like this. Michael Owen ran it back in reverse some years later and although the strength of feeling is enough to prevent direct movement between the clubs, neither fanbase is satisfied. As far as Manchester United were concerned Ince was *persona non grata*. Any lingering goodwill that there was surrounding his time at Old Trafford was eaten up by the sentiment offered by Ferguson himself. He doesn't admit to mistakes, in public certainly. But for so long Ince was defined by a nickname coined by his former manager: Big Time Charlie. Recorded in the dressing room for a documentary, the idea that he would feel the need to make a comment like that speaks volumes in and of itself. In a way it's the biggest compliment Ince ever received. To play for the clubs he had, it's essentially a prerequisite.

Confidence at the highest level is never in short supply. Players who don't have it don't make it. Success at Liverpool would have been the ultimate retort to the idea that he needed to be moved on from Old Trafford and given the weight of history, there's a self-belief that goes above and beyond to relish that kind of challenge. But it would take more than just one person to change the circumstances at Anfield. There were positive moments and bandages around the bigger picture. Ince celebrating against his old employers after scoring against them was one. It also opens up the stark parallel between those players who refuse to join in with any post-goal revelry. Some – Ince included – absolutely hate that aspect of the game. There is a fine line between respect and performative humbleness. When there was a point to prove this was his way of doing so. It didn't matter that it cost him the support of a fanbase who had all but discarded him anyway.

The overall under-achievment at Anfield came to a head when Gérard Houllier came in. Roy Evans had done well enough to steer the club after the disaster that was the Graeme Souness era and make them competitive but in terms of going up a level the time had come to move on. Ince was among his first casualties in that regard. After Ince had gone off injured in an FA Cup game at Old Trafford in which Liverpool surrendered a one-goal lead late on, the manager waited until the midfielder tried to challenge him about his training methods before asserting his authority. Already earmarked as part of the disappointments in previous years, Ince was then moved on in the summer.

Middlesbrough and Bryan Robson offered another chance and a familiar face with which to make a fresh start. Whether it was a sign of the times or just a slowing down of his favourable style of play, there were yellow cards in abundance during his time at the Riverside. A midfield consisting of Andy Townsend and Paul Gascoigne might have blossomed into something special some years earlier, but not in 2000. Of all the cards Ince received during that three-year spell, there was one in particular that hurt more than the rest, which meant he missed out on the FA Cup semi-final in 2001 and watched on as Arsenal got over the line 1-0. Those were the kind of games he lived for but they weren't coming along as regularly as they had been.

After leaving Middlesbrough for Wolverhampton Wanderers, the goal there was very clear: lifting Wolves up into the Premier League after so many years of trying. They were a club that had been left behind. The old gold in years gone by had been able to leave a much bigger mark in English football and needed some help getting back to where they belonged. Falling at the play-off hurdle on two separate occasions in between not even making it into the top six, this team had enough to run the gauntlet. Their demolition job of Sheffield United to win the 2003 play-off final at the Millennium Stadium left no room for ambiguity. They had a fanbase and a team ready for top-flight football. Wolves were back.

When it comes to the battle-hardened veteran, there's always one last job. One more time to roll up the sleeves and rediscover the magic that once was there. Despite possessing a team filled with talent more than good enough to make a mark, one by one they all went down. Joleon Lescott and Matt Murray were both out for the season, Mark Kennedy and Kenny Miller on the sidelines for extended patches. This left Paul Ince and his former Old Trafford colleague Denis Irwin outnumbered and outgunned. There was still time for one last hurrah in terms of a 1-0 victory over Manchester United at Molineux but it was a season all but rooted to the bottom.

Passion can't win matches alone. Without it though, there's no way of getting through to the point where victory is in sight. There are many unwritten rules of English football. Addendums that amount to nothing and yet are treated as gospel. Chief among them is the need for that kind of desire. Sometimes losing isn't the worst thing that can happen to a team. It's abandoning the fight. Paul Ince was more than just that, his influence bigger than any of the reputations he gained throughout that early part of his career. Fans need someone to go into battle with them. He was right there.

23

Darren Bent

BELIEF IS the current on which the game flows. It charges and changes everything. Whether it comes from the stands or someone closer to the action who refuses to accept defeat, that kind of spirit is contagious. When all else appears lost, a few defiant voices can change the mood. The first step towards any success is a conviction that it can be done and is the last thing to go. Fans lose faith in their team from time to time just as players do in their own ability. Only one of those has long-lasting effects, however.

The mechanics of a superstar are all very uninteresting. Repeating the same small processes over and over, to the point where they become second nature. Training is all about rhythm and making sure that when it comes to the game itself, thought processes are clear. The head overrules the heart. Form can become the adversary of this practice. When those same repetitive motions do not reap the same rewards, some go looking for it. Having a crisis of confidence has nothing to do with skill. It's all about reaching for something elusive that was there last week but isn't now. Strikers fall foul of this most of all, going from club to club as their reputation fluctuates. They don't change so much as the circumstances around them do.

Difficult times often find unique solutions, which maybe don't necessarily solve a problem in the moment but allow for much brighter things to come further down the road. There are few positives to be drawn from relegation, especially one that comes in the immediate aftermath of a season of such great pride and achievement. In 2002 Ipswich came crashing down just a year after having flown close to the summit of the Premier League table. Though Darren Bent's chances were limited, he still managed to score his first goal in the top flight and was on the bench when the Tractor Boys beat Inter Milan in a UEFA Cup tie earlier on that season. Over the next few years those crumbs of first-team football grew and grew, just as he began to hone his eye for goal. After four years and nearly 50 league goals for Ipswich as they were increasingly unable to get out of the Championship, Bent was ready for another chance at the top level.

Charlton were in theory the perfect club. They had stable management and a good team, exactly the environment for any young talent to come in and thrive. In that sense this was the ideal meeting of player and environment as Bent hit the ground running in spectacular fashion. A dream debut at the Stadium of Light in helping the Addicks to an impressive 3-1 win over Sunderland was followed up with a goal in each of his next three games. Out of the blocks and running, to say that the season revolved around him is almost an understatement. The rest of the team combined only scored four more than him in the league, with his 18 goals behind only Ruud van Nistelrooy and Thierry Henry in the rest of the division. With a World Cup on the horizon, there was room for an emerging Premier League talent to break through on to the international stage.

Sven-Göran Eriksson thought something similar, but had a completely different way of going about it.

It wasn't necessarily the inclusion of Theo Walcott in England's World Cup squad that hung over so many at the end of that season. Every major tournament has surprise selections but this one took that to an extreme. Picking a player who hadn't yet played a single Premier League game to join up with an international squad raised some eyebrows. What made it even worse for the likes of Bent, however, was that Walcott didn't play a single minute in the tournament. Being overlooked for someone considered to be a talent that couldn't be ignored is painful, less so if that player then completely gets discarded.

After the disappointment of the summer came the disaster of 2006/07. In trying to move in a different direction following the departure of long-serving manager Alan Curbishley, Charlton found themselves cut adrift. Once again Bent was their top scorer, albeit his tally was not quite as high as it had been previously, but once again he was far and away their only consistent threat. Thirteen league goals alone isn't quite enough to save a side from relegation but when the next best record is just three, it more than illustrates not just the gap in the squad at the time but also why they subsequently fell down collectively as a club.

Thirty-seven goals in two years at Charlton following on from his haul in the years prior at Ipswich should have been enough for the next step up to have been obvious. By the mid-2000s the distinction between buying from abroad versus paying more for domestic based players had already been set. English players, when they do move around the top flight, tend to break the bank much more than their continental counterparts. Bent's transfer to Tottenham seemed to fly in the face of this understanding.

Maybe it was part of the more modest nature of his previous club. There was also a critical cog in the hype machine – as it would become – notable by its absence. If Bent had scored at the rate he'd scored in the years later, when both the media cycle became much more rampant and social media played its part, then perhaps he would have enjoyed much more of the fanfare that his record warranted. As it was, Bent failed to capture the imagination like some of the other transfers going around at the time.

Up until this point, he had been the main man as far as his Premier League career had gone. At White Hart Lane he was very much part of a squad and trying to break through ahead of Robbie Keane and Dimitar Berbatov meant that he was going to have to hit the ground running in a matter of minutes. Playing in the last quarter of an hour of games meant either contributing when victories had already been secured or being unable to take what little chances came in the short time available. Not even getting on to the pitch as Tottenham beat Chelsea in the League Cup in March 2008 summed up his faded importance within the team, having been their record signing not seven months earlier. Being thrust into the spotlight while being sat on the bench didn't do much for anyone.

The 2008/09 season represented at the very least more opportunity. Both of the star strikers ahead of him in the pecking order departed, Keane to Liverpool and Berbatov to Manchester United. With those moves, more playing time meant more goals for Bent with 17 in all competitions as Spurs made their way back to Wembley for the League Cup Final. There was disappointment for a second year in terms of losing on penalties to Manchester United but at least this time he got on to the pitch. League form swung incredibly, for Spurs' poor start to the season left them potentially in the midst of a relegation battle before Harry Redknapp galvanised the squad and took them up to a respectable eighth position. Famous for a particular style of jovial man-management and always one for a quote, there were some choice words for Bent before the season was over.

The greed that strikers are often said to possess reflects beyond themselves. No matter how many they score, there will always be room for more. Whatever there is, it's never enough. It's an unquenchable thirst that permeates every level of football. The board expects it. Managers demand it. Fans want it. Below that, there is a baseline level of expectation. Week after week, finish after finish; right up until something glaring happens. Misses of a particular nature shock the system. A glitch in among the hat-tricks. When Bent headed wide late on during Spurs' 1-1 draw with Portsmouth in January 2009, it almost defied explanation. With all of the goal to aim at, in some ways it was harder to nod the ball past the post than it was to score. As ever in regard to such chances, there's no guarantee but it's highly likely that was the victory spurned. Games are decided by fine margins and forward players will always have to be within them.

Redknapp's demeanour when it came to talking to the media was one of a kind, especially for a manager during that time. Whereas so many want to give so little away, he cannot help himself. The iconic line 'My missus could have scored it' was nothing more than a throwaway. Not malicious within its intent and yet these things stick. Come the summer Bent would be moving away from White Hart Lane and in need of a rebrand. Sunderland and the Stadium of Light in particular would provide a welcome return to the emphasis and playing style he had enjoyed earlier on in his career. Once again a clear focal point rather than being on the periphery, the goals would return.

As a sign of the times, it took Twitter to make the move happen. Absent for Spurs' pre-season tour to China while protracted negotiations wore on, Bent took to social media to pour out his frustrations in no more than 140 characters, 'Do I wanna go to Hull? No. Do I wanna go to Stoke? No. Do I wanna go to Sunderland? Yes.' After a frustrating wait for the transfer to go through, there was no stopping him when the season actually started. Twenty-four goals in the Premier League blew away both the competition and expectations. If nothing else this season will be remembered for a single goal technically scored by Bent but assisted in the most bizarre way imaginable. During a game against Liverpool in late October, the result was settled by a strike that veered off course, having struck an inflatable beach ball thrown on to the pitch. On the whole there was a lot less to laugh about for Steve Bruce as inconsistencies at the other end of the pitch tempered Sunderland's hot form in front of goal. In spite of how Bent had performed, the team as a whole only managed to finish 13th.

Picking up from where Bent had left off in 2010/11, Sunderland's progress continued even further. With Asamoah Gyan having been brought in from Rennes and Danny Welbeck on loan from Manchester United, the Black Cats had a real attacking threat. Right at the point where everything looked rosy for Bruce, it all changed. Gérard Houllier and Aston Villa made their interest in taking Bent to Villa Park in January known. Seemingly overnight, the deal was done. A shock transfer request, bids approaching and then in excess of £20m and before anyone could catch their breath, Bent was heading to the Midlands.

Within a broken structure there has become an ugliness to spending. As the payments went up, the punishment for failure became alarmingly steep. The desperation to hang on to what was available as TV deals bloated became very palpable. At the heart of every transfer lies a balancing act. Every single one in the eyes of those watching from the stands only see it in a particular direction. Ability commands a fee and performance has its price, but the juxtaposition of the two don't always correlate. Aston Villa did the maths in regard to what relegation would do to them versus taking Bent from Sunderland and this was much more productive and cost-effective.

Exaggerated though the fee might have been, it worked. A winner on debut at home against Manchester City as well as a flurry of goals in April was enough to ensure Villa were well-placed come the end of the season. Bent had gone from a joke to a man in demand. As far as English Premier League strikers were concerned, the last two years had put him in the top category. Fabio Capello had overlooked his breakout season at Sunderland in terms of the 2010 World Cup but had suggested that he would be getting his chance afterwards. A ruptured ankle ligament in March 2012 and change in management for England cruelly closed that door.

Bent had arrived at Villa Park to do a specific job. As it turned out, that was all he was able to do. The 2012/13 season saw the emergence of Christian Benteke; all the while persistent injuries kept Bent from either challenging for a place or forming any kind of partnership. A season-long loan to Fulham never promised to see a return to the form he had previously been capable of. He did still manage to score a dramatic last-gasp equaliser at Old Trafford in a game that had been headlined by the sheer number of crosses David Moyes's team had thrown into the box. It was the breaking point in terms of the aura that Manchester United had built over the years, that a side who would finish 19th could do this to them at home. Goals in the Championship followed but this would be his last contribution in a Premier League game.

Darren Bent's story is as much about all of the clubs he played for and what they were going through as it was his own capacity for scoring goals. If anything, that part of his game has severely been overlooked as his record stands for itself, with six over the benchmark century that grants him membership of the Premier League 100 club. This puts him above the likes of Didier Drogba, Ruud van Nistelrooy and Fernando Torres. When it comes to getting the right amount of respect and potential reasons why, it goes a lot further than what Harry Redknapp's wife would do in front of goal.

24

Craig Bellamy

HOME IS more than where the heart is. It's a comfort that cannot be replicated elsewhere. That yearning for belonging extends to more than just football for without it nowhere is safe. It's more than just a place on a map, although that plays a very distinct part of it. The where matters much more than who ever will. There's a collective belief that regardless of what happens over the course of a football career, you'll always be tied to a certain place, and that place isn't necessarily the badge you wear on a shirt.

Identity goes so much deeper than the surface and it will not fully blossom in the absence of understanding or acceptance. In its place is a front, a visage of a personality that serves to protect and uphold whatever ideals matter the most. Every day there are standards to uphold. How they are set and how deep they go will vary constantly. Underneath all the conventions there is always a certain level of pride that people carry with them throughout the day, regardless of profession. Athletes of all distinctions often talk of being their harshest critic, having spent a lifetime abiding by a very specific set of values. At times these beliefs are all they have left.

Those who appear to be the most confrontational and antagonistic on face value are often looking for somewhere they can feel welcome. A place where they can be themselves, warts and all. Acceptance is the very foundation of how people operate on a day-to-day basis and that level of peace brings out the very best. Coaching is about cultivating personalities just as well as talent. Some have an abundance of both.

There will always be a disconnect between what came before and what comes after. As practices differ, the sense of something being lost along the way prevails. Either that or that the present generation will take it all for granted. Schoolboy and youth team contracts involved so much more than football and this was the last crop of players that would in addition to their training have to do things like clean boots, help out around the stadium and run any other errands that the club required. As coarse as this process could be at times, it left a mark on Craig Bellamy that would last for an entire career.

Being obsessed with the game means more than just watching highlights on a Saturday night or being able to go through the names of everyone on a specific team sheet. It's watching, studying, playing and learning. Even as a schoolboy absorbing the scraps of information given by those he was playing against, from the streets of Cardiff to the Bristol Rovers academy at nine years old. Two years later Bellamy transferred into the Norwich setup. This is where that formal training began, 'The hardest year of my life' as he later described it in his autobiography. Kids who go through football setups from an early age have a very different upbringing. This is the other side to the trade-off that is seen as so glamorous.

In dealing with those strong emotions running through Bellamy at the time, there are choices. Along with that severe longing for being closer to family, there was a sense of being seriously demoralised by the senior pro he was paired with. As a result, he began lashing out. Multiple breaches of discipline included breaking the arm of a goalkeeper during a training ground fight. Norwich spared his contract, not through any kind of mercy but because of the potential that he was showing as a player. Graduation through to the reserve side wasn't the only thing going on in his life at the time. Still a teenager himself, Bellamy was about to become a father. While the prospect of parenthood was apparently that which would turn his life around in one sense, it certainly wouldn't quieten him down.

Foregoing a regular life for that of a footballer is such a face-value trade. The rewards outweigh most of the obligations by quite some distance. Sacrifices have to be worth it and as such there remains a line. Bellamy was an extremist in this sense. His effort, talent and motivation would pay off because of the life he had given up as much as what was promised. It's not so much a sense of entitlement as it is an understanding that perseverance pays off. By the time he was in and around the Norwich first team, there were those who would try and bring him down a peg. They wouldn't be the first.

As high as the ceiling was for Bellamy at Carrow Road, he never played a single Premier League game for Norwich. The ultimate traveller – in terms of his record of the teams he played for – took a while to step into the wider footballing world. Injury took away the ability to make an impact upon the Norwich first team in the way that might have been a given. By the time he was ready to come back, it was time to leave. Coventry had sold one bright young talent in the form of Robbie Keane and were looking for another.

John Fashanu was a true character. In this story, the former Wimbledon striker played a key role in regard to events at Highfield Road, if only to push Bellamy in that direction. Without an agent, his advisers spoke with Fash ahead of a meeting with Coventry manager Gordon Strachan, which Fashanu then decided to attend. This apparently twisted Bellamy's arm and he became the Sky Blues' record signing in August 2000. If the way in which the transfer itself had gone through was absurd, it was certainly in line with what would happen for the rest of that season.

Coventry were performing Premier League escape acts long before Wigan came along and made it fashionable, but in 2000/01 the only magic left was to disappear completely. Four games across December was the longest unbeaten streak they managed to string together. With defeats coming thick and fast at the start of the season, they were in trouble from the very beginning. Aside from the absence of a few talismanic players and no one stepping into that mantle, the solidity that had kept them out in previous years had now cracked. Bellamy clashed with older members of the squad, being such a high-profile signing at such a young age. Strachan did his best to bring out the footballing qualities that were underneath all those layers, which included trying to break out of the fear that he would be re-injured. Fellow Welshman John Hartson arrived in January to provide some form of backup both on and off the pitch. Results never quite picked up at the rate they would need to, however, and Coventry were comfortably relegated come the end of the season. With the club needing to get his high wages off the books, Bellamy was off to Newcastle.

For all those who live and breathe football, few are as respected as Sir Bobby Robson. He had an incredible career both as a player and manager, travelling all across Europe. Coupled with his warmth of personality, his passing left a huge hole within the English game that can never be filled. He deserved more, certainly in terms of the team that was built during his time at St James' Park. Putting together the right amount of ability unfortunately is no guarantee of success. Even more damning, the wrong combination can undo a lot of hard work. There is no easy explanation for what happened during that period. Bellamy gets a nominal amount of the condemnation. Stories of dissension combine with a plausible level of opposition to create something powerful. If his reputation off the pitch lent itself to a very specific judgement, what happened on it was enough to come to a similar verdict.

Of all the modern mutations that make up European football, the Champions League somehow managed to pair together the esteem of a competition steeped in tradition as well as the excitement and allure that came with an increased level of prominence between those taking part. Their exploits during the 2002/03 season underline that. At a time where there were two group stages, progress was a lot more protracted just as failure was a lot more forgiving. Losing the first three games meant they were down but not quite out. Bellamy didn't even play a part until the very end thanks to a retrospective red card following a headbutt that wasn't spotted in real time. Victories over Juventus and Dynamo Kyiv gave them all a platform. It wasn't until Feyenoord that revival became reality.

Going away and needing to win is always a daunting prospect, especially when Feyenoord could have punched their own ticket to the next round with victory themselves. The home side were dumped from the competition even after having staged an improbable comeback. Throwing away a two-goal lead, Newcastle were still able to have the last laugh with Bellamy's late effort that somehow snuck into Patrick Lodewijks' near post after he had spilled Kieron Dyer's effort. Most teams think that their side doesn't do things the easy way. For Newcastle it's a way of life.

Another group stage, another red card. The fastest in Champions League history at the time, no less. There's a point about being competitive and having a certain amount of aggressive spirit, especially in these types of games, but this was indicative of a growing problem. Part of the failure for Newcastle to make that big leap was seen as the indiscipline of this young team. Luckily, Bellamy's second ban of the season didn't prove decisive in terms of their progress. With two games of the second group phase to go, Inter Milan and Barcelona would prove the sternest of tests. A point in Italy was good enough and showcased all the talents of Shearer and Bellamy as a duo. Defeat at home to the Spaniards saw Newcastle exit the tournament and left them once again cut off from reaching a higher level.

Bobby Robson's departure from St James' Park was both sombre and inevitable. Well before the days of Mike Ashley, Freddie Shepherd's attitude and running of the club was abrasive and cut-throat. Sir Bobby had been seen to have given his team too much freedom and that they needed to have a more authoritarian setup in order to get the best out of them. Graeme Souness was given the job of laying down the law. From the minute he arrived, a clash between him and Bellamy was inevitable. Public gestures and behind-the-scenes altercations were just the beginning.

In January 2005 everything came to a head. Souness claimed that Bellamy wasn't fit for Newcastle's 1-0 defeat to Arsenal. The story then became that he had refused to play on the wing. There was an immediate retort in front of the TV cameras, claiming that his manager was trying to get the fans to turn on him. A war of words being played out in public, hinging on Bellamy's displeasure at playing out of position and saying that he would fabricate injury to avoid doing so again. It was an impossible situation to come back from. A loan move to Celtic was green-lit as Souness stated that he would never play for Newcastle again. Things remained chaotic while the Welshman was in Scotland, with Dyer and Lee Bowyer coming to blows on the pitch during a game against Aston Villa. Problems at St James' went deeper than one player, yet his confrontational personality and off-field issues were alarmingly prominent.

Blackburn offered more than just another chance. With his former international manager Mark Hughes at the helm and international team-mate Robbie Savage in the squad, there were familiar faces who were able to get the best out of him. In a stop-start season, from the spring onward both Rovers and Bellamy hit top gear. A sixth-place finish in the league was more than had been previously expected. European football would return to Ewood Park but the lure of the Champions League and Liverpool proved too much to turn down. A £6m release clause in his contract allowed Rafa Benítez to take

Bellamy to Anfield. After delivering on the promise he had shown earlier on in his career, the Reds were hoping that his off-field antics were behind him. John Arne Riise would have loved for that to be the case.

Separating what are career and personal decisions can be difficult. Growing up supporting Liverpool meant the pull was always going to be too much for Bellamy to resist. A single year at Anfield, with a manager who didn't always see eye to eye with him, wasn't the dream he had in mind. Rafa was very different to Souness in that regard. There were no physical confrontations, quite the opposite. Never the most personable character, Benítez kept his distance, which can be off-putting. In terms of coaching and results, there was plenty of emotion on display as once again Liverpool were making their way through the Champions League. An infamous night out in Barcelona awaited, with a scoreline and scorers that couldn't have been scripted.

Team bonding nights out can either be tedious or nefarious affairs, depending on how much alcohol is involved. For Liverpool, just before their round of 16 tie, it was the latter. After an evening of politely – and then not so politely – trying to coerce Riise to sing karaoke, Bellamy burst into his hotel room later that evening with a golf club. One of the wildest conceits to football glory in history. After all of this, Liverpool defeated the reigning champions 2-1 at the Camp Nou. The goalscorers that night were, of course, Bellamy and Riise. Getting through that tie sent the Reds on course for another final and a rematch with AC Milan just two years after beating them to win a fifth European Cup in Istanbul. Bellamy was on the bench for the Athens showpiece and failed to make it on to the pitch even with the Reds trailing 2-0. That summer Liverpool were dipping into the transfer market once again, opening the exit door and allowing him to go to West Ham.

Muscle tears and strains meant for very little in terms of playing time at Upton Park, and a year and a half spent more with the physio than his team-mates. Four goals in the winter months of 2008 suggested all that was behind him and prompted interest from both Spurs and Manchester City. Bellamy reunited with Mark Hughes at the City of Manchester Stadium, as it was then known, for a project and a team looking to make waves at the upper reaches of the Premier League table. City been in the shadows for too long, having the perfect – or rather the worst kind of – seat to watch as Alex Ferguson conquered all before him. The job was now to draw the line. City had beaten Manchester United before in the Premier League but this wasn't about winning or losing, it was about sending a message and giving them something to think about in the future. Starved of – and craving – attention, Bellamy was the perfect player to give them an edge and put them into the spotlight.

As time ticks on, people get left behind. Manchester City's fifth-place finish in 2009/10 was the first time they had been in the top five since the early 1990s. The sheer amount of money involved meant expectations were high and margins were thin, making the departure of Hughes inevitable. Not for the first time, in Roberto Mancini City had a manager who did not mesh well with Bellamy. On the periphery of an ever-growing squad and being frozen out, he went back to the only place he knew he would be welcome.

Cardiff City were caught in a holding pattern; good enough throughout the Championship season but found wanting in the play-offs. Bellamy's arrival was seen as a catalyst that could change their fortunes and his late-season form got them to the brink of automatic promotion. Five points from the last four games ended that chance, after which Reading visited the Cardiff City Stadium and finished them off for another season. The wait for promotion continued. In the meantime, a face from the past offered another chance at a former club. When Kenny Dalglish and Liverpool showed their interest, this was more the boyhood dream Bellamy had been envisioning.

Liverpool were a very different prospect in 2011 compared to 2007. Although no longer competing for the top prize in Europe, there was still enough pride and talent there to try and reclaim some of the ground that had been lost in between. The cup competitions that year saw Bellamy at his very best. Days after the passing of Gary Speed, Liverpool travelled to Chelsea in the quarter-final of the League Cup. His emotions were brought to bear in the immediate aftermath of that. It was impossible not to.

The performances he put in during that time were of a rawness that spoke to the panacea that football can provide. Emotions are overwhelmingly complicated; the game itself is very simple. He was hurting and wanting to take it out on Chelsea. Nothing could have stopped him that night. Very similar was the semi-final second leg against Manchester City, where Bellamy poured every single drop he had left that night into getting the Reds over the line and through to Wembley. Later on that season in the FA Cup the stage was set again. To assist Andy Carroll for a winner in the sem-final was sweet enough; that it was against Everton only added to the joy.

After Kenny Dalglish was dismissed at Liverpool and Brendan Rodgers came in, there was a decision to make. After all the emotion following the death of his Wales team-mate, Bellamy made the choice that he would come home for good. This time it was for real. Cardiff could no longer be held back after topping the table from November onwards. There were no standout heroics, no need for any dramatic turnarounds, just a team and a fanbase that had finally been granted their tilt at the top. The rebranding of the Bluebirds to playing in red was seen as a strange decision to say the least but the Welsh capital would finally be hosting Premier League football for the first time in 2013.

That last season was the closing of a book that had seen it all. Scoring against Norwich in February 2014 made

Bellamy the first player to score for seven different clubs in the Premier League.

Outspoken, unconstrained and unapologetic. Since retirement, Bellamy has opened up about the issues that plagued his career and the motivations behind what were often impudent actions. It was that stubborn mentality that allowed him to be the player he was and to go to the places he did. After all that, he got to go home.

25

Nigel Martyn

POPULARITY IS not a referendum on quality. Talent has a voice and it speaks for itself. Between the two exists a fine line. Holding on to credibility is difficult in a game that is prepared to punish at a moment's notice. Every would-be hero is but a moment away from becoming the villain. The longer you stay the more likely that is. All the pressures and ever-changing minutiae, along with the physical betrayal that comes with ageing, reduce those chances down to near zero.

In a sense it's easier to dislike than it is to like, certainly based on sheer volume of experience. There are boundless opportunities to sour on someone, whereas atonement in the mind's eye is a lot harder. Careers are what happens when perfectly good footballers are put through the grind of frustration, angst and disappointment, especially if you're a goalkeeper.

Partly because of their proximity, they are the last line of defence but the first line of abuse. Nowhere to hide with challenges coming from all angles. That's when those cries of derision from the opposition fans can become like badges of honour. Nothing ever stuck to Nigel Martyn in terms of vilification. The level of respect he carried around with him throughout his career wasn't limited to partisan support, not that it mattered one way or the other. Universal acclaim is almost unobtainable to those whose only goal is not to concede any. Almost.

Every team needs a player that makes everything feel easier, even if it isn't all that simple in the moment. Asking questions of a team requires – at times – desperate answers. Whether it be a brief period of a game or sustained throughout the 90 minutes, someone will have to put their hand up eventually. These responses don't need to be perfect, though they need to be consistent, for the job is more about composure than capacity. Being able to hold out one end for just long enough to pose something decisive at the other.

The value of a goalkeeper has always been hard to measure in that ideally they would not be called into action enough. In between the qualities required to consistently perform the role itself, the reliance on those in front and that particular balancing act mean that teams need to pay for a lot more than just a safe pair of hands. Then there's the mentality that comes into play; fully gauging the temperament of someone that needs to be able to deal with a bombardment of pressure or be called upon for one crucial moment. The rare few who can keep their heads above all else and command those in front of them with a weight of authority are worth their weight in gold.

Though it's probably one of the most important positions on the pitch to buy for, it's not a signing that holds the same kind of glamour as unveiling a potential superstar striker. As such, there's not ever quite the same amount of money invested in those whose job it is to stop goals as there is those who score them, which makes Martyn becoming British football's first £1m goalkeeper when joining Crystal Palace from Bristol Rovers in 1989 all the more impressive. If there were any doubts about that investment, none would be left by the time he moved on from Selhurst Park after 272 games for the Eagles during a frenetic time for the club. Even before the Premier League came into existence, he was a part of the Palace side that got to the 1990 FA Cup Final. The 3-3 draw that set up Manchester

United winning in a replay still remains – for very different reasons – a vital moment in the history of both clubs. Incredibly, this was the closest Martyn got to a major trophy (with all due respect to the Zenith Data Systems Cup victory in 1991).

The Premier League came and went. Relegation in 1993 was followed by promotion in 1994 and then another exit ensued in 1995. Both times will have stung particularly harshly for two wild sets of circumstances. The first involved an extraordinary turnaround by Oldham with three games to go that saw Crystal Palace go down on goal difference whereas the latter demotion came about due to a restructuring of the division to reduce the number of teams in it. Going from 22 teams down to just 20 meant widening the drop zone up to four places. Somebody had to be that unfortunate extra; it just had to be Palace.

Another opportunity to return to the top flight wouldn't be long in coming. Finishing third in the First Division as it was then in 1996, once Palace had dispatched Charlton in the play-off semi-final, Wembley was the reward. Leicester represented a big challenge, with a fair share of what would come to be recognisable faces in and around their line-up. Emile Heskey, Muzzy Izzet, Neil Lennon, even the manager Martin O'Neill himself, all had a much larger part to play. In order to do that they would have to overcome a Palace side filled with experience and one that took the lead early and held onto it until the end was nearly in sight. With only 15 minutes left on the clock as the game entered its final phase, the Foxes would be presented with a chance for an equaliser from the penalty spot. Martyn got a hand to the shot but not enough to prevent Garry Parker's strike from reaching the bottom corner. If the timing of their first goal was painful, how it ended will have been excruciating.

Approaching the very end of extra time, penalties were looming, to the point where O'Neill had taken off Kevin Poole in goal and brought on the imposing frame of Zeljko Kalac. At the other end, Martyn could have been looking to get even closer to the upcoming spot kicks than he had done earlier, only to see the ball flying past him into the top corner of his net. Martyn was rooted to his spot with the ball beyond him in a flash. Steve Claridge with virtually the last kick of the game had decided it for everyone else. It would be Leicester who would be playing Premier League football in 1996/97. So too – as it turned out – would Martyn.

Leeds United were the team of the past that were building for the future. As the last side to win the top flight before it morphed into the Premier League, they were bringing Martyn in to help a new generation aim for something similar. Whatever promise there was, it all went to pieces rather dramatically over the course of a September afternoon against Manchester United. The fallout of a 4-0 beatdown was the departure of Howard Wilkinson, whose place in football remains frozen in time. In guiding Leeds to that 1992 First Division title, he remains the last English manager to win the English top flight at the time of publication and will likely have that record through the 2020s and beyond.

If Wilkinson was removed from his position because by 1996 time had passed him by, his replacement wasn't exactly someone who had new ideas. Fundamentals remain the same by definition. George Graham had successfully coached a very defined, old-school style at Arsenal and imprinted it on Leeds. Coming in partway through a season and taking Leeds to a finish of 11th, with just 38 goals conceded, showed how quickly these methods had been adopted. But it was the goals scored column that raised the most eyebrows with 28 across a whole campaign. Essentially whenever Leeds played that year, between Martyn and his opposite number – whomever that may have been each week – one of them was all but guaranteed a clean sheet.

The space left behind when certain people vacate it can lead to a particularly astonishing set of circumstances. David O'Leary became front and centre of a timeline that could never have been foreseen. Differences in the dugout often led to polarising attitudes on the pitch. Partly due to the players that they had at their disposal – specifically those coming through from the youth team – this particular upturn was more than just a new manager bounce. Dynamism up front and integrity at the back was provided by Lucas Radebe, Ian Harte, Alf-Inge Haaland and an emerging Jonathan Woodgate playing their part ahead of an ever-consistent Martyn. Despite the brakes being loosened at one end in terms of scoring over double the amount of goals they had managed the previous season, Leeds were still resolute at the back and conceded fewer than eventual champions Manchester United. Their fourth-placed finish in 1998/99 also unlocked the door to European football. And so began the story of how a team that flew so high could come crashing down so badly.

Of all the things that were either introduced or evolved during the early 21st century, the idea of becoming at one with a club's finances ranks among the very worst. Just as the figures climbed so high that the everyday fan could no longer keep up, they became an integral part of the conversation. What was once a discussion about form, ability and everything that took place on the pitch soon gave way to wage bills and balance sheets. The need to qualify for the Champions League idealistically grew out of an idea to play in the biggest competition and compete against the best in Europe. For the fans it was about a packed-out Elland Road showcased in front of the whole world. As far as the hierarchy were concerned, it had nothing to do with prestige and everything to do with money. Over the years there have been many teams that have gambled with their future in terms of paying over the odds for a specific player or selecting a particular manager. Never had the phrase been so literal.

Leeds were far from a long shot in terms of Champions League football. They were one of the most exciting teams in the country, if not the continent, and up until Christmas 1999 it was looking like a Premier League title challenge was in the offing. Michael Bridges was having a breakthrough season before injuries took their toll, with 19 league goals to put Leeds in a position alongside Manchester United and Arsenal. Over the course of the season their league form would tail off but not enough to see them ever really out of the top four. But what happened in the Premier League after April took a back seat to genuine tragedy.

Tribalism flows through football, touching almost every aspect of it. With that there is aggression and intimidation; a hostile atmosphere, making sure that opponents don't feel welcome or comfortable. It's all very primal. Where that behaviour should end is before it develops into violence. There should be no circumstance in which people go to watch a game and don't come back. Kevin Speight and Chris Loftus travelled to Istanbul in the run up to Leeds' 2000 UEFA Cup semi-final with Galatasaray and were stabbed to death. What played out paled in comparison. It was a game that shouldn't have been played. Leeds were knocked out after an emotional return leg in which the club banned all travelling support. The grief from such a horrific event encompasses more than just the passage of time and what happened in the hereafter. That despicable side of the game is as far removed from the comfort it can bring and the connections it can make. Football moved on, the game continued apace as it ever does. Leeds, marching on together, progressed into a campaign in whichever small way they could possibly help the healing process.

A year later Leeds hosted Deportivo La Coruña and their players put them on the verge of greatness. Belief was in the air that night. It could almost be touched. In reaching the semi-finals of the Champions League they had risen to a height few had thought possible. It wasn't losing to Valencia that brought them back down. Not qualifying for the competition the following season was about to take its toll. Rio Ferdinand arriving for £18m in the summer of 2000 wasn't what broke the bank. A year later, Seth Johnson's contract talks were much more indicative. Johnson was earning £5,000 per week at Derby but the heavily reputed £30,000 that he was offered gave more of an indication of just how much the club itself was ready to burst.

From the Champions League to the First Division in just three years, and Martyn was long gone by the time relegation was confirmed. The emergence of Paul Robinson meant he had been pushed down to the bench. Leeds fans would eventually honour Martyn with a place in their all-time team, with his inclusion being the only player from after Don Revie's tenure. Moving on to Everton wasn't meant to be the start of another glorious chapter. Having been playing for 16 years at this point, the idea at Goodison was initially to be the understudy to Richard Wright, but the young stopper's season-long injury thrust Martyn back into the action. After making such an impression at his previous two clubs, Martyn was ready for a hat-trick.

Finishing just one place above the relegation zone in 2003/04 – even if they weren't in immediate danger – everyone at Goodison Park knew that there had to be a recovery. The sale of Wayne Rooney to Manchester United before the new season left a sense of trepidation as to what would await and how far they could really go. Gatecrashing the top four might not have been predicted by even the most ardent Toffees, but doing so came on the back of an immense defensive performance. Marytn only conceded 26 goals that season. Four of them came in the opening game. Fourteen clean sheets was an emphatic lockdown of the opposition attacks but also enough to obtain fourth spot and a place in the Champions League. At the age of 38, it was to be Martyn's last full season before calling it a day.

As the Premier League grew and hyperbole increased, there's something to be said for those players who just got on with it and deserved much greater fanfare but had little time for it. Sitting behind David Seaman throughout the 1990s denied Martyn the chance to do for England what he had done at club level but at no point did his standards or attitude ever drop. Every team should have someone like Nigel Martyn but only a fortunate few do. Similarly every player is lucky if he is well remembered at one club, let alone all of them.

26

Jermain Defoe

SWIPE THROUGH a catalogue of history and you'll notice what changes. There's something to be said within that, however, in terms of what stays the same. Longevity means a lot, especially for a position that has no time for the passing of time, both in terms of players getting older and actual minutes left on the clock. It's a game of self-imposed deception. Chances come and go, but they have to believe there will always be another one. Be ready for something that will in all likelihood never come in the knowledge that in the small margin where it does, it has to be taken. Even then the mantra has to be, they will get to have another go.

Roles are varied, on and off the pitch. Even the player who does the same thing throughout can be multiple different things to many different people, all within a single fanbase. Rival supporters will typecast even the most amiable personality as the villain by default. In the theatre of football you can be the starring role or a bit-part player, antagonist or protagonist, all within the space of a single 90 minutes. The longer a career spans, the more people they become. With all these preconceptions and misconceptions it would be hard for an individual to stay true to themselves. Hard, but not impossible.

Jermain Defoe broke records from the very beginning. Not long after making his first-team debut for West Ham in 2000, he joined up with a Bournemouth side in need of something special. Scoring away at Stoke in a 2-1 defeat was not the most auspicious of starts but it began a run of consecutive games with a goal that equalled the post-war record of ten in a row. Nearly two decades later he would be reunited with Bournemouth in the Premier League but in that moment, 18 goals for the season foretold of a bright future and going back to Upton Park to be integrated into a side that boasted a plethora of bright young English talent. The idea that this all ended with relegation seems unfathomable.

Rio Ferdinand was the first domino to fall. This – among other things – led to Harry Redknapp's departure. At the top end of the Premier League, money was beginning to talk louder than it ever had before. The Hammers had cultivated and assembled a team that would go on to win so much, just not in the famous claret and blue. The £18m offered by Leeds for Ferdinand was even for the time such an eye-watering figure. By the time Defoe returned and was ready to contribute, Glenn Roeder was in the dugout. Redknapp voiced his concerns about the money available to improve the team very publicly, which prompted alarm bells even before his departure. In the summer of 2001, Frank Lampard left for Chelsea, later followed to Stamford Bridge by Joe Cole and Glen Johnson, while Michael Carrick eventually moved to Tottenham. What was even more remarkable about the relegation of a side that was supposedly too good to go down was just that. The last of those names were all still there when it happened, in addition to Defoe, Paolo Di Canio and David James. Sure enough the fruits of the West Ham academy were to be picked by others, but it wasn't until everything had gone rotten in the first place.

On the face of it everything had carried on as normal. Defoe was the perfect impact player, being used mainly as an option from off the bench but still scoring enough to lead them in the league in 2001/02. Coupled with West Ham's seventh-place finish there was very little indication of what was to come.

From the start it seemed inconceivable that West Ham could go down, even in spite of their horrible beginning. Two points from the first six games, including back-to-back home defeats to Charlton and West Brom, meant that they had not so much stumbled out the blocks as outright fallen over. Teams have poor starts all the time and are able to restore a sense of balance, yet West Ham never seemed to get upright again until it was too late. The relegation itself was remarkable, not least of all because their tally of 42 points remains the highest that has ever seen a team go down after the Premier League became a 20-team division. If their fans were struggling to accept what had happened, 24 hours later came another hammer blow. Defoe wanted out.

From the outside looking in, there was an abundance of talent that deserved to be playing at a higher level. As far as West Ham fans were concerned they were simply being abandoned. Even the most begrudging of supporters might have come around to the exodus that was to come, but not in the immediate aftermath of an already open wound. Cole, Johnson, James, Frédéric Kanouté and Trevor Sinclair all left that summer. Defoe not only stayed for the first half of the season but ended up being their top scorer in the First Division. There was also the curious case of a bizarre spate of disciplinary issues that led to him accumulating the majority of his career red cards in just six months. The eventual move to White Hart Lane in January finally put a line under a period of which he later spoke about his deep regret.

For a variety of reasons, Tottenham in the 2000s were a level above what had come before. Defoe joined at very much a bridge that would eventually see them shake off certain bad habits and tendencies, potentially only to form others at a higher level. To start with David Pleat in the 21st century – as respected as he was – only underlined what needed to change. Jacques Santini is another who falls down a particular rabbit hole to join the most obscure Premier League managers of all time. The man who replaced him may very well have set something in motion.

Martin Jol might very well be too amiable to get any credit. Football is such a cut-throat game with heartless people making ruthless decisions. His Tottenham team were moulded in his image to some degree. Certainly the football they played and the players who were at the club began to turn the tide of relative mid-table mediocrity. The problem for Defoe was that for every advancement they made, there was another face added to a crowd looking to replace him. First there was Robbie Keane. His eventual partnership with Dimitar Berbatov became impenetrable. Alongside them were a rotating cast of characters who were left with nothing more than taking Defoe's minutes from the bench. Despite having vowed to fight for his place upon the arrival of Darren Bent, he was very much in the shop window. Now at Portsmouth, Harry Redknapp – known for his more serious browsing – was very much interested.

There was no element of Defoe having to prove himself as a Premier League striker, yet his start to life at Fratton Park was about as emphatic as it could have been. Eight goals in the first seven games underlined an ability that may have been overlooked during his time coming off the bench for Spurs. At Portsmouth there were no such restrictions, other than the one that prevented him from contributing to their FA Cup triumph. Cup-tied after having played in a previous round, Defoe had to sit out and watch as Pompey went the distance. Not only that, his old Spurs team-mates were celebrating beating Chelsea in the League Cup Final little over a month after he left them. If there was a disconnect between the player and the team that had done so well to bring silverware to Fratton Park, in the eyes of the fans it was one that was only going to get bigger.

Even before Defoe decided to take his leave in January and head back to Tottenham, a sorry chapter in Portsmouth's history had already been set in motion as they fell from FA Cup glory to the fourth tier of English football in just six seasons. Seen as turning his back on the fans who had taken to him after such a quick turnaround and following Redknapp leaving a sinking ship, Defoe's opinion was that Pompey didn't try that hard to keep him. After ankle trouble kept him out of what remained of 2008/09, by the next season both he and Spurs were ready to go. This time with no horrific start to recover from, all the focus was on landing a Champions League berth. Competing with them in that regard would be a Manchester City side rapidly on the rise. Forever the immaculate finisher, Defoe helped himself to 18 league goals, including being the first person since Alan Shearer to help himself to five in a Premier League game as Tottenham destroyed Wigan 9-1. What's more, being able to rekindle the partnership that began at Fratton Park, Peter Crouch's inclusion in the team was enough to push them on to fourth spot, including a stirring performance at the Etihad that got them over the line.

Defoe's remaining years at Tottenham continued as they had before he left. Manchester City leapfrogged them – as well as everyone else – and pushed them to the outside looking in as far as the top four was concerned. The goals kept coming even as the cast around him changed. Emmanuel Adebayor still had something left to prove and Gareth Bale emerged as a world-class talent. At this point the idea that Redknapp could take Spurs no further meant a different direction entirely. André Villas-Boas came in with a dented reputation and a point to prove. There was also the matter of a heavy chunk of change in Tottenham's back pocket following the transfer of Bale. Replacing one player of elite level quality with four or five just below that is fine in theory but of all the transfers that came through at the time only Christian Eriksen made the grade. With such a renovation going on at White Hart Lane, the call came out to see if Defoe would like a change of scenery himself.

Drake's presence in football is a surprising one. Involved with Toronto FC, the rapper himself ushered Defoe to come over and make a name for himself across the Atlantic. While his goal record there was more than favourable, it didn't carry the weight it might have done elsewhere. Moving out of England carries with it a certain disregard. Part of the arrogance of the Premier League means that when players leave, they disappear from relevance. Coupled with the impression that MLS is seen as somewhere just before retirement and for a few months there was a disconnect. A year later he was back, this time at the Stadium of Light. Sunderland needed assistance in getting clear of the drop zone and all eyes were on Defoe to see whether he still had it. One strike was all he needed to prove any doubters wrong.

In a nothing encounter it would have been incredible. During a must-win game against Newcastle, it took off on to a whole other level. He even teared up after burying it, the emotion of everything becoming too strong. Sunderland rejuvenated Defoe in a way that few could have ever predicted. It wasn't just about a player coming to the latter stages of his career and showing he still had the finishing touches. Not about reclaiming a place in the England squad or any long-lost milestone that he continue to attain. It was about a little boy. Bradley Lowery was a mascot at the Stadium of Light when they first met. The two struck up a friendship that warmed the hearts of a nation. The time they spent together helped to raise money but more importantly helped fill those moments with a special bond, a meaningful connection. Whenever Jermain Defoe talked about him that was what always stood out. Football shelters from that sort of pain, or at least it tries.

27

Ruud Gullit

A SINGLE spark is all it takes. Given the right amount of fuel and space to breathe, a fire can rise that engulfs all that before it. The Premier League was a new lick of paint. Nothing much had changed in terms of the football being played and the teams themselves. It was high in profile but not in substance. The level of talent and coaching available at the time had potential but was ultimately limited. What it needed was that ignition, something to propel it forth into the modern age. That was the arrival of Ruud Gullit.

Whether it be defiance or flat-out ignorance, where the continent led England followed, eventually. What tactical gridlock that previously existed relied on what was readily available at the time. There just weren't anywhere near the number of players to play in any of the ways that were readily on show from the 2010s and beyond. During the course of that evolution that gap has narrowed. English football culture remains very headstrong in the kind of football it collectively enjoys, yet it has adapted and embraced some of the differing ways of playing that have brought joy to a variety of setup. The cultivation of cosmopolitan ideals mixing with more traditional values in such a way has become part of a process that once initiated cannot be halted. Which begs the question: how did it all start?

Glenn Hoddle matters. Not least of all because he was one of the few who played to such a different rhythm that he could lay claim to being among the forefathers of the technical transition which was to come. His time at Chelsea occupies a quaint period in their history which if nothing else exists to unintentionally set the groundwork for what was to come. Of all the pieces that could ever have been put into place, Gullit was arguably the most important. What he did personally was enough; the impact of his arrival spoke volumes and events that transpired afterwards carved a very different path, all of which add up to one of the single most influential transfers in English football history.

In 1995 the Premier League was still in its infancy. Eyes of an eager, envious public – or at least those with a vested interest – perhaps for the only time ever, looked abroad. The sentiment around Italian football during this time was a mixture of many things. Partly due to a warm feeling from Italia '90, partly due to the very legitimate fact of the talent that was on show – it really did have everything. There was also still just enough in the way of a lack of common knowledge for it to hold a very exotic, intoxicating place within the heart of the average fan. Channel 4 has a lot to do with that. James Richardson having a coffee while rifling through the iconic pink pages of *La Gazzetta dello Sport* (among others) remains a fond memory for all those of a certain age.

Securing a signing of such significance meant a lot to the league as a whole but it carried more weight for Chelsea. The club they became was very much not that which they were, to the point that this was such an important step in that direction. Winning is a potent force, contagious to the point that those who don't possess certain skills are still able to fill a trophy cabinet. Different from the idea of having a specific mental strength while still reflecting on a singular mindset. Though it can be taught, the method is very much real-time. As such, bringing in players with the required credentials is key. With numerous league titles in both Holland and Italy, Gullit was the perfect candidate. A former Ballon d'Or winner could add an ingredient to the setup at Stamford Bridge that no one else at the club had. Even in being moved out of AC Milan a year before and going to Sampdoria to help them win the Italian Cup, on par with his playing ability was the crucial fact that he knew what it took.

The hardest thing to do when it comes to making the leap as a football club is that initial jump. By default, there are going to be a few teams with similar ideas that are also better equipped to win things, even before getting to those with vast resources that are trying to continue the process rather than get it started. That first season was very much an adjustment period in the sense that Gullit's ability was slightly held back by a lack of it around him. If not necessarily skill, certainly the kind of anticipation and understanding that he was used to. Playing out across the training sessions at Chelsea that season was a drop in the ocean of what was to come.

Chelsea finishing 11th in 1996 was par for the course at the time. Nearly three decades later and they've yet to again finish outside the top ten. It was the FA Cup that offered possibilities. Knockout competition presents the scope for disruption. At the semi-final stage everything is up for grabs. Across the course of a season, there was little hope at the time of reaching the level of a team like Manchester United. In a one-off game, however, anything can happen. As it was, Andy Cole and David Beckham would cancel out Gullit's opening effort. The following season, not only would he be back but have a greater say in matters than anyone could ever have predicted.

Hoddle leaving to take over the England team could easily have been such a backward step. Rather than disrupting what was being built at the time, it accelerated progress. Appointing a player-manager from within rather than trying to secure one of the bigger names elsewhere presented a dilemma. How many bigger names were there than Gullit at the time? If nothing else, the list of players who joined the club over the course of the next six months would have been enough to demonstrate

Gullit's influence over the transformation that was about to occur: Gianluca Vialli, Roberto Di Matteo, Frank Leboeuf and Gianfranco Zola. During a time without transfer windows, this still has to go down as one of the most successful set of signings a club could ever make.

There are many different paths to victory. In football, the first and only real criteria that must be filled is that key factor. Within the margins for error come questions of style. Defensive, cautious managers will try and drag their team over the line by any means necessary. Gullit didn't play the game like that, nor would his teams. The term 'sexy football' was something he had originated during his time as a pundit for the BBC in 1996 and would follow him around for the rest of his career. At the very least it was something different, playing with a blend of continental flair and nonchalance that very much went against the hard-nosed rigours of English football. Whether it was taken lightly or seen as something of a fad, the impact this solitary season would have on Chelsea was groundbreaking.

In May 1997, Gullit broke the mould. Not only did he end Chelsea's 26-year wait for a trophy by winning the FA Cup, he also became the first black manager to win a major British trophy as well as the first from outside of the UK. Among the vast swathes of changes that were to come in terms of the globalisation of English football, Gullit was the very first. Finals can be tense, tentative affairs that really draw out the pressure. Di Matteo made sure this wouldn't be the case for Chelsea, driving through the heart of the Middlesbrough team and scoring after just 42 seconds. In a season in which little went right for Boro, having already lost one cup final and being relegated due to a points deduction, the sight of Fabrizio Ravanelli going off after 24 minutes might have been the end of it. As it was, the scoreline remained close until Eddie Newton capped off a famous victory ten minutes before time. As fans, the team and the manager celebrated at Wembley that day, it was impossible to contemplate the idea that ten months later Gullit would be sacked.

On top of what winning does to the rest of the team, it should also buy time with the board. Managers go through dips in form just like players do, except the consequences are much greater. With a trophy or two in the bank, there should always be some credit available, however. All of this and Chelsea weren't even in trouble. In fact they were second in the table when Gullit was dismissed. Ken Bates was a very different owner to the man who would come in next at Stamford Bridge but one of the things they had in common was a ruthlessness when it came to chopping and changing managers. This sacking – as shocking as it was – set the tone for what was to become a recurring theme.

It didn't take long for Gullit to be back in management. Newcastle had a reputation earlier in the 1990s for being the great entertainers and as such, Gullit's brand of football on paper was the perfect fit. After having been discarded in such a way at Chelsea, there might have been more of a point to prove than in normal circumstances. As ever it was the FA Cup that provided the biggest cause for optimism during that 1998/99 season. For both the club and the manager it was a chance to right some wrongs. Things might have still spiralled out of control as they did but at the very least Newcastle would have had their success. Having gone so close so many times during the decade, for Gullit to be the one to get them over the line and end that trophy drought would have been so sweet. To prevent one leg of the 1999 Manchester United treble, consequences roll out in a different direction. As it was, the game was indicative of what had happened between the two, with Newcastle on the receiving end of a dispiriting 2-0 defeat.

In terms of the wider implications of Gullit's reign, the defeat at Wembley was probably the high point. Rob Lee's ostracisation, to the point of even not giving him a squad number, left a sour taste. Results failed to pick up in the way they would have been expected to, eventually finishing that first season in 13th. In terms of building for the future, there was an almost inversely successful hit rate at St James' Park in terms of transfer success, with Stéphane Guivarc'h, Marcelino and Silvio Marić going from forgettable to much more.

It got worse during the start of the 1999/2000 season. One point from the first four games saw Gullit on the brink. Something had to give but not in the way that anyone could have predicted. Newcastle were going into a Tyne–Wear derby but that took second stage to a clash between player and manager.

Alan Shearer is, was and forever will be a big deal at St James' Park. Even among the rapid change that is sure to occur over the next few years with the investment to come, it's hard to believe that anyone will ever come close to his level of influence. The game against Sunderland was a civil war, fought between the entire Toon army and an army of one. In that sense it was only ever going to be decided one way. Going into a club certain decisions are necessary and challenges that require a different perspective are the very reason why someone new has been brought in. Creating new problems is where this all falls down. Of all the things that were going on at Newcastle at the time, Shearer wasn't the person to be challenged. Even if Newcastle had beaten Sunderland that night, the reaction was such that it probably would have counted for nothing. A week later, Gullit resigned.

Gullit's place in football history was assured long before he had ever kicked a ball on English shores. The Premier League needed a talent like his to raise its profile; he did that and so much more. To be remembered for such a short spell as a manager is a testament to the hunger for controversy and derision that exists within English culture. Gullit cited the British media during his final press conference; whatever impact they had within that time, when things are going wrong those vultures have been known to circle. For what he did at Chelsea alone, in terms of starting a process, his star should burn brighter. A legacy should be more than just a single game, more than a manager leaving out his star player and then later going on to regret it. Football in the early 1990s was – at times – bad haircuts, terrible pitches and very limited play. Kids grew up looking for the kind of flair and style that he brought, changing the English game from within. The Premier League needed sexy football. We needed Ruud Gullit.

28

Ade Akinbiyi

LANGUAGE CAN evolve but numbers stay the same. What words mean – or even the context to certain phrases – will ebb and flow with the changing of time. Five remains five, as it was then and as it will be forever. It's striking, then, that when it comes to financial matters the meaning behind the former grew to matter more than the latter. The price to pay in a physical sense, both as wages have increased during the last 30 years in addition to transfers, has risen. Money itself doesn't change.

Trevor Francis became a name to drag through a certain part of history. The idea of him being a million-pound player both educated and disenfranchised what was to come. At the point where the fanbase cannot fathom the numbers, they cease to be important. These kind of financial figures skew everything, well before the Premier League began to inflate everything to a degree that was so cut off from the everyday concept of earnings and what players were paid.

Following on from Francis's move to Nottingham Forest in 1979, the British transfer record was broken two more times in the same year. The bar was raised on five separate occasions during the 1980s. A few months before the 1992/93 season, Paul Gascoigne left Tottenham for Lazio and a £5.5m fee. In 13 years it had gone from a solitary million to five times that amount. By

1996 it would be £15m, a world record at the time. Underneath Alan Shearer, however, there were nine other players who would have broken the pre-Premier League record. It's not that it was spiralling out of control at the top but rather as those numbers kept rising, eventually there would come a point where previously astonishing figures were being paid for those who may not be necessarily able to match up to them.

It's hard – impossible even – to justify transfer fees in an ever-increasing monopoly, not least of all because the transfer system is within itself imperfect. Scouting, negotiations, personal alignment; they all can point to one thing and yet the end result be the other. With the ever-ballooning finances, it wasn't just those at the top who were splashing the cash. The issue here is that with great purse strings comes great responsibility, especially for those clubs that really need every single recruit to be a hit.

Football is merciless in terms of punishing those who stand still. Unfortunately it has a similar track record with those that attempt to rectify change and ultimately get it wrong. The transfer market is full of dominos that tumble in quick succession once that first one falls. One club filling a need usually means another has to do the same, especially when these moves come from up on high. Emile Heskey moving to Liverpool for £11m created a situation where Leicester had both money and motive. In came one of the most talked-about figures in Premier League history. Ade Akinbiyi coming in by himself wasn't so much the issue as the £5.5m that Leicester paid for him.

Being guilty of breaking the entire transfer system is a decision that cannot rest upon a single case. Not only is every step forward a risk, even the attempt itself is fraught with danger. Choosing to move in a particular direction allows for the possibility of getting it wrong. This makes every decision a planted foot. When it comes to the trial of a single purchase and how it went awry, there is always more to the story than that which has forever been crystallised. Those single instances that go on to become infamous for the wrong reasons are only ever teachable after the fact. Looking back allows the opportunity to apportion reason as well as blame. Whatever cosmic force doomed this particular purchase to failure, the verdict rests on neither party.

To look upon an instance of the power that money holds over the game is to rewind everything. All the way back to the beginning, the grassroots of English football is such a fertile ground from which everything else comes forth. Akinbiyi is one of many to come through a particular pathway. Senrab FC in Forest Gate means a lot down south, as do a lot of the teams in that area. London itself has such a consistent production line in part due to the catchment area being so big. There are clubs like it all over the city and what they offer these players is more than just a chance at a career. As ever the grassroots supplies talent so rich in potential that they can go on to be fully grown internationals and yet not see much of anything in return. Far beyond the 92, this is football at its most commercial. Over the years money has been poured into the game from every angle. Down at that level, there is not a drop.

Grassroots football has an ever more questionable future as teams move further away. So much of what happens at the top of the game gives off the hint that final body blows are close. For all that modern football purportedly takes away, if these kinds of teams are left to ruin, it will be from the bottom down that everything dies. There have been many points in Premier League history where it's been blatantly obvious what's going on. When the bubble bursts, it will be a collective responsibility. The writing had been on the wall for some time.

Ade Akinbiyi became caught up in a system that broke the connection between those on the pitch and those in the stands. His breakthrough and progression up until that point, however, is a rise that's much less cynical and much more wholesome. From one capital to another – via the academy at Carrow Road – in 1993 the journey from a London suburb to the Olympic

Stadium in Munich is enough of a story. A second-half substitute in one of the most iconic games in Norwich's history is at once an apex and an afterthought.

Relegation at the end of 1993/94 meant First Division football, whereby over the course of a couple of seasons Akinbiyi worked his way into the first team – Gillingham's. Moving over to the Priestfield Stadium and stepping down a level, by 1997 he had found the scoring touch. Twenty-one goals in 44 games was more than enough to repay a large amount of the £250,000 they had paid for him but was not quite enough for the Gills to crash into the Second Division play-offs, missing out by goal difference alone. It was from here that things started to accelerate rapidly.

While Akinbiyi hadn't managed to attain promotion with Gillingham, Bristol City had seen enough to take him along with them as they went up to the second tier. A transfer of £1.2m in 1998 between two teams far outside the reaches of the endless money pit that was the Premier League was very much a sign of the times. In what was a miserable season for the Robins, Akinbiyi was one of few bright spots. Relegated in 23rd place and firmly sent back down whence they came, his 19 league goals at the very least backed up the idea that he was an emerging talent who knew where the goal was. For the second time in two seasons, his signature was in demand.

In signing on the dotted line at Wolverhampton Wanderers, Akinbiyi had another price tag. This time it was £3.5m. Up until this point everything had worked out. In this instance not only was there for the first time a monetary replacement but also a hole in the squad itself. Robbie Keane leaving Wolves for Coventry created a significant void, which the increasingly enlarged compensation had to fill. As all of these pieces began to fall into place, this was just another example of how business was done. Even at this stage there was enough in the way of productivity to look over what came next. Had Wolves managed to work their way into the play-offs and beyond rather than being denied by two points, perhaps things would have been different.

Regardless of circumstance, players who are brought into a situation have more on their shoulders than those already in place. Promotion with Wolves would have been a natural progression, with a fanbase who by default would have cherished someone to put them in that position. As it was, the sharks were circling. Constant activity in terms of prestige and responsibility registered with those above, just as they had done so many times before. In among all this was an ever-growing amount of capital. Akinbiyi moving to Leicester became held up as indicative of the frivolousness that detached itself from the match-going fan.

It was an inevitability of movement. Someone would have had to suffer the pains of a transfer gone wrong. With the money being put in there also grew an ever-widening lens and a much more intense focus. Even so, such a notorious narrative doesn't happen overnight. Akinbiyi's plight became intertwined with a Leicester side that rose and then fell in spectacular fashion. On top of this was a manager who looked golden when things were going well but appeared equally helpless when it was going wrong. Peter Taylor suffered from the backlash that was to come, not quite as much as Akinbiyi himself but the two were to become forever linked. Incredibly, it all started with a blistering run to start a season.

The Foxes sitting top of the Premier League eight games into 2000/01 was impressive enough; doing so while only scoring seven goals went one step further. Defence was key in that period. New signings Gary Rowett and Calum Davidson helped bolster a back line that conceded just two before the middle of October. Akinbiyi himself had even begun to settle in, scoring a couple of what would be a decent return that campaign. Nine goals in a season doesn't necessarily hit the headlines but it's certainly not terrible, especially given the fact that the player he replaced – who had his own image issues – hadn't even managed that in either of the two seasons prior.

Expectations for the expensive striker rose once the performances of the team as a whole began to suffer, and 2001/02 was an all-round catastrophe for Leicester from the very beginning. Without the cushion of a good start they were cut adrift at the bottom of the table for the majority of the season. Even so, there were still depths to plumb. A single game cannot ever define a player, either positively or negatively, but Akinbiyi's performance against Liverpool in October 2001 became symbolic of everything that was going wrong at the time. It wasn't that chances were missed, they were never close. Some strikers get no service and are unable to make a difference because it rarely comes to them. This wasn't that. An unwelcome hat-trick of misses and any indifference gone along with it. Well before Leicester were finally relegated to the First Division, Akinbiyi had been transferred down there himself to Crystal Palace.

Reputations form quickly and are inexorably harder to change. What followed was a very public degradation along with a complete abandonment of form. The demand that had been there in his earlier years in the second tier had been replaced by a revulsion. Too heavy was the baggage that came with such a high-profile disappointment. Even with that he still managed to contribute. Saving Stoke from relegation with the only goal in their 1-0 last-day victory over Reading allowed Tony Pulis to put into motion what would be their eventual rise. Twice Akinbiyi went to Turf Moor and managed to win over the Burnley fans, including an unbelievable victory on penalties over Chelsea in the League Cup at Stamford Bridge. Sandwiched in between those two spells was his time at Sheffield United. Joining in late January for £1.75m, it was a world away from the so-called outrageous fee he had previously gone for. Even so, the Blades hit the jackpot. Scoring on his debut against Sheffield Wednesday and ending up helping the team to second place wasn't bad for a player written off across the board.

As far as out-of-control finances went, this was only the prologue. Prices rose and clubs began to trade in increasingly higher figures. Almost overnight the whole process became divorced from reality. For Ade Akinbiyi, what happened to him and everything that is now attached to his name speaks more of a system that escalated too quickly than of a manager who overpaid and a club that suffered the consequences. Numbers are incapable of lying. They are also not equipped to tell the full story.

29

Matt Holland

TO LET go is to love. The gift of fandom is just that. Offering up support in the often broken optimism that in exchange for such devotion, what follows matches up with either hope or expectation. Every season, every game, every silent prayer offered up for another corner that doesn't clear the first man, a piece of those watching goes with it. For the majority it can feel like a weekly surrender that rarely satisfies. On those special occasions where it does, that's what seduces supporters all over again.

For an unwritten bond the roles of both sides are very clear, although the idea of it even being a two-way relationship is a concept that has weathered over time. At its very best the symbiotic alliance between those in the stands and those on the pitch yields victory in the most remarkable of places. The power of support, transferred through all that wear the badge. If only it were that simple.

Everyone who has ever passed through a turnstile brings with them their own footballing baggage. Over the course of 90-plus minutes it all gets emptied out on to the pitch and then repacked all over again, sometimes with a souvenir to bring along to the next game. Severe though it may be, all the goodwill in the world sometimes cannot counteract one awful afternoon. The idea is to encourage and accept everyone equally.

It's not one that will ever bear fruit. Over the course of a season, too much can and will happen. That early sunlit optimism often disappears into the darkness as winter and spring roll around. No amount of rain can wash away the water that has no bridge to go under.

Implementing the long-held dreams of so many onlookers sounds about as strange as it is daunting. What lies beyond pride and pay grade for those on the pitch is a responsibility that isn't always able to be picked up, let alone shouldered. There's enough going on practically to be concerned with any more loftier ambitions. The bottom line for any player is that if they do their job well enough then everything else falls into place by default. Some do it so well that they are able to carry all that weight forward, into a much brighter tomorrow.

When everyone pulls in the same direction, with enough quality – and a sprinkling of luck – anything is possible. That wistful thinking doesn't just materialise out of nothing, it must be channelled. To buy into a specific point in the future is to punch a ticket to an unknown destination. This can be regressive as well as progressive. Only a select few can fulfil that initial bargain of forward momentum. Their reward is not just a professional one. It's a place in the hearts and minds of those who not just charted that progression but willed it along every step of the way.

Finding the way means having enough inner strength to not worry about a route. West Ham's academy might have eventually found a place for Matt Holland to thrive, but at 21 he was more concerned about first-team football in the immediate future. Over a century of games for Bournemouth in the two and a half years that followed proved that taking a step down the leagues for a step up in opportunities was a worthy trade-off. So trusted was he down at Dean Court, despite his young age and relative first-team inexperience, Holland was appointed as captain.

Of all the symbolic gestures in football, the armband may very well be the most fraught. It's a responsibility that at least one will carry yet few make proper use of. Being a leader consists of many things. To corral the chaos and ride the wave of emotion. Heading up a group of people in any context is a complicated, ever-changing conundrum. With captaincy consistency becomes imperative. To do it effectively is to have the utmost grasp of oneself, regardless of what that may consist of. Holland was the epitome of all those things, leading by example.

The only way to be present when it matters most in football terms is to always be there. No one knows which game will define a season because they all mean something. To have the discipline and focus to be constantly available relies on a certain amount of luck when it comes to injuries. Signing for Ipswich in 1997 and playing 59 games in league and cup over that first season is a truly astonishing feat for a player who very quickly gained the respect and admiration of the Portman Road faithful. That it ended in heartbreak at the end of that season after losing in the play-offs to Charlton only set up what was to be the next chapter of Holland's career. The challenge, to guide them into the promised land, wasn't without a few bumps in the road.

Experiences bring people together, bonding through the good and the bad, enduring immediate pain in order to taste success in the future. Football is a little more barbarous than that, however. Continued setbacks can break a team. Eventually there will be nothing left to give. Earning the right to go again after having given everything can leave both players and fans empty. Certainly that's how Ipswich might have been feeling after three successive play-off defeats. George Burley and his team clearly had the talent within their ranks to win, but never quite enough. Kieron Dyer, Richard Wright, Marcus Stewart and James Scowcroft all played their parts throughout those years (and beyond) alongside Holland, yet the end result was always the same.

All those years of being close but not close enough could easily have seen everyone give up hope or had the team broken apart, Dyer being the only meaningful exit in moving to Newcastle

United. For all it takes emotionally, football will always present another chance. As the new millennium dawned across the 1999/2000 season, Ipswich once again found themselves in the play-off spots. If the three seasons of torment wasn't enough, the three games that stood between them and promotion were absolute pandemonium.

Superstitions don't have any real effect on proceedings but they definitely influence attitudes surrounding them. Third place playing sixth first up has a built-in hierarchy, yet coming up against a Bolton side who had lost one game in 13 and had reached the semi-finals of both the League Cup and FA Cup wasn't exactly a reward. With half an hour gone of the first leg and already two goals down, the Premier League may have never seemed so far away for Ipswich. Stewart stepped up to score either side of the break but the drama was only just beginning. In front of a packed Portman Road crowd, one of the all-time great play-off encounters played out. Jim Magilton's hat-trick only scratches the surface of a truly extraordinary game. Bolton took the lead on three separate occasions that night and Magilton also had a penalty saved just before half-time. When Allan Johnston smashed one in for the Trotters immediately after Ipswich's second equaliser, once again the Tractor Boys were on the ropes. Having suffered so often in recent years, it was time for those inside Portman Road to be on the other end of it for a change. A hopeful long ball was headed into the path of Magilton, who proceeded to slot home and send the crowd into delirium. Still there was more to come.

Two more goals in extra time finally put Bolton to the sword but as emotionally exhausting as those first two play-off games were, Barnsley awaited at Wembley in the final. Having beaten them home and away already that season there would have been great optimism but without top scorer Scowcroft, it would have been of the cautious variety. Once again Ipswich had to start on the back foot. Barely had the game got going when Craig Hignett drove forward for Barnsley and struck one off the bar, only for it to come straight back down and go in off goalkeeper Wright. If ever there was a time to fold, this may well have been it. But Ipswich had come too far to give up now.

The 15 minutes before half-time swung the game completely. Tony Mowbray headed in from a Magilton corner to level it up on the half-hour mark, before Wright was adjudged to have brought down Hignett in the penalty area. Saving the resulting penalty set up a second half in which it looked as though the Tractor Boys had finally pulled ahead. Richard Naylor and Stewart looked to have put things beyond Barnsley's reach, until yet another penalty brought the Tykes within one. Nerves shredded, nails bitten beyond all comprehension, at one end those last ten minutes will have felt like an eternity while at the other it will all have gone by far too fast. Martijn Reuser put an exclamation point on events to ensure that Ipswich could be denied no further. His 90th-minute strike meant that they would be playing Premier League football.

If their run to the top was difficult, when they actually got there Ipswich made light work of it. It had been a few years since a side had come up from the second tier and adapted so well but having been through so much to simply get to that point, the feel-good factor lasted all the way through a phenomenal 2000/01 season. Only three teams came to Portman Road that year and won; just one of them finished above Ipswich. Memorable wins at Liverpool, Leeds and West Ham and a run to the semi-finals of the League Cup; virtually everything clicked into place. After years of relative adversity this was the reward. As far as the league was concerned, one year was all they got.

On top of all the plaudits Ipswich were getting, a run in Europe was a much more tangible sweetener. The UEFA Cup in 2001/02 held no group stages and was a straight knockout all the way. With so many teams involved, those early rounds can provide some intriguing away days if not quite the match-ups fans dream of. After the Tractor Boys had seen off Torpedo Moscow and Helsingborgs, the draw smiled kindly on them.

Playing against Inter Milan would evoke memories of Bobby Robson's Ipswich during the late 1970s and early '80s as they eventually won the competition. Ipswich even managed to draw first blood as Alun Armstrong's solo effort ten minutes from time was enough to record a famous victory in front of their own fans. The return leg held no quarter in terms of romance. Christian Vieri's hat-trick put away any chances of a giant-killing as the Italian side strode into the next round with a 4-1 win on the night. With the European dream now over, it was very much time to return to a domestic nightmare.

Second season syndrome is a simple and easy phrase that covers a variety of different things. For Ipswich there was a lot going on. Firstly the sales of Wright and Scowcroft left gaps in the squad that weren't plugged. The addition of Finidi George is often cited as one of the main reasons but his underperformance alone wasn't enough to make a team go from fifth to 18th. The other thing that gets lost in the details is that with ten games to go Ipswich were safe. They had done the hard yards in December and January to pull away from relegation before a 6-0 hammering at home to Liverpool triggered a run that saw them back in the First Division. At the end of this season, Matt Holland went off to Japan and Korea. From one crisis, to another.

Roy Keane was a very different style of player. Both he and Holland were captains of their respective clubs, each with a distinct approach to how they went about their business both on and off the pitch. There was even something of an issue there in regard to Holland singing 'God Save the Queen' which Keane wrote about in an autobiography. As far as the 2002 World Cup went, as far as the Manchester United man was concerned, there were standards all around not being met. Deciding to go home didn't change the fact that those who were left still had to play. Holland's goal against Cameroon in their opening game didn't erase all that had gone before but at least allowed the conversation to move on. Robbie Keane's equaliser against

Germany gave them hope of competing against anyone. That strength of spirit was enough to see them take Spain all the way to the wire in the last 16 but the Republic of Ireland were to be knocked out. Being seen as so dependable, Matt Holland's missed penalty in the shoot-out stung all the more.

As far as Ipswich were concerned, fortunately there would be no further play-off torment in 2002/03. Finishing just four points outside the top six sparked a 17-year run in the second tier. During the following summer, Charlton paid £750,000 to take Holland down to The Valley. Alan Curbishley had spent years putting together the perfect functional team. Unfancied and without pretension, yet every year they performed above expectation. Fans can often point to a particular season or a period of time in which everything was going well but so rarely can that be distilled down into one game. A Boxing Day 2003 clash with Chelsea that certainly packed a lot of punch. Overcoming Claudio Ranieiri's Chelsea was a very different prospect compared to what would follow a year later but they were a huge scalp all the same.

The scoreline – as dramatic as it was – couldn't capture just how big of a victory it was. Charlton 4 Chelsea 2 on paper meant a lot, but it was much more than that: the power of the performance at the heart of it, an aggregation of a side assembled and put together, with both hard work and more than a little bit of skill. Alongside Holland, Scott Parker ran the show that day. It was very much a headline-grabbing performance. Certainly it got Chelsea's attention and four days later Parker signed for them. Charlton didn't fall apart after this but a stark reality had dawned, if it wasn't clear already. There was no way through a glass ceiling if every time they were to get close, someone from above it could come down and take out a key piece at will.

Parker's absence was covered. It wasn't as though he left and they began to dip. In the years that followed, both Charlton and Holland remained as consistent as ever. After finishing seventh in 2004, just three points outside of a European place and seven behind the top four, they never quite reached those heights again. At the moment the Addicks were poised to take that next leap, they were given a firm shove back down and existed in a form of mid-table purgatory for some years. No matter how well oiled it may be, not all cogs in the machine are replaceable. When Curbishley left Charlton, there was both a recognition of all the hard work that had been put in but also a false sense of something more that lay ahead. That kind of stability, that kind of consistency, it all comes from the top down. Unfortunately, you can never take anything for granted in the Premier League. No matter how strong and stable the foundations seem set, it only ever takes a small number of things to go wrong for it all to spiral.

Years of hard work can be undone in a matter of months. All that effort for naught, but not so. At the time with the resources they had – and even knowing everything else since – there can be no denying the incredible achievement of everyone at The Valley during that time. However, looking back at some of the points tallies and the gaps between their finishes and something taking that one extra step further then it feels like an extra kick in the gut. Holland finished his career at Charlton, staying with them until a very bitter end whereby they were relegated from the Championship. He had taken Ipswich up to the promised land and led by example as captain at both Portman Road and The Valley. He is the kind of player that the fans can put their trust in and know that it won't be misplaced.

30

Stan Collymore

AFTER THREE decades, there's a pitfall that stands before the next generation of football fans. Something which exists within the present to the point where so much has already been lost to a particularly poisonous form of nostalgia. The naivety of youth coupled with fixed perspectives forms a barricade over context. This is just the process as it ever was, in that all anyone has ever known grows to be as important as anything can ever be.

At the very centre of the schism that separated the old First Division from the Premier League is the idea that football was created in 1992. Abolishing the past and ignoring what came before is to break up the path that led to the present. English football history is so rich precisely because of the wealth of stories that exist long before this point. History continues to be created all the way through to the present day. If only the achievements of today matter then ultimately nothing matters.

Aside from a long-term erasure, there's another form of football cancellation in regard to the idea that anything not involving a set few clubs is irrelevant. Records and statistics are retconned, filtered through the lens of modern football rather than the game as a whole. This kind of self-imposed barrier fails to recognise, let alone appreciate the full picture. Like a wave of selective nostalgia, cherry-picking teams and moments from a recent past without allowing for the full significance.

The game will continue to innovate as it goes; not necessarily change for the better but react to an ever different set of circumstances and the players that then come through as a result. Advances in tactics, dietary requirements and general physical health as well as the continual search for an extra yard or two means the standard of play theoretically will get higher with each generation that passes. Similarly, because this process doesn't ever slow down, the present will always be as good as it's ever been.

Nottingham Forest come with a very specific nostalgic label. An image to cast the mind back, should you remember. That's why drawing such an obvious line through history is ignorant and harsh in equal measure. There are always going to be those who fall on the other side of it. The exploits of Brian Clough and Forest dwarf what the team could possibly have hoped to achieve in the Premier League. That it remains but a distant memory now is down to a variety of factors. But one thing is for sure, the Forest side of 1994/95 exploded into the Premier League. When people now talk about teams coming up from the second tier, the idea of having a good season is to finish in the top ten. Forest – and Newcastle before them – defied that theory even before it came into existence.

It took until the 12th game of the season for Collymore and Forest to taste defeat, having won eight of the previous 11. Though they had a less-than-stellar middle patch over the season, the incredible winning runs at both the start and the end proved they were a match for anyone. Third place in the table and back into Europe for the first time for ten years and on face value it appeared as though the good times were on their way back to the City Ground. That kind of sentiment was all but immediately cut short when Liverpool put their hands into their pockets to break the British transfer record in order to take Collymore to Anfield. £8.5m in 1995 was astronomical money, the kind of offer that could not be refused.

Though Liverpool didn't have the same kind of lustre they enjoyed in times gone by, this was quite the purchase on paper. There were no doubts around the talent Collymore possessed and the anticipation of what was possible playing in such an attacking team was palpable. At the very least, in the advanced areas of the park, Roy Evans had a team that was much more credible than the reputation that would follow them. Adding Collymore to a team that already contain Jamie Redknapp, Steve McManaman and Robbie Fowler gave more fuel to the fire in terms of the eternal power struggle that lay at the heart of the Premier League. As one had risen, one had faded. Perhaps now with the required firepower, the red sides of both Merseyside and Manchester would play out their battle for supremacy.

In Liverpool's two most important moments that year, Manchester United were the immediate beneficiaries. Anfield played host to the greatest single game in Premier League history on 3 April 1996. Seven goals in 90 minutes only begins to scratch the surface of a breathless, absurd match: Liverpool 4 Newcastle 3. Classics like these have a certain rhythm to them. If all the goals were scored in the first half, it certainly would have made for an even more frenetic 45 but ultimately the excitement would have deflated as the game wore on. It didn't take long for the madness to materialise. Fowler's second-minute strike was almost immediately cancelled out by Les Ferdinand's equaliser, and moments later David Ginola gave Newcastle the lead. When it comes to epic encounters, a fast start is not a necessary ingredient but an always-welcome one.

For a game to tick all the boxes, it needs to have the ability to twist and turn within the pre-existing narrative. Effectively a winner-take-all situation for who could carry on their title challenge, even if the maths said different things to both teams. To that end, the second half lived up to that billing and then some. Another three goals in quick succession, this time between Fowler, Faustino Asprilla and Collymore, brought everything to a heady stand-off at 3-3 with 20 minutes left to play. With the clock now the enemy and the draw no use to either of them, every second that ticked by increased the odds of a single goal being that ultimate knockout blow.

Collymore closing in. As late as the 92nd minute, he broke Newcastle's resistance and spirit. The goal – as good of a finish as it was – doesn't say as much as the reactions do. Kevin Keegan slumped over the advertising hoardings, as if he had been previously held up by strings and they had suddenly been cut. Collymore racing off with an expression that combined elation and bemusement at what exactly was happening. Both of those images come closer to explaining the emotions of a game that went down in history. That applies to both that particular 90 minutes and football itself. Newcastle tripped up in the title race in the most joyously brutal fashion imaginable.

As ever with Liverpool during that period, consistency wasn't their greatest strength. To make that last-gasp Newcastle victory count for anything themselves, it would have to be followed up near flawlessly. Defeat away to Coventry just a few days later ended that possibility very swiftly. Still there was the chance for silverware and a date at Wembley against Manchester United awaited in the FA Cup Final. A game less famous for it being a clash of two of English football's greatest rivals and certainly not for the football on display but instead for what one of the two sides were dressed like in the build-up.

The Spice Boys were a very 1990s contrivance. A snapshot in time. It became heavily associated not only with failures of a particular team but also in the generation as a whole that were dealing with unprecedented levels of fame and fortune. Nobody would have cared about the white suits had Liverpool gone on to win but Eric Cantona ended the game as a contest, pouncing on a soft punch from David James following a late corner. Part of the feeling behind the disparaging label that was put upon them was based upon the potential for more. That feeling that success wasn't that far away for the Reds and yet they would continually find a way to come up short.

Another season that began in promise ended with disappointment. Fowler and Collymore were again playing their part, aided by McManaman, John Barnes and Patrik Berger. A brilliant start consisting of six wins and two draws from the first eight in 1996/97 gave hope that things were finally coming into place. The remaining 30 were full of inconsistencies which proved otherwise. Defeats to Manchester United and Blackburn were unwanted but understandable; losing to Sheffield Wednesday and Coventry later down the line less so. No matter how many they scored nor how good the attacking play looked, championships are built on the kind of defensive solidity that Liverpool simply did not possess. Evans's dilemma was clear, yet breaking up what had worked as an effective striking partnership wasn't necessarily on the cards. The emergence of one Michael Owen rather forced the issue. After a summer of sales, Aston Villa found the funds and the choice was clear. Collymore was going to play for his boyhood club.

In a more sugar-coated existence, the story wraps up here. The sentimental significance of donning the famous claret and blue and finding a greater sense of self among childhood dreams. Maybe even a last-gasp trophy or two, to etch his name along with those he cheered as a child. Reality is rarely that simple. Rather than finding his footing, Collymore drifted out of form and eventually out of favour. He had his moments, most notably in the UEFA Cup quarter-final as Villa looked to throw caution to the wind in order to come back against Atlético Madrid. Needing three goals to progress, Ian Taylor and Collymore scored in successive minutes to electrify Villa Park and set up a potential late winner that never arrived. There were also impressive performances against Tottenham and Liverpool in the league that showed glimpses of the player who had exploded on to the scene.

Footballers live in a different world. It's a bubble that shields them from most, but not everything. What's more, most players come from backgrounds and upbringings whereby certain things are set well before their wage packet becomes such that it's difficult to reach out. Talking about mental health issues in the 1990s was an impossibility. A toxic combination of faux masculinity, the British ideal of keeping a stiff upper lip and football being infamous for preying on any perceived weakness meant that for the longest time there was silence. This isn't to excuse or to ignore any harmful behaviour, but when an exasperated John Gregory equated wages to depression it reinforced this idea that these players weren't entitled to feel. Collymore was released from his Aston Villa contract after some time away on loan and eventually signed for Leicester City on a pay-as-you-play deal. Martin O'Neill's words before signing him in a press conference loomed large. This would be his last chance. It didn't take long for things to go the way everyone might have predicted.

Leicester and La Manga, with the 2000 League Cup Final on the horizon. Taking the squad away to both relax and to bond them is something that many teams do. O'Neill was meant to be joining up with the players later on, leaving them – along with a few of the coaching staff – to their own devices. Within 24 hours the team had been ordered back and news of yet another incident spread across the British media like wildfire. Collymore had gotten hold of a fire extinguisher and sprayed it in the middle of a piano bar; the kind of rowdiness seen among many a group of travelling young men. Even then, before the age of smartphones and social media, the speed with which even the whiff of a scandal forced the entire team to come home was rapid. Collymore was fined, ordered to undertake community service and threatened with having his contract terminated.

After injury hampered any onfield action and O'Neill departed north of the border, Leicester's new manager, Peter Taylor, didn't appear to want to shoulder the same kind of responsibility as far as Collymore was concerned. Played out of position or not at all, it wasn't long before he was allowed to leave the club. Bradford had narrowly escaped relegation from the top division the previous season and were desperate to avoid being pulled down in 2000/01. The injections of cash that the Premier League provided had made certain teams react obsessively, throwing money at anything that moved. Collymore wasn't their only big signing; Benito Carbone, Dan Petrescu, Ashley Ward and David Hopkin all arrived in quick succession. None of them were on particularly low wages but Carbone in particular became a weight around their necks in the not-too-distant future.

Apart from an acrobatic overhead kick on his debut against Leeds United, Bradford provided very little solace for Collymore. Much like most of the second half of his career his spell there was too short and there was too little in the way of any actual footballing promise. Such was the folly of the hierarchy at Valley Parade that Collymore and a few others were placed on the transfer list to try and reduce the club's wage bill just months after arriving. By the end of the season he had already moved to Spain to play for Real Oviedo, left them and retired. It was an empty end to a career that once promised so much.

As the Premier League gets older, those first ten years stand out more, both in terms of what became different but also in terms of how much still needed to change.

31

Jussi Jääskeläinen

WHETHER ANY convincing balance ever truly existed or not, over the last 30 years the Premier League has become an exercise in selfishness over selflessness. The spotlight never shifted, its glare just intensified. With an ever-increasing superstardom came a horizon beyond the here and now. Players could see past their current situation – to a point where everything from the fans to their team and their team-mates were all behind them.

The excesses of the 1990s exacerbated all this ten-fold. Prominence is one thing and money another; the Premier League had excesses of both. There's always been an unwritten understanding among fans that players will move on. Such was the transfer market as it was, there was a conditioning and acceptance that they would leave as soon as the wind blew in a different direction. Players transferred with such speed and frequency that it wasn't worth ever trying to feel an attachment to those who would just leave anyway.

We expect those born in the area to show a degree of loyalty; to embrace the culture and know the ins and outs of the club. As such fans can be very guarded about outsiders. They're either going to hurt us by not caring – or even worse – we'll care about them and they'll leave. This is why it means so much when someone manages to break through and fully endear themselves to a club.

Staying is only part of the formula. Virtually anyone can remain long enough and pick up a pay cheque. It's about quite literally having a hand in matters. Their affability is what endears but no one grows to become too attached to a player who never actually gets out on to the pitch. Loyalty and support are two sides of the same coin. They are so often seen as absolutes but there is as ever some nuance within that. Loyalties are tested. Support wanes, or becomes disillusioned. The difference between the player and the fan is that their time at the club is even more of a microcosm. Everyone knows there will come a time when they don't don any particular colours and in an increasingly frantic transfer market that moment always feels close. Supporters' journeys never waver. Whatever happens, they're in it for the long haul.

Reliance isn't just something that's needed in terms of staying true to a particular team. A player has to go out there and do their job, especially when it comes to something as important as goalkeeping. The confidence that they radiate throughout the team cannot be generated elsewhere. That one player can have such a ripple effect everyone else around them, when it comes to goalkeeping, is quite astounding. Unconvincing or erratic keepers seem to radiate fragility. This in turn infects the defence who then make more unforeseen errors which then makes more work for someone who has shown themselves incapable of dealing with it. This also goes into the crowd and makes them fearful of what might happen next, making the whole thing a vicious cycle.

Not every team is blessed with a good defence. Most of the time you have to deal with a passable one. It's the last area of the pitch that gets any attention, if it gets any attention at all. As such, those in and around it have to suffer. Fans watch perfectly good games ruined by an individual mistake or a lapse in concentration. It's this mismatch of misfits that make you really enjoy the good players.

What's in a name? Jussi Jääskeläinen became a byword for solidity during the 2000s. His stature and presence as one of those players who never quite got the same plaudits as those who had a lot less to do but played for clubs with higher esteem only further solidified his reputation within the Bolton faithful at the very least. Arriving at the Reebok Stadium – as it was called at the time – in 1997 at the age of 22 for the inconceivable sum of just £100,000, at the very least it proves that in an era of players costing increasingly extravagant sums of money there were still bargains to be found.

Incidental events during a career can have long-lasting effects. Colin Todd may have been the one who brought Jussi to the club; it would be Sam Allardyce who would get the very best of him. Coming together in the First Division in October 1999, it would be the start of a seven-year adventure in which Big Sam would turn Bolton into one of the more daunting Premier League opponents on their day. Throughout it all, the big Finn at the back was there to inject a degree of calmness into the storms that were raging elsewhere on the pitch. This wasn't always the case, however. Those two years in the First Division after he came in were an unforgivable proving ground, which forged the steel that was to come.

Young goalkeepers are inexperienced in more important ways than those of their outfield counterparts. Because of the fragile nature of the position as a whole, it doesn't take a lot in among the constant bombardment that is football for a burgeoning career to get lost. It's all too easy and all too frequent for those looking to the weather in order to excuse certain things but as far as a fledgling Jääskeläinen was concerned, having known nothing but the temperature and snow of Finnish football, the almost permanent rain in the north of England came as something of a hurdle to get over. What's more, he was fifth choice at a club that was looking to get back to the Premier League. In order to take that number one spot and for his employers to make that step up, the answer – as with so much in football – was in coaching.

It takes more than just one pair of hands to mould a player. Managers go to great lengths in order to keep the same team around them throughout the years and it stands to bear that they are very much a part of taking those separate pieces and bringing them all together as one. For goalkeepers though it's much more isolated, much like every other part of the game. Understudies get put through their paces at a very different level to those trying to break through into the outfield positions. After moving to England as a 22-year-old to try and make the breakthrough, this is where Jääskeläinen met 'The Devil'.

Ability needs to be shaped in much the same way that determination can be channelled. No footballer has ever reached the very top by themselves. Throughout Jääskeläinen's journey at Bolton, he had someone pushing him every step of the way. At the end of a nearly 20-year playing career, Fred Barber joined the Bolton coaching staff in 1996. When Jääskeläinen arrived, there was work to do. So rigorous were the training sessions that the soft-spoken Finn referred to Barber in his native tongue. Somehow, even after Barber discovered that he was being called 'The Devil', the two formed an indelible bond that helped build Jääskeläinen into the figure he would become. It wasn't just in the goalkeeping department that Bolton were growing, however. Allardyce wanted every advantage his team could get.

Reputations change over time, most notably at the beginning and end of a career, where at once there is nothing established and then latterly when those expectations are measured. Allardyce remained himself throughout his time as a manager and yet there were very different phases of notoriety. Veering in the direction of becoming a caricature in his later years, what has become buried under the rubble of a combative career was some of the more progressive ideas he brought to the table during those early days at Bolton.

Forever looking for those marginal gains, the use of computer tracking software that would become essential to clubs of all sizes was used to plot out the best method of survival once they had arrived in the Premier League. They were always going to be underestimated, and this played into their hands to a degree. Allardyce always liked his teams to be in the faces of their opponents, to make sure that they never gave them an inch. It made them a pain to play against, even when the results didn't quite back it up. Before they could put down roots within the top flight, it was all about continuity and endurance. Getting to the heralded 40-point mark that so often safeguards against relegation and then going from there was the target.

It took just two years for Bolton to acclimatise to the Premier League. After having hung on by a thread, the team that was being assembled allowed for a higher ceiling. Bruno Ngotty was the first, adding more than just name value to their defence. Next up was Jay-Jay Okocha, whose talent and trickery mesmerised and made him a favourite far beyond the reaches of the Reebok Stadium. Youri Djorkaeff was not that far removed from setting up Zinedine Zidane in the 1998 World Cup Final, yet he too came to the Trotters. Stelios Giannakopoulos, Iván Campo and Kevin Davies arrived a year later and added yet another layer of solidity and competitive quality. Bolton's secret weapon was their ability to not just go under the radar but to get under the skin. Not one of the traditional footballing powers, four successive top-eight finishes made the rest of the league sit up and pay attention.

As the top teams embraced a more open and fluid style of play, Allardyce remained true to form. Their adaptability came in the form of the players he would allow free rein. The technically gifted that would add the finishing touches to the solidity behind them. Okocha and Djorkaeff transitioned it over to El Hadji Diouf. Homegrown Kevin Nolan even got in on the act. All the while, Jääskeläinen remained an ever-permanent fixture behind them. The one they could all rely on.

The established order will always pretend to embrace something new. They might even actually be sincere, so long as it never threatens to tangibly change anything. Clubs that like to punch above their weight are held up as a shining example at one end of the scale and derided as a nuisance by those at the other. It all depends on how often they get the upper hand. With everything Bolton were doing there was also a distinct layer of bitterness, specifically when it came to Arsène Wenger. He had created something of a revolution of his own down at Arsenal and even though they and Bolton were looking into areas that others weren't, both managers were very much at opposite ends when it came down to the games themselves. During a time where Arsenal were beating everyone, Allardyce and his team made sure their presence was felt every time.

Bolton's growth wasn't restricted to the Premier League. Being able to play in European competitions meant the chance to showcase their particular brand of football as well as hosting some of the burgeoning understudies across the continent. Sevilla were en route to the first of their six triumphant UEFA Cup/Europa League campaigns when they visited the Reebok Stadium to fight for a point in 2005/06. Though Jääskeläinen wasn't in goal that night, he was when it came to the clash with Marseille following the group stage. Bolton managed to hold a side containing Franck Ribery and Samir Nasri to a goalless draw at home before succumbing to a 2-1 defeat in the Stade Vélodrome. It was a long way to come from losing away to Southend some ten years earlier.

But all good things come to an end. While the rest of the Premier League would debate on the favourable qualities of Big Sam at the time, this would have been more than a testament to how good Bolton had become during his tenure. Certainly it would have been a relief to many up and down the league when he decided to step aside. Passing the baton down to Sammy Lee seemed like a reasonable choice of successor, if for no other reason than he had been there alongside Allardyce for so long. Just one victory in 11 league games either side of the summer of 2007 sent that train of thought very much off the tracks. Gary Megson came in with the remit of keeping Bolton in the Premier

League, a responsibility he put over everything else, even to the detriment of what could have been something special.

Rotation was a concept viewed with contempt in the late 2000s. Only the bigger teams could afford to do it in the first instance and even then, there had been a history of managers being mocked for making too many changes to their team. Claudio Ranieri at Chelsea had been a 'tinkerman' and Rafael Benítez at Liverpool confounded the critics by making changes to his team for 99 straight games, only to keep the same line-up before arriving at the century. Cup competitions had gone from a distraction to an unwelcome disruption, especially playing in Europe. The UEFA Cup became particularly inconvenient. Teams wanting to qualify for the domestic top four would play a mixture of their regular first team and reserve players, all in the hope to keep them fit enough to qualify for Europe the following season. It was a perpetual cycle of inertia, with the fans themselves losing out. Bolton had no such ambitions in 2008. Their league form did indeed need tending to. Game after game, Megson ignored the UEFA Cup. Yet results kept coming.

Bayern Munich at the Allianz Arena with world-class talent all over the park. Yet it was no match for Ricardo Gardner and Kevin Davies. Getting a draw at such a famous stadium would have been the highlight for any English team. So too would be going to Atlético Madrid and holding them to a goalless draw to knock them out 1-0 on aggregate. By the time Bolton travelled to Lisbon, a place in the quarter-finals was up for grabs. These are the kind of opportunities that come along once in a lifetime. Yet Megson thought a trip away to Wigan was the higher priority of the two. He fielded a reserve side in Portugal and Bolton lost. They also lost to Wigan a few days later. Bolton managed to pick up enough points between then and the end of the season to survive in the Premier League. Whatever might have happened had they gone down will never be known. When they will get another shot in Europe like that, however, is what fans must wonder.

Throughout all that happened at the Reebok in between Bolton's highs and the relegation that followed, Jääskeläinen stayed until the bitter end. He was forever linked with moves to different clubs because of both his high stature and the perception that he would be easy pickings, yet he remained constant all the way through Bolton's 11-year stay in the Premier League. His loyalty extended even further than to just the club. When Owen Coyle joined in 2010 and wanted to bring in his own coaching staff, Jääskeläinen stuck up for his old mentor and insisted that Fred Barber be brought back into the fold. Two years later, as Bolton were being relegated, Jääskeläinen watched from the bench. The club had moved on; it was finally time for him to do the same.

Joining Allardyce at West Ham made for a comforting reunion and a clean slate all the same. In the three years that Jääskeläinen spent there, everything was winding down. All the work they had both done at Bolton was a long way behind them by 2012. Things had moved on. Big Sam's tenure at Upton Park was ill-fitting throughout. By proxy Jääskeläinen had one good year before Adrián came along and pushed him down the pecking order. It was a hollow end to what had been a staunch career. Players and managers move through different clubs and situations all the time. Every now and then, everything comes together. The right club at the right time. Make those moments special and the connections will last forever.

32

Andrew Johnson

PAIN IS – or rather becomes – any number of platitudes. Making it more about the mind than the matter can be a dangerous default. Trying to move forward, to persevere and find a way through; that becomes the goal. It's not always glory that awaits on the other side. The tools that were at once necessary can become detrimental. Determination and courage are essential in the climb. Standing tall opposing those who either underestimated or gave up, overcoming adversity; these are all the required qualities that necessitate success. This line of thinking has a breaking point, however. The human body can only be pushed so far. In a contact sport, getting hurt physically is a part of the job. Unforeseen and all but unavoidable, these consequences of actions in turn have long-lasting ramifications.

Being in the stands for a cup final is meant to be something to celebrate, especially in those instances where simply getting there in the first place has been as impressive as the achievement of lifting the trophy itself. Far from the promise and potential of a day out like no other when it comes to most of those in attendance, missing out as part of the playing staff comes with a significant serving of anguish. The sentiment of it being once in a lifetime becomes rather sinister in this regard.

As frustrating as it can be looking on, knowing that there's little you can do to affect the result, it must pale in comparison to taking a very similar seat and knowing you should be out there. After proving the ability to be able to take the field to compete, the worst seat in the house must be all of them. The role of luck in football can be overplayed at times but the length of time on the treatment table plays into the eventual outcomes of many a career. Missing one game in particular can shadow a lifetime, let alone significant periods. Andrew Johnson had the misfortune of both.

Wednesday, 12 May 2010; Fulham in the Europa League Final, locking horns with an Atlético Madrid side on their way to having a formidable reputation at home and abroad. Among their number were a list of players who either were or would be familiar to the Premier League. The likes of Sergio Agüero and David de Gea as well as José Antonio Reyes were matched by Roy Hodgson's resolute Cottagers all the way up until Diego Forlán killed the dream for Fulham in extra time. European heartbreak for Andrew Johnson didn't even begin to sum up a few months that had lasting effects on a career that never quite got going.

The immediate appears worth sacrificing, not least of all because the future is unwritten, so by the time any consequences arise, it will already be too late. Already having suffered a dislocated collarbone against Amkar Perm in the earlier rounds of the Europa League as well as a groin strain that required an operation, a third setback became too much. Knee surgery ruled Johnson out for the rest of the season, begrudgingly watching his team-mates on crutches but encouraging them all the same as they made that incredible run to the final in Hamburg that included a truly mesmeric night against Juventus at Craven Cottage.

Injuries take from tomorrow just as much as they take from today. Losing time during that incredible run – difficult though it may have been – doesn't compare to the frustration of being back in the team and not quite up to speed. By 2011 it had all become too much. Every period of being sidelined meant even more time to find the pace of a game that had already moved on. It began during Johnson's time at Everton a few years prior. One or two knocks forcing him out of contention became more and more frequent as the years went on. What's more, he had become the face of something much bigger, something that changed his game and cursed the second half of his career even more than any tackle ever could.

Arriving at Everton in the summer of 2006 very much at the peak of his powers, Johnson had been as prolific a goalscorer as anyone within the English game over the last few years. His problem was that for two of them he had been in the second tier. Regardless of level, 63 goals in three seasons for a 25-year-old meant that he was very much in demand. Whatever his promise was, the start to life at Goodison was even better. With six goals in his first seven games, including a double in a Merseyside derby which Everton won 3-0, things couldn't have gone much better. Things turned for Johnson a few months later after Chelsea had come to town and just about escaped with three points. Though he didn't get on the scoresheet that day, José Mourinho had some thoughts about his playing style.

To be accused of being a diver, and by proxy a cheat, is a heavy accusation to be on the receiving end of. Mourinho chose his words much more carefully, describing the forward as 'untrustworthy'. Still, it upset the Everton management so much that they threatened the Chelsea manager with legal action, after which his comments were gradually walked back. There seems to be an unwritten acceptance throughout the course of Premier League history that there is a dividing line and English players fall on the right side of it. Gamesmanship, clever play, looking to make contact. As with anything in football, it's much more complicated than it first appears.

Diving is a very particular action, filled with complication and nuance, all of which are removed from the thought processes of fans depending on the player and the club in question.

Refereeing standards have also made the lines less clear and much more blurred in somewhat forcing a necessity of going down in order to get a decision. Trying to con the referee and break the rules is one thing; understanding that staying up and not going down is a false honesty that will not be rewarded is another. Unfortunately because of the double standards at play all around, there's never going to be an obvious answer. A year later the head of refereeing, Keith Hackett, admitted that Johnson should have been awarded more penalties than he had been given. It didn't matter. Even after Mourinho withdrew his words or otherwise, their intention stuck.

Those last few years were an uphill battle, just trying to find form in the shape of consecutive minutes rather than goals. After trying to recuperate and get back into the plans at Craven Cottage, a switch from one west London club to another offered a new chance. Queens Park Rangers had enough players coming and going between 2012 and 2015 to keep up with those on the sideline, as Harry Redknapp and Mark Hughes bloated the squad on their way to multiple Premier League relegations. Even in the Championship, Johnson was on the books while being written out of contention. It wasn't the end but it was very much in sight.

Looking for a happy ending becomes increasingly difficult when things start going south from the halfway point, yet there is sometimes room for sentiment. It wasn't a perfect farewell, not least because losing 3-2 to Newcastle in a third round League Cup tie is no way to wrap it all up. But in terms of 24 September 2014, it was still a final run out at Selhurst Park. This was where he made his mark; where he burst on to the scene a dozen years earlier. Before the injuries, before all that time missed. Back when time was on his side.

Promotion came at a cost. After Birmingham City claimed their place in the top flight in 2002, after nearly two decades away, they were immediately on the lookout for a striker to bolster their squad. Johnson by this time had already been at St Andrew's for four years but Steve Bruce had eyes on someone. Clinton Morrison would be the man chosen to lead the line and so a package involving some £3m would go to Crystal Palace in addition to the two players swapping clubs. A fairly uneventful season for the Eagles would play out, save for the sacking of Trevor Francis that purportedly stunned the former England man into silence save for the words, 'But it's my birthday.' Happier times for Palace at the very least were on the horizon.

The top scorer in every single season Johnson played at Selhurst Park – save for that end-of-career cameo – things took a massive step up in 2003/04 with 30 goals in all competitions, by far the top scorer in the First Division, and yet the Premier League seemed a world away. A Boxing Day defeat to Millwall and Palace hovering just above the relegation zone meant the immediate future was much more about stability than any further ambitions. With a new manager in place, it wasn't necessarily about turning around Johnson's form as it was about the rest of the team. Even so, he was about to reach another level entirely and take Palace with him. Propelled by nine goals in six games across the early part of 2004, Iain Dowie's team began to move up the table. Four defeats in the second half of that season led to an unlikely play-off berth.

When an opportunity like this presents itself, modesty realises that whatever happens from here on in, an achievement has been made. Desire and ambition demand it go on that much further. Sunderland came to Selhurst Park and fell to the firepower that was now self-evident. Neil Shipperley and Danny Butterfield had put Palace ahead before Kevin Kyle looked to have spared Sunderland, only for Johnson once more to come to the fore. There were heroes for the Eagles all over the team at that stage. Never did they need one more than in the dying embers of the return leg at the Stadium of Light. A goal down on aggregate and a man light in the game itself thanks to Julian Gray's red card, only for Darren Powell to head home in injury time to eventually send the tie to penalties. After some late-stage nerves in which four consecutive penalties were missed, Michael Hughes wrapped it up for Palace and in turn booked a date at the Millennium Stadium with West Ham. For the team it was the opportunity of a lifetime. For Johnson, it was also a chance to bury some demons.

Before they reunited at Selhurst Park, the enduring image of Trevor Francis and Andrew Johnson is one of commiseration and abject despair. Emotions got the better of the manager and tears flowed as he attempted to console his player having just missed the penalty that gave Liverpool the 2001 League Cup during their time together at Birmingham. Johnson's response was one of apology. Twenty years old at the time, immediately after the most important kick of his career to date, he found time to say the words, 'I'm sorry.' Fast forward three years and there were no tears and no penalties, no pain nor any need to feel anything other than pure joy. With half an hour of the game to go, Johnson picked up the ball some 40 yards out. Running towards the West Ham goal, all that was needed was enough of a gap to get a shot off. Tracked by both a defender and someone from midfield that had followed him all the way, the only effort he could manage was a weak one. Stephen Bywater in the Hammers' goal inexplicably parried the paltry attempt straight to Shipperley, who made no mistake. This time there was no denying Johnson his place in the Premier League. Palace had their promotion.

When it came time to finally show what he was made of at the top level, Johnson delivered. Only Thierry Henry scored more goals than he did in the 2004/05 season. Finding the net 21 times in a season for a side that still ends up being relegated remains a Premier League record. His goals might not have been enough to get Palace to safety but without them they would have been washed away long before it eventually came to pass. It all came right down to the wire. Coming from behind against Charlton at The Valley, with 20 minutes to go, Johnson looked to have accomplished the gargantuan task of keeping Palace up virtually all by himself, but fate had other plans. Jonathan Fortune's 82nd-minute leveller floored the Eagles and they would be heading back down to the First Division.

In another time and with a little more luck it could all have been so different. All of that early promise cut short over time. When players get hurt and are forced on to the sideline most of the consideration goes to the team. Everyone misses out in those circumstances in terms of what could have been but they are the ones that suffer because of what is. Losing is a part of football. It hurts, but it's the kind of anguish that will heal. Not being able to get on the pitch to play in the first place, that's real pain.

33

Sol Campbell

OBSTACLES DON'T consider their own existence. If the job is to restrict, then that is what they are designed to do. What impedes can even have a sense of righteousness. It's a responsibility to ensure someone else doesn't reach a particular goal. When it comes to the art of defending, this is all part and parcel of the game. Far from prejudiced, nobody gets through. It is only afterwards that certain barriers are somehow still imposed by those who are completely oblivious that they're holding them in the first place.

Sol Campbell was much better than the stories of him are capable of telling. So many defenders have come to the fore since and the standard to which they are held grew with the television audiences and hype that came with them. Playing in the era just before a litany of incredible centre-halves does him no favours, yet he stood toe to toe with them all. Realistically he should not be a polarising figure to those outside of the Tottenham fanbase but football is a game that revolves around certain kind of lines. Crossing those divides can be as crucial as a match-winning tackle and preventing the ball from going in or something much more unthinkable.

The rivals are meant to be the enemy, the antithesis of everything. Such language is both excessive and nowhere near representative of how so many feel. There are multiple factors that play into what happened in regard to Campbell moving from Tottenham to Arsenal for it to be as simple as an issue of allegiance, but for so many that's all it can ever be.

Hate is a very strong word. To have such depth of feeling for what ultimately amounts to strangers is an extreme example of a game that shouldn't matter that much yet still does. Even a milder form of hostility doesn't change the person or the reality, but distorts them to such a degree. What's happened in regard to Campbell's reputation following his playing career is a more unique set of circumstances. Some of his political views, including running for mayor of London for the Conservative Party and loosely being in favour of Brexit, can be divisive to say the least. In a sense it's hard to think of Campbell in just footballing terms. But ultimately that's what it should be all about.

The idea that only characters who are universally likeable get their dues is exceptionally naive. Forgetting the idea that a contingent of Campbell's peers have been able to take jobs at a higher level, it's the idea that any failure is permanent. As such what happened at Macclesfield and Southend should be evidence that might prevent him from ever being given another managerial offer. Taking a side five points adrift and keeping them up in six months is anything but. What happened at Roots Hall was much more complicated, long before the season was halted for Covid.

The elephant in the room is not what Campbell has done but what he represents. Attitudes towards his managerial ability may only be a minor form of prejudice but they all count the same. Personalities clash, people don't always get things right. Macclesfield fans will point to him wanting the club to be wound up for what amounted to a paltry sum of money, similarly taking Portsmouth to court when they were at an all-time low. Southend players felt cut off from him during the lockdown and Spurs fans have a more obvious objection. Dislike him for who he is if you have to, but not for the caricature that many are desperate to portray him as.

The imposing figure that became an imperious centre-half. Long before St George's Park there was Lilleshall, the football school that lies at the heart of so much of a particular generation of players. Closed in 1999, by this stage it was already considered well behind the times. Though it did not fulfil the purposes of bringing through a collection of players good enough to bring England back to glory on the international stage, there were more than a few familiar faces who passed through its ranks and went on to be key for both club and country. Few of them won more than Campbell.

Good players can survive being thrown in at the deep end. Having the ability is all well and good but it's also about keeping a certain level as the challenges get harder. Being thrust into the Tottenham first team at 18 years of age against Chelsea in September 1992 and scoring is certainly a way to make waves. It wasn't enough for Terry Venables, however, who didn't play Campbell again for the entire season. It would be the first of over 250 Premier League appearances for Spurs, during a time of massive upheaval that ended largely the same way. Though optimism persisted throughout the 1990s, there was little in terms of tangible hope for those at White Hart Lane. It was home to some fantastic players down the years, who for whatever reason never quite put all the pieces together.

Campbell the captain was never much of a doubt. The role befits the position of centre-half perfectly, with all the leadership across the defence that is already entailed. Beyond that the way he played with composure and assurance, it wasn't possible to create a more ideal candidate. In 1999 he won the League Cup at Wembley with Tottenham to become the first black captain to lift a major trophy underneath those old twin towers having already been the second youngest player to wear the armband for England during the summer prior. Gaining in stature and status all the time, this was maybe where a crossroads appeared before him. As far as the White Hart Lane faithful were concerned he was at the very heart of Tottenham

Hotspur. What followed was the incredible process of having it ripped out.

Leaving in the first instance would have stung. Running down a contract and signing somewhere else on a free would have hurt even more. Explicitly stating that would not happen adds an extra layer. Every step along the way felt specifically designed to enrage Tottenham fans. There is also a question of loyalty. Supporters often lean on this concept, as though clubs and managers don't cast players aside in an equally fickle manner. In this instance it goes deeper than that. In October 1998 Campbell was accused of breaking a steward's hand after an altercation following Spurs' 1-0 win at Derby County. The club's lawyers wanted him to have the case bound over, effectively admitting guilt with no further consequences. He wanted to directly contest the charge and was informed he would have to pay for his own legal defence and that Tottenham themselves would have nothing to do with it. The case was dropped during the summer of 1999; Campbell's sense of abandonment lingered.

This is where football blurs that line between business and personal. On one side it's an impenetrable barrier; it doesn't exist on the other. Campbell made a choice about his career in the same way everyone else does. At the same time those who adored him and cheered him have a right to feel aggrieved. Those divisions that exist have the capacity to consume. Feelings above all else. While all the emotions that Tottenham fans have felt are valid, it's the abuse – both at the time and ever since – that becomes too much. Not that moving club is something that should ever require it in the first place; forgiveness in football remains then as it is now, very much in short order.

As for what became of Campbell at Arsenal, that may have been even more insulting. Plugging a player of that ability into the team that Arsène Wenger was building made both go up another level. With Tony Adams on the verge of retirement, the transition between the two was seamless. Over the course of the

1990s the Gunners had become synonymous with a rigid and determined set of defenders that Campbell was at the perfect point in his career, that didn't also mean that there was any need to wait for trophies. A commanding second half of the 2001/02 season meant that Arsenal were well placed to take back the Premier League trophy. Included in that run was a powerful performance at Old Trafford that won it outright. With the FA Cup already having been secured a few days beforehand, it meant that for the second time in three years Arsenal had done the double. Taking the title in the home of their fiercest championship rivals set the bar incredibly high but it wouldn't take them long to clear it.

Campbell the leader was by this point very well established. But in 2003/04, in among all that was going on at the time, at the epicentre of the Arsenal defence there wasn't the kind of famous partnerships that had populated it in years gone by. Alongside him for what would be one of the most memorable seasons in Premier League history was Kolo Touré. Going through the whole season unbeaten, the emphasis lies very much more on the defence rather than it does the attack. The idea of breaking Arsenal's resilience in terms of holding on to their record – especially down the latter stretch – was built upon the solidity of that defence. Just 26 goals conceded in 2003/04 would have been enough of a foundation for success in any season.

Nothing lasts forever. In October 2004, invincibility would be stripped from the Gunners in cruel fashion, all from the dangling leg of Campbell. He clearly tried to move his leg back and out of the way of Wayne Rooney as he drove into the penalty area but the Manchester United man made sure of the contact. Impossible though it was for things to get any better than they had been previously, that whole season became one of real discontent. By its end Campbell was watching from the sideline as Philippe Senderos partnered Kolo Touré at the heart of that Arsenal back line. All the effort and hard work put in over the years to maintain such high standards seemed to be coming to the fore. There's never any room for a break at that level, no opportunity to take a breath. The following year Campbell took matters into his own hands. After a dismal performance at home to West Ham, he asked to be substituted at half-time and then left the ground. Wenger gave him time off – albeit reluctantly – and the defender flew to Brussels to clear his mind. He didn't return for a month.

Coming back into the Arsenal fold, remarkably there was yet more drama to play out. The Champions League Final in Paris pitted if not the two best footballing sides then certainly the more aesthetically pleasing sides in the world against each other. This wasn't the all-encompassing Barcelona team that was to come and the Gunners were more than a match for Frank Rijkaard's team, if not better. After years of stamping their authority on the English game, getting their hands on the Champions League would not only emphasise their place in world football but underline the Wenger era as a whole. Rather than being decided by tactics, the game was determined by administration.

When there is ambiguity to a situation, the men in the middle have a lofty track record of making less than straightforward decisions. Jens Lehmann's challenge on Samuel Eto'o appeared to be mitigated by the fact that Ludovic Giuly put the ball in the net for Barcelona. Referee Terje Hauge decided to rule out the goal and instead force Arsenal to play with ten men for 70 minutes than rather than play with a full complement. Somehow, the Gunners took the lead. Thierry Henry's free kick was bulleted into the top corner by Campbell. Now they had something to hold on to.

The second half was an inspired performance, showcasing none of the things that made this team great but all that was needed to try and get over the line. With 15 minutes to go Eto'o slotted home an agonising equaliser having been played in down the left-hand side. With barely any time for Arsenal to gather themselves, Juliano Belletti snuck into the box and fired through the legs of Manuel Almunia. Barcelona had their hands on the trophy for a second time, denying Arsenal their first. Campbell, having scored the goal earlier on in the night, was forced to rue yet another instance of his attacking exploits being for nothing.

David Beckham's red card was the overarching headline of a tumultuous World Cup second round tie in 1998. It could so easily have been Campbell dominating the back pages. With the game deadlocked at 2-2 and destined for penalties, his disallowed goal late on would have almost certainly given the win to England. Something similar happened again in the European Championship in Portugal six years later. Beckham's free kick was headed on to the bar by Michael Owen only for it to loop high into the air. Campbell put it home with ease but a very generous foul was called. If either one of those had gone the other way, they could have changed everything.

Leaving Arsenal in 2006, the suggestion of Campbell playing abroad lingered before he eventually signed for Portsmouth. Harry Redknapp's collection of seasoned pros gelled perfectly and were able to punch well above their weight. After Pompey finished eighth in 2006/07, Campbell was announced as captain and led them into the new season looking for further glory. Different victories mean different things. When it came to lifting the FA Cup in May against Cardiff, this was the kind of esteem and importance he was used to. Portsmouth's definitive cup win that season came a few rounds before, however. Going to Manchester United and putting Alex Ferguson's side out was of a difficulty few could ever conquer. During the 101 FA Cup ties over the course of his Old Trafford career, United only ever lost four at home. Redknapp and Campbell were each involved in two of them.

With 15 minutes to go thoughts might have turned to simply trying to claim the replay but when Tomasz Kuszczak was sent off for taking out Milan Baroš, the complexion of the game swung dramatically. Not only did Portsmouth have a penalty but there was no goalkeeper to call upon for United, with Edwin van der Sar having already been subbed off injured at half-time. Rio Ferdinand donned the gloves for what time remained. His first job was to pick the ball out of the net after Sulley Muntari dispatched the penalty perfectly in the right corner. Knocking out Manchester United left Portsmouth with an open path through to the final and gave Campbell one more chance to lift the FA Cup high above his head at Wembley.

The wheels fell off very quickly at Fratton Park shortly afterwards. Redknapp left along with a host of players and those who stayed weren't being paid. At the end of a challenging season Campbell too left the club. Things were getting worse as legal action continued in the background while Pompey's Premier League existence was being extinguished. Money matters of a very different kind involved Campbell signing for fourth-tier Notts County of all places. Sven-Göran Eriksson's influence – along with plans for an incredible amount of investment – encouraged him to sign on the dotted line. It didn't last long. The whole project fell apart very quickly and Campbell only ever ended up playing one game for the club. Still it did allow him to enjoy a late stage resurgence, going from League Two to the Premier League again and being welcomed back in by Arsenal.

If it was to be a farewell tour then at least Campbell got to say goodbye properly. A goal in the Champions League helped Arsenal into the quarter-finals against Porto and a real run in the side followed as they closed out the 2009/10 season. He wasn't finished yet. The briefest of runs at St James' Park in a Newcastle shirt even saw him take the armband briefly.

Sol Campbell was a giant of English football, an ever-present right the way through from the inception of the Premier League until 2011. His transfer across north London in the summer of 2001 remains the most contentious move the league has ever seen. Possibly will ever see. The divide between rivals is strong. Campbell was stronger.

34

Jan Åge Fjørtoft

AS PART of its many magnificent contradictions, the experience of being a fan is both singular and composite all the same. Regardless of allegiance, everyone brings with them a perpetuity of opinion. All well-intentioned and all with a particular common goal in mind, the only consensus here is within a mutual victory. Even in the face of division, this is the great unifying factor of football. No matter what other exterior or interior factors in this world may tell us apart, we are all at home – rain or shine – under this particular umbrella.

Pure joy cannot be found in solitary. Witnessing even the greatest of triumphs alone means very little, for it becomes those moments shared within the gaze or embrace of a stranger that form the foundations of our deep-rooted connections. Stories don't have to be written down if they can be experienced in such a way. It's how myths and legends are made. Every generation passing down a version of events, all told through their own particular vantage point.

Perhaps the largest universal truth in football is that no fan would swap their experiences of that with another club, regardless of how large the respective success discrepancy of the two teams. The league table never lies, so they say. But those lines are so fragile and frenetic that ever-changing rankings allow for some untruths to slip through the cracks. Finishing sixth is nothing to lord over seventh without context. When only one team can ever stand out on top, this doesn't mean that there isn't anything left to play for or anything left to feel. Up and down the leagues there are a multitude of experiences left to be had.

Fanbases exist within bubbles, as a result of which nobody knows as to where any other teams stand. League tables and cup competitions tell us of a hierarchy; season tickets and watching the games can contradict all of that information. Devotion exists at such a baseline level as to overrule objectivity. That kind of allegiance means more than any kind of professional jealousy. Up and down the league setup as it is, there exists 92 separate groups who – in spite of whatever flaws – all believe in that singular vision. They wouldn't have it any other way.

No one can have it all, from the obscenely wealthy to those fallen on harder times. Success can take as much as it gives; hardship through pain can bring people together. The Premier League has grown in the past 30 years to a point which for some renders the game itself unrecognisable. That disconnect between generations of fans has led to – at least on the surface – a very soulless experience. Global giants from way upon high can look down upon those below them but to do so is to misunderstand the togetherness beneath.

When stripped bare, following football is meant to be about something bigger than just trophies stored away in a cabinet. They help signpost certain destinations but in and of themselves they are hollow trinkets. Winning is the driving force behind so much; the prizes on the other side of any given season are always what motivate. Rewards come in many different forms. The joy is in the process as much as it is the end result. Rather than simply being ushered through, having a grip on the future is to be in control, even if what turns out to be on the other side isn't all it's cracked up to be.

Whatever happens, happens. There's no alternative reality, no second chances. Part of the beauty of supporting is that no matter what, nobody has to go through it alone. Agonising heartbreak or unbridled joy. Being able to share those feelings, that's what the beautiful game really is. Everyone has stories of countless days out and the people around them who under other circumstances are complete strangers. Faces that are only ever seen in passing. Yet this is them at their very best and worst. Whether watching in the stands, out with friends or at home with relatives. They are all family.

The system is always in need of a slap, something to keep everyone on their toes. A league set up primarily to fuel the greed of those at the top needs some variety to keep it in check. Those humblings come in the form of participants that don't fit the traditional mould. The financiers and sponsors of the 2020s would simultaneously paint them as unwelcome guests and plucky underdogs all the same. Where the Premier League has become a repetition of the same old servings, looking back they are the colour that fills in the lines.

Swindon Town joined the Premier League in 1993. Ten months later they were relegated having finished at the bottom of the table. In between those points in time, a record was set which will take some going before it is ever beaten. Admittedly, this feat owes more to the fact that there were two more teams in the league and as such four more games in which to play but conceding 100 goals in a campaign isn't something that can accidentally be broken. For context, Derby County shipped 89 goals in 2007/08 and this would only get to 98 if extended across 42 games.

When the talk surrounding promotion is one of simply being happy to be there, it can become inconsequential very quickly. Swindon earned the right to play in the top flight for the first time in their history by virtue of overcoming Leicester City in the First Division play-off final. It was the second time in four years they had won at Wembley, having been previously involved in a scandal that would eventually see chairman Brian Hillier jailed. A tax fraud case was brought against the club throughout 1989/90 with allegations of money being placed on them winning the Third Division two years earlier and yet somehow Ossie Ardiles managed to guide them into the play-offs and promotion to the First Division. Ten days after securing their place in the top tier, an admittance of 36 breaches of league rules saw them stay down rather than go up. With fan protests to ratify their elevation unsuccessful, regardless of how emphatically they were cast aside in 1993/94, at the very least they had their fate decided on the pitch. Even in that sense it was still off-field changes that set the tone for what was to be Swindon's solitary season in the Premier League.

John Gorman is a face from football past, where all the old adages apply. The kind of man who loves the game so much and for whom it is poorer that there are fewer and fewer of his kind. It was under him that Swindon went 17 games from the start of the season without a single win, saw a century of goals against and were firmly rooted to the bottom throughout. Despite it all, no significant amount of blame could be pointed in his direction. Everything could have been so different.

In all probability it would have all been too much, but having such an integral part of what had taken them to that point ripped away made what was to be a crowning achievement so bittersweet. Glenn Hoddle joined Swindon as a player-manager in 1991. Further player sales prompted a feeling of a potential downfall. These fears turned out to be unwarranted. It wasn't so much a case of turning around a sinking ship as it was steadying the course. He did such a good job that upon beating Leicester in the play-offs, Chelsea took notice and chose Hoddle to take them forward. Incredibly this was then the point that high-profile players began to depart. Broken and divided, Gorman stepped in to hold it all together.

When everything appears to be going wrong there's always something to cling to. Regardless of how facile it may seem, hope can be found in the most unforeseen of circumstances. Jan Åge Fjørtoft arrived at Swindon as their most expensive signing of all time; nearly 30 years later his position on that list has only moved down to third. The idea that someone could come from a village in Norway (via Austria) to spearhead the attack of an unfancied Robins side encapsulates the scope and speed with which English football was continuing to expand. That he ingratiated himself in such a way as to be still remembered is a testament to a time that had a very unbalanced proportion of highs and lows, but it was still worthy all the same. Looking back, there is also a distinct possibility that things could have worked out differently. If only Fjørtoft had managed to start scoring earlier.

Form is a remarkable intangible. When it's apparent there's no mistaking it. Finding it can feel as futile as pouring smoke into a keyhole. Twelve league goals from the end of January onwards represents one of the better six months of scoring throughout all of the Premier League years. The problem arises when this is on the back of a six-month dry spell immediately prior. No individual turnaround could have helped Swindon to such a degree as to ensure their safety but there are always those games that hang in the balance and can be decided by a prolific striker, which Fjørtoft absolutely was after the turn of the year. As ever with strikers there is no switch that could have been flipped, no key differences that are made. All it takes is one moment.

After half a season without even a glimmer of success and with a World Cup on the horizon, Fjørtoft was looking to ensure his place within the Norway team that year. If that meant leaving Swindon then so be it. A cup game against Ipswich changed all that. Scoring – even in defeat – at the very least alleviated the short-term worries. What happened next was that sense of communal belonging in action. Something as simple as going into the city centre to run errands and seeing the cry from the local paper for him to stay, that kind of acceptance and affection goes a long way. Though it wasn't to ultimately end with a reprieve for Swindon – bittersweet though it may be – was still enough to form a lasting bond between a club and player that remains to this day.

Following relegation, things continued to escalate in the wrong direction at the County Ground, which meant a change of scenery was needed. Swapping Swindon for Middlesbrough has its own sense of glamour, even before the idea that Fjørtoft lived in a castle during his early days. This was a Boro side that, with Bryan Robson in 1995, needed just that little extra to see themselves over the top of a restructured First Division that only had room for one automatic promotion place. One year after dropping out of the Premier League, Fjørtoft had found a way back. Unlike his previous spell, however, this time around his team had a lot more in the way of creative firepower.

Moving away from Ayresome Park to the Riverside Stadium in 1995, at the same moment as stepping into the top tier, everything about Middlesbrough in the mid-1990s felt very much like a step forward. Fjørtoft christening their new home with a goal in a 2-0 victory over Chelsea, even as early as August set the tone for a team that even in spite of a horrific second half of the season were never in any trouble of going back down again. This was an exciting, exuberant group of players that caught the eye for all the right reasons. Adding Fabrizio Ravanelli from Juventus a year later to a side that already contained one of the most enigmatic young talents in Juninho was a salivating prospect. By the time they went down in 1997, however, Fjørtoft had already been moved on.

From the outside of the top flight looking in once more, a year at Bramall Lane split over two seasons that produced 19 goals may very well have been the most fruitful spell. Losing to Crystal Palace in the 1997 play-off final prevented this particular arc from being fulfilled but there was to be one more chance. The parallels between Barnsley in 1997 and Swindon in 1993 don't quite mesh completely, yet there was more than an element of resemblance in their respective journeys. Part of an exclusive club to remain in the Premier League for a single season, both have had their day in the sun. Rather than be forgotten or cast aside, for that alone they should be celebrated.

Barnsley Football Club – like so many others – wears its heart on its sleeve. Its rise to the top of the English football pyramid was a once-in-a-generation event. Everything clicked in such a way that makes a mockery of tactics, planning and foresight. What Danny Wilson and those players came together to do was to allow for a peek behind the velvet rope. Those six months Fjørtoft played at Oakwell in the Premier League, when it was likely already too late to stage a resurrection, was a time that meant something. There's so much that doesn't matter to so many. Years in which nothing at all happens. This kind of success means more than that which transpired over a short space in time. If not for the moment itself then for that which led up to it.

These are the kind of accomplishments that mean little to those above them. They have never had to overcome odds in such a way. Putting together an assortment of talent from across the globe for an enormous amount is one thing. Getting over that line is one of inevitability. Doing it without those resources, being able to get to a point that was never promised, that's really special. Supporting a team is meant to be a relief, that which alleviates the pain of everyday life. It's not so much entertainment as it is a world away. To grab the attention of those who would rather pretend you're not there. The ability to bring the eyes of the world to Swindon or Barnsley and to acknowledge their existence. There has been so much taken away from these fanbases in the years that have followed. This can never be.

35

Sergi Canós

SO MUCH of football is entrenched in the when. Every second asks a question, every answer requires more time. Nameless faces not only can but will come and go, as a parade of insignificance marches ever backward. For the most part, the characters that matter live in the shadows. Echoing the lore of certain comic book counterparts, masked until the point they make a significant mark.

Irrespective of ability, price tag or even circumstance, the identity of those who will bring the most joy is kept secret. A multitude of candidates will come and go, many of whom tick all of the boxes, only to be left with a half-baked selection of failed opportunities. Few get the storybook ending they deserve and as a result their legacy doesn't taste as sweet. When fan favourites don't correspond directly with periods of success, remembering them is without distinction.

Euphoria gives as much even if it's expected. The prospect of a first game in the top flight for over half a century is enough to enthral multiple generations, all of whom barring a select few were entering unknown territory. Adding to the lure that was dangled out there so tantalisingly was a wounded opponent. Simultaneously an amalgamation of the comedy and tragedy masks that supposedly represent all of drama, Arsenal have –

since the latter 2010s – provided much of both for their own and opposition fans alike. With both absences from Covid and injury, the Gunners were lacking firepower in every sense. Not that Brentford needed any motivation or indeed levelling of the playing field; it all made for an occasion that would reflect the jubilant mood. Nothing could have truly dampened the atmosphere. As things were about to play out, everything was about to be go up several notches.

Regardless of their availability, Arsenal went into a game waiting to be picked off by their opponents. Sacrificed at the hands of the banter gods to an expectant and willing audience. For those who stood inside the Brentford Community Stadium and wondered. For those who were there that day and witnessed. It only took twenty minutes to have that first taste of what was a seemingly inevitable victory.

Pressure comes in many forms. Whether it was the way in which Brentford pushed their opponents back or that difficult feeling of excitement and anxiety that blanketed everyone in attendance, the home fans needed a release almost as much as the Arsenal defence. Bryan Mbeumo hung a cross in the air that was scrambled clear in a desperate attempt to not give away a corner. Within an instant the ball was put back in. Almost as if it had been fated. Sergi Canós picked it up just on the corner of the penalty area. Shaking off the token attempt to close him down while cutting inside, in an instant his shot had been fizzed into the back of the net. Christian Nørgaard came on late to seal the win and settle any nerves; everything that had started some time beforehand could reach its climax.

Plotting the way back from that moment goes through a lot for both Brentford and Canós respectively. Two years before the two had even met, a move from La Masia to Melwood set a certain future in motion. Joining Liverpool from Barcelona in 2013, progression was slow and steady but continually constant as Canós went through the ranks under the youth team setup at Anfield for two years and it was clear a career lay ahead. It's not so much that the loan system has fallen out of favour in the last decade, more that there are so many prospective players on hand at any given time that giving them the proper focus can be difficult. In terms of gaining first-team experience, this can be more of a stalling process than anything else. Canós joining Brentford in 2015/16 wasn't meant to be decisive. Along with other factors going on at the club at the time, building blocks were being put into place.

The sums required to ascend right the way up to the top of English football are as complicated as they are large. Whether it be as simple as goals or assists or a formula much more complex, ultimately the numbers that matter are financial. To operate independently of the ever-changing landscape that is within the EFL, clubs often find themselves on the wrong side of a group or an individual boldly broadcasting a desire to propel them through the leagues. Within that too there are those who have bottlenecked the top of the Championship having gorged on a solid diet of Premier League parachute payment. Even before thoughts can turn to any kind of ascension, simply trying to stay afloat among all of this in some instances requires a different set of thinking.

Matthew Benham didn't do it all single-handedly. No one person could have. Yet whenever the rise of Brentford is discussed, his is the name that comes up. It didn't happen overnight either. Scouting and dealing in transfer fees both in and out is an imperfect process, one which Brentford have been fortunate enough to be on the right side of more often than not. There have been mistakes, however. From the outside it was a meteoric rise that ignores the fallout with Mark Warbuton and a continued scepticism that this model – however the media were prepared to label it – would ever work.

Marinus Dijkhuizen isn't necessarily going into Brentford folklore, to the point that Dean Smith's tenure is much more about three years of correcting an unfortunate miscalculation. Within that time a squad had been assembled and stripped in equal measure. Plenty of sides have made it to the Premier League and then found themselves in a situation whereby teams higher up look at them through the eyes of a child in a sweet shop; very few of them make it through that process lower down and maintain progress.

Ezri Konsa, Neal Maupay, Ollie Watkins and Saïd Benrahma had all been identified by metrics and then subsequently been plucked out in a very similar way for much higher fees. Being able to pinpoint talent at the right time and develop them into something that will benefit long term either financially or on the pitch, is about as complete a process as scouting gets.

When Canós arrived in England, he was 16 and the Bees were in the third tier. Players brought into high-profile setups at a young age, only to find that particular door shut on them, face a difficult choice. It's hard to rebuild a career that hasn't even fully started yet.

Over the years as progress sputtered and stalled, loan moves to Norwich and then the initial period with Brentford that piqued their interest, the likelihood of first-team football at Anfield diminished. With so many drafted in to try and fill any and every hole that a side could possibly need, very little attention is paid to those that come out the other side and have to start again. Staring down that particular career cliff edge, however, there is another way.

Cutting those ties isn't easy. The blanket of being able to hide within the fringes on higher wages, hoping to get one last opportunity will call to some. A one-off game at the end of the 2015/16 season as Jürgen Klopp hugely rotated ahead of the Europa League Final might have offered enough of a reason to stay. It's the ultimate test of talent, appetite and application. Only if you have the first will you be able to make it back and even then that relies on the other two not being slowly taken away. Canós took the leap of faith to change what was meant to be the main story into the prologue and make what came next the narrative that mattered.

After Dean Smith came Thomas Frank. The culmination of a specific period in history was coming, that much was clear, and 2019/20 would be the final season Brentford would play at their traditional home ground. Signing off with promotion to the Premier League would have been the ideal ending but football has never been that straightforward. At first it was form that got in the way, then trying to recover from a less-than-ideal start was made even more difficult by the fact that Canós would be absent. An injury sustained in October 2019 away at Nottingham Forest all but put an end to his season. He wouldn't be back ready to play again at all until the following summer, by which time Brentford's season still hadn't finished.

Recovering from knee ligament damage as Covid-19 put a stop to all football represented both a light at the end of the tunnel and also illuminated the emptiness. The escape that the game usually provides was put into stark contrast for everyone. Canós made his comeback albeit tentatively, sitting on the bench, ready to make an impact on a surreal season that was about to take another turn. West Brom continuously faltered in their attempt to secure automatic promotion, with Brentford unable to capitalise in painfully helpless fashion. On the final day with the Baggies drawing at home to QPR, everything appeared to have opened up perfectly. All they had to do was get over the line against relegation-threatened Barnsley, in what was the last game at Griffin Park. With no fans in the ground, what should have been a raucous finish instead evaporated into nothing. A draw wasn't good enough anyway, so only a last-minute winner for the Tykes would tangibly affect anything. Barnsley got their reward and Brentford would have to go again to fight for theirs.

It's not so much superstition as it is mentality when it comes to the play-offs. The sides grateful to get in at the lower end are playing with a freedom that those who have just missed out on the top two places often cannot. An entire season of work with such a prize being dangled in front of them all to be condensed into three games. Swansea City weren't in perfect form going into their semi-final with Brentford but with 16 goals in their last ten games had found a dangerous attacking edge. A 1-0 win for Swansea at the Liberty Stadium wasn't quite the free-scoring encounter that might have been envisaged but once again it leant into the idea that Brentford had completely blown it. Yet another chance to bow out at Griffin Park awaited in the second leg. To see them off in the perfect circumstances.

By the time Canós took to the field with 15 minutes to go, it was all over. Brentford's three-goal blitz in the first half had erased Swansea's lead and then some. Rhian Brewster managed to get one back to set up a nervy last ten minutes but part one of the job was done. Fulham lay in wait for them at Wembley as Brentford looked to finish it. The rawness of a one-off game like this is that all it takes is one mistake to end it, especially when it is tight enough to go to extra time. David Raya stepping off his line in anticipation of a cross, only for Joe Bryan to sneak a free kick in behind him, doesn't sound out of the ordinary in principle. That the shot in question was from 35 yards and still somehow managed to find its way into the net puts into perspective how out of position the Brentford keeper was in the first place. Chasing the game meant a second Bryan goal followed before an arbitrary consolation in added time. The final whistle confirmed Fulham's ascendency and condemned the Bees to have to start all over again. They wouldn't have to wait for long.

Setbacks in football provoke a feeling of impatience. There's no room for sitting back and collectively sulking, just an insistence on getting back out there to try and put those troubles to one side. In different circumstances Brentford might have had more time to mourn what had just happened, but because of how Covid-19 had affected the schedules there were just 39 days between their defeat to Fulham and the opening day of the new Championship season. Form-wise, it took a while as a club to get into a groove again, just as Canós himself was getting closer and closer to being fully match fit. During the winter both the player and the team found themselves again. A Canós hat-trick away at Cardiff on Boxing Day as Brentford won 3-2 elevated what was already a good run of form into something that could see them challenge for automatic promotion once more. Wycombe were hammered 7-2 a few weeks later and Brentford now looked unstoppable but three defeats in February proved otherwise. Once again the play-offs were where it would all be decided.

At the very least, this time there would be some fans in the ground, albeit not quite the contingent that would have made the kind of noise and atmosphere that games like this deserve. Another semi-final, another first-leg defeat. Bournemouth had been through a disappointing campaign to date given their hopes of bouncing back to the Premier League at the first attempt but trying to deny them that chance was going to take a lot, especially when they doubled their lead in the opening exchanges of the return leg. In a breathless half of football, the future of both clubs hung in the balance. Ivan Toney levelled from the penalty spot to cut the deficit in half before the game was even ten minutes old. Chances kept coming at both ends before the game turned on a red card dished out to Chris Mepham. Despite the disadvantage, Bournemouth continued to pose a threat, knowing that one goal would leave Brentford needing three. The second half took little time to warm up as Vitaly Janelt levelled the tie with a stunning finish from outside the box. Marcus Forss added a third to put Brentford ahead for the first time with ten to go and from there it was a case of holding off any last-minute surprises. For the second season running, one game was all that stood between Brentford and Premier League football.

Promotion itself is never easy. The accumulation of so many little moments along the way, distilled into a season or a single game. There was little time for drama this time around, with Toney and Emiliano Marcondes putting the Bees 2-0 up within the first 20 minutes of the final against Swansea and never looking back. Into the top flight for the first time since the late

1940s, generations of Brentford fans waited in anticipation for the campaign that was to follow. Very few players get the chance to write their place in history so vividly. It's usually only after the dust has settled and context can be applied that the full picture appears. With Canós scoring that goal against Arsenal, however, right there in that moment, the picture was organically complete. Regardless of what else happens in the future this will remain a snapshot in time, which Brentford fans will be able to take with them and cherish forever.

36

Ashley Young

NO MATTER how progressive a certain time feels, it will always be put to shame with what's to come. After the turn of the 21st century, being stuck in the past was even more of an error than it already had been previously. Preconceived notions of playing styles had moved on very quickly yet certain ideas remained.

Of all the flawed tactical notions that have continually circled the drain it's the insistence of physicality at an early age. It helps, there's no mistaking that. But there remained a notion that it was easier to teach technique to overdeveloped teenagers than anything else. This of course ignores a famous photo with three figures standing together for a youth game. Two of them completely dwarf the other and one of them is the referee. The shorter figure in this instance was none other than Andrés Iniesta, one of the most technically gifted players of his generation.

Who knows how many players were discarded in favour of those with a temporary advantage. Ashley Young was very nearly one among them. Released from Watford's academy at 16, there aren't many for whom that wouldn't have been the end of their journey. Not everyone gets another chance to prove themselves again. He did. Being able to stay on part-time and look those same coaches in the eye and prove them wrong takes a level of mental toughness that few possess. Add that to close control and a breathless turn of pace and therein lies a potential superstar.

Over two decades now, the Hornets have always carried with them something of a sting in the tail. Their first foray into Premier League football in 1999 served – if nothing else – to resolve Graham Taylor's standing after his England humiliation. In the subsequent years Watford spent more time avoiding second-tier relegation than any flirtation with going back up before Aidy Boothroyd's team was able to put together a promotion campaign that defied all expectations.

The pitfalls of the Championship play-offs all incur how a team arrives there in the first instance. There are those who miss out on going up automatically and can't get over that setback, and alternatively there is always a side that sneaks in at the last minute and rides that wave to glory. Somehow Watford managed to avoid both, having finished third comfortably but so far behind second place that it didn't matter too much. Dispatching Crystal Palace with their all too recent Premier League history in the semi-finals was a feat in itself. One game from dreamland, an even bigger challenge lay in wait. Leeds were a side that had heritage on their side even if not those history makers within it. Beating them wasn't necessarily on the cards or even something that anyone could have predicted. Watford didn't care much for predictions and emerged victorious, 3-0. Back in the big time.

Teams don't arrive in the Premier League as perfect; far from it. Unfortunately for Aidy Boothroyd and the Hornets there was a long road to go to even get to imperfect. Young in 2006/07 was a solitary comfort to everyone at Vicarage Road, to the point where his talent became so obvious that leaving was on the cards. With him they were doomed, so the choice to cash in during January of that particular season felt as inevitable as their slide back into the league below. Martin O'Neill and Aston Villa were very much putting together a side to be reckoned with and there was no doubt that Young would fit in with that.

Everything was set up. Through a succession of smart transfers and a bold young English core, surely it would belong to them. The future is promised to no one.

Breaking into the top four and the Champions League places was a challenge for so many teams during the 2000s. As difficult as it would be in terms of resources and quality in any other era, Villa's task grew exponentially because of just how much their collective opponents – Manchester United, Arsenal, Liverpool and Chelsea – had about them. They were not just vying for prizes domestically at this point and the coveted Champions League places but looking to take that particular trophy home too. Trying to force one of them out was always going to be a monumental proposition.

Villa reinforced as best they could. There was no denying the team they had built had some real substance to it, yet the levels above were always going to be too much. By 2008 they were more of a top-four pretender than contender. That year Young was the only outfielder to make the team of the year outside of the aforementioned cabal of clubs. Even within that, Villa finished in sixth place some 16 points away from all of them and were still shut out of prospective Champions League football. As hard an undertaking as this was already, what really hurt O'Neill at this point was the growing disinterest from above. Having tried, tried and tried again, there was to be no more money forthcoming from owner Randy Lerner. Though this challenge proved too much for Villa, for Young there was another level to go.

For a player that had spent so long in his career to date delivering so much for very little in return, moving to Manchester United ahead of the 2011/12 season was very much a welcome change. Having been outside of a very specific bubble looking in, his first goal at Old Trafford represented what he had been previously up against as well as another one that was forming. Beating Arsenal 8-2 early in that campaign stands out now as it did then as a result that ended an era. Though success abounded in the immediate future, an old warning from that game still rings true. Being left behind happens rapidly, quicker than anyone could possibly ever expect it.

Transformation is a big idea contained within a single word. Either weighed down or let loose by what came before, going in a different direction is fraught with danger. There was no doubt that Sir Alex Ferguson's retirement two years later would leave a hole that would prove difficult in filling. Things very quickly went from bad to worse. Part of this is a fallacy of stability, in that change is inevitable. What matters is to be able to ride the waves of revolution in real time. A longer delay or outright denial of it, makes the eventuality of what is to come so much harder.

The United standard was for so long the very best any team could ever get; something only they could maintain and that other clubs looked on with envy. Ferguson had steered that particular ship through both calm and choppy waters, picking up all manner of treasures along the way. An empire that was built to last that then began to dissipate. There are a myriad of factors as to why it didn't go well for all those that followed but the cold hard truth is that they couldn't measure up to all that which had gone before. It was an impossible ask, with an answer all too obvious to those looking on. With both aura and manager departed, there remained a group of players with the experiences and knowhow from those lofty days. Slowly but surely, they too began to leave. Young was by no means in the Class of '92, and nor would he go down among Fergie's most important signings, but he knew what it took and once again had to dig deep. To fight for his place, he would have to evolve again.

Formations and set positions have come to mean less and less. Maybe they never meant anything at all and were solely a way of simplifying everything to such a degree that anyone would be able to understand it. Truth lies somewhere in the middle. So it's not a new thing that players possessed of a certain understanding would be coached into new roles. What's become fascinating is that this process has continued to speed up as the roles themselves have become ever more demanding.

Most forward-thinking players go on a journey as they get older, usually in a backwards direction. This is more due to physical demands of attacking areas and an ever-increasing insistence on flexibility. What helps these transitions, however – and makes them seem more frequent – is pulling from a footballing knowledge base that they have drilled into them from day one.

It's not quite total football. Even now, players having to play in every position is some way away from modern Premier League tactics boards. But as demands for wingers have increasingly become more about their proclivity for tracking back in addition to their attacking prowess, so too has a focus on full-back play become more and more about not just defending. As a generation has grown up with an upturn in multi-position productivity it's now easier and less eye-opening to see someone who used to be an all-out attacker become a solid defender.

There will always be room in the England squad for a tricky winger. Whether any dazzling skill or dynamic driving runs would have been showcased in a Roy Hodgson team is another matter entirely. Having been a mainstay in that Euro 2012 side, Young's international career came to something of a halt, however. That was until his role had been redefined. The Three Lions' run in the 2018 World Cup presented something of a second chance and it was one he relished. It seems also there will always be room in the England side for a solid professional who knows his job and can work within a system. This too would ultimately end in disappointment, having been taken off after 90 minutes and watching on as Croatia completed their turnaround in the semi-final.

With age comes responsibility. There are very few in a footballing sense bigger than that of being the captain of Manchester United. Having been there through and beyond a failed revival or two, compensation for Young's hard work and commitment came in 2019. It was a far cry from the team he joined some seven years prior but the distinction still remained the same. There was even still time for one last hurrah and one final moment of magic to savour, Young wearing the armband in Paris the night Ole Gunnar Solskjaer and his team wrote another page into Manchester United folklore with a dramatic victory in the 2018/19 Champions League round of 16. Regardless of the long-term repercussions of this result, it still goes down as an all-time performance for a club built on them.

With playing time dwindling and the glory days seemingly in the rear view mirror, certain challenges have more appeal than perhaps they would have in previous years. Taking the leap to join Inter Milan at 34 years of age would have been a bold call for anyone. Those kinds of risks are the reward in and of themselves; simply being in sufficient demand to even have the opportunity to play in Italy was a testament to Young's application and ability. Antonio Conte demands a lot from his charges and it certainly wouldn't have been a tranquil couple of years of Young soaking in the sun simply waiting for retirement. Scoring in the final game of the 2020/21 season was the cherry on top. This was already a game in which he had staked his claim to fame by becoming the first English player to win both the Premier League and Serie A.

There is still to be an epilogue written for Ashley Young. Having rejoined Aston Villa in the summer of 2021, a project that appeared to be stalling has a new lease of life under Steven Gerrard. Champions League football may not be the ask this time around but even so, Young's career has been one filled with defying expectations and rising to any challenge. Whatever happens next, however he bows out, there are few who could have accomplished more given his initial circumstances. The boy who was cut from Watford's academy came a long way.

37

Edin Džeko

OF ALL the sacrifices that are to be made on the way to glory, notoriety might be the most negligible. Trophy rooms contain achievements and not accreditations. The team is bigger than any one person. Every input matters, though not all are made equal. There's always going to be some discrepancy within the squad as a whole and those that actually added the finishing touches to drag everyone over the line.

There have always been superstars, the players that shaped the game during the second half of the 20th century. As the years passed and generations followed, those who became legends in their own lifetime were still around to witness their mythology grow. When Diego Maradona passed away in late 2020 it felt like even with everything that had moved on within the game, no one individual could ever have that kind of impact again.

Collective kudos has taken something of a back seat over the 2010s as the game became increasingly more devoted to the singular. Applications of team spirit are eventually applauded but the contributions that add up are often missed in either the sum of events or the overbearing weight of a moment that can only ever be determined by a lone striking of the ball. Of all the adulation that's there to be given, it will always be goalscorers who get theirs first. From the back to the front, no matter what the achievement, those that put the ball in the net will gain the most attention.

The very best goals are meaningful. Regardless of the way in which they are scored or the intricacy of the build-up, even the most aesthetically pleasing goal flatters to deceive if it ends in defeat. They all count, but the ones that really matter are those that go in when the situation calls for it the most. Cup final goals are always looked back on with more fondness than the 30-yard screamer under the lights against a team that was comfortably relegated. Not only is there a certain significance in terms of winning trophies important but timing is key too. The last-minute effort draws out a much better reaction than any other, creating scenes in the stands as much as they do ripple effects in time. Combine them both and you have a recipe for something beyond incredible. Under the right circumstances, even a conventional finish can go down in the record books for all time.

When it comes down to what happened at the Etihad Stadium on 13 May 2012, one word describes a whole range of emotions and events: Agüero. Admittedly it needs the Martin Tyler spin on it and heavy emphasis on that last syllable, but those who were there to see it know how futile any attempt to describe it may be. In that regard, here's what happened. Going into the final game of 2011/12, the destination of the Premier League championship had already been decided. Manchester was where it was heading; it was just a matter of whether it would be the blue or the red half. Both sides had relatively winnable games given the form they had been in over the course of that season. Manchester City hosted relegation-threatened Queens Park Rangers while Manchester United travelled to the Stadium of Light to take on a Sunderland side with nothing to play for. The Red Devils would have to beat their local rivals' result in order to snatch the trophy from under them. Any City win would see them crowned champions. Even with that, no one could have ever imagined the events that would play out.

The role of spoiler is a unique one for a team to be in. Supporters often embrace it; inflicting pain on another group of fans can offer a cruel momentary satisfaction. Sunderland did enough to keep the scoreline down and the contest alive before eventually falling 1-0. QPR, meanwhile, tore up all expectations in a way that defied belief. They had their own ambitions in regard to not winning the league but simply staying afloat in it. To guarantee such a place, they needed to get something out of this fixture themselves. Of all the talk of a turnaround that instantly went into footballing folklore, the rollercoaster ride for QPR in terms of how this day played out will have been equally exhilarating.

For the first half at least, this was nothing more than a routine home game. City carried with them the impetus and all the threat, while Mark Hughes's QPR team went about the task of trying to keep it as tight as possible for as long as possible and then see what played out. By the time Pablo Zabaleta opened the scoring, already too much time had passed. A few minutes before half-time is typically referred to as a great moment to break the deadlock; in this case this was more than just a cliche. People were breathing a sigh of relief when the real tension was still to come.

Collective mentality means more than just a side having the will to win. In City's case there was an integral split between the players on the pitch that day and certain sections of the fanbase. Having experienced certain highs and more frequent lows over the decades, those who spent the last 20 years watching their neighbours win everything in sight while they were once languishing in the third tier had a certain sense of disbelief. Not in terms of any mistrust in the players or the manager who had taken them this far, just a horrible sense of impending doom.

'Typical City'. A two-word phrase that can be applied to many clubs up and down the country. If they're going to achieve anything at all, it's not going to be easy. Djibril Cissé scored for QPR just after half-time. Instantly the tension that hung around the stadium before the interval increased ten-fold. Joey Barton then decided that things weren't dramatic enough and so kicked out at Agüero before half-heartedly trying to headbutt Vincent Kompany; all of this after he had been sent off for an elbow on Carlos Tevez. The dichotomy of a football match when it becomes 11 v 10 can often embolden the defending side into completely frustrating their opponents. Things got even worse for the home side when Armand Traoré capitalised on some space in behind on the left and picked out an unmarked Jamie Mackie to give QPR an incredible lead. Even with everything they had been through, for Manchester City this was far from typical.

From the pit of despair came the inevitable response. Trailing 2-1 with just over 20 minutes to go, all the while Manchester United holding firm against Sunderland meant they would need a turnaround the likes of which didn't feel plausible, let alone possible. Goals change everything. One of the more forgotten aspects of what was about to play out didn't happen in the north-east of England but rather in the Midlands. Stoke had staged their own comeback against Bolton and Jon Walters' penalty meant that QPR would be safe even if they lost at City. How much word goes round in these situations and how great a say they have in them is down to the players themselves. But with so much hanging in the balance and things changing so quickly, they would all have been acutely aware of what was at stake. At the very least the mood would have changed in the away end. Soon the whole stadium would be celebrating.

What's more important, the winning moment or the collective opportunities that led to it? The culmination of either a game or an entire campaign – especially a triumphant one – owes much to so many different factors that attributing it to just one is both obvious and oblivious. Last-minute winners don't exist without the equaliser, it's just that in this case Manchester City needed both. Paddy Kenny in goal for QPR was on the verge of something remarkable; a Manchester United hero without ever putting on the shirt. As the clock ticked down it looked destined to be but in a plight such as this, all it takes is one moment.

Set pieces add to the drama, both in terms of the possibilities they could lead to and the pause in action to allow that pressure to build. Edin Džeko's goal is a perfect illustration of everything he brought to the table for Manchester City: tall, imposing and with a perfect head but also with just enough movement so as to not rely on physical presence alone. The roar around the Etihad was one of pain and promise. They had come so far and now the equation was very simple – a single goal and nothing else would matter. A single chance for everything to matter.

Then the clock read 93:20. Bedlam. Football at its most incredible. Layer upon layer of meaning. Heartache and heartbreak with the single swing of a boot, all to a level that can never quite be put into context. That's for Manchester City fans to do. Neutrals are fortunate enough in having witnessed it but those emotions are only on the surface value. What value it was. Given everything that had gone before, there's no scenario in which anyone outside of their own support will feel sorry for Manchester United in the way things panned out but it will be hard for them to add the required sentiment from something that everyone else saw through the same lens. Teams lose trophies, rivals beat them. Never quite like that.

Aside from the work put into that one result to conclude the season, so much more had to be put into place in order for that fantastical finish. Last-minute heroics dragged Manchester City to a title that was decided on goal difference. Other leagues settle these kinds of scores on a head-to-head basis, which that season fell in City's favour too. Their superior goal difference was underlined at Old Trafford where Džeko came off the bench to score twice and change the narrative of a derby defeat to that of a changing of the guard in a 6-1 scoreline. The line between Mario Balotelli's 'Why Always Me?' and Martin Tyler's 'Drink it in' isn't a straightforward one. It goes through Vincent Kompany's winner against United at the Etihad before ultimately stopping at Agüero and euphoria. With ten goals in his first 11 games, Džeko helped as much at the beginning as he did in the end.

For what it's worth, 2012 wasn't even the only time Džeko played a pivotal part in bringing the title to the Etihad. The 2013/14 season presented a different opponent. There were also more trophies to play for; not content with just challenging for the league alone, this was now a team that could compete on all fronts. Twenty-six goals in all competitions that season included a central role in their victorious League Cup campaign. Still it wasn't enough to outshine a certain Argentinian. Once again Agüero was dominating the headlines and the affections of Manchester City fans. There was another weapon at their disposal this time around, someone who added an extra dimension and took them up a level. When questions were asked of their consistency going into the final straight, he allowed them to pull ahead and never look back.

Yaya Touré dominated the league in 2013/14 to a degree that few have ever done before or since. Not even an hour after Steven Gerrard's slip and Chelsea's 2-0 win at Liverpool, Manchester City took to the field against a Crystal Palace side at Selhurst Park desperate to (and later to) have their say on proceedings. Both hindsight and a very specific narrative make the following result seem a foregone conclusion. Palace had built up a head of steam and if ever there were an opportunity for another twist in the title race, this was it. After four minutes Touré found Džeko with a beautiful cross to make it 1-0. Before the break Touré burst through to shrug off Damien Delaney and put City firmly on course for a second title.

Information and access go hand in hand with propaganda and deception. As the quality of the Premier League began to mature and flourish during its adolescence, so too did the scope. Quite literally, a whole world opened up. Somewhere along the way this became a point of supremacy, a melting pot of talent, collectively lauded for their competition as a whole. The Best

League In The World™ may have been born in 1992 but it wasn't christened until much later.

On the surface it was mainly about protecting an investment. Sky TV footed the bill so naturally they would be eager to laud the results. At first when UEFA opened a door, results on the continent were mixed. For as much as would change domestically, the collective addition of multiple teams from a single nation to the Champions League would ultimately play out consequences that no one could have ever seen coming. That collision of clubs that would see an unprecedented amount of footballing prize fights, it made a mockery of the World Cup.

The greatest gathering of players was no longer restricted to every four years on the global stage, it was transmitted into our living rooms on an almost weekly basis. Pitched against the backdrop of a golden generation and successive European Cup finalists – including an all-English final – and the narrative was set. That's how you can end up a Bundesliga title winner without playing for Bayern Munich and it doesn't matter. Why scoring 29 goals in Serie A to guide your team into the Champions League and then helping them towards one of the greatest comebacks of all time is an irrelevance. Reducing Edin Džeko's contribution to the Premier League alone is to do him a disservice but at the same time still does more than enough in the time he was here. Others may have the attention; without Džeko they wouldn't have as many medals.

38

Titus Bramble

CRUEL IS the finger that points, ruthless is the laughter. At the sharp end football can be overtly painful. Not just in the traditional heartbreak of a one-off result or season that ends in tragedy. It's a mandatory ritual of humiliation, weighted heavily from one end of the pitch to the other. Attack versus defence not only conjures images of a very precise setup but also how the whole game becomes defined. Childhood dreams are made of scoring a last-minute winner and not running back to make a goal-saving tackle after all.

On top of the idealistic divide there is also a more pragmatic problem. In addition to the aesthetic advantages that forwards will always enjoy from up in the stands, it's a duel that will end one-sidedly. A goal can be threatened multiple times and in turn that danger can be dealt with. It only takes one defensive error to undo all that good work.

From an entertainment perspective, perfection is boring. Annibale Frossi is a name that resonates more in Italy than it does on English shores but he – and many others – helped shape the game across Europe during the the 20th century. The tactical breakdown between what is known as 'Catenaccio' and simply parking the bus may be frivolous at best but the defensive ethos remains the same. Frossi's philosophy was that a completely flawless game of football would finish goalless. In his eyes it was the ultimate balance between the two sides. If that is the case, football should be more thankful to the flawed.

Defending is hard enough as it is. The communication, positioning, physicality and reading of the game all at the same time, all nullified by one bobble of the ball. To a degree, mistakes are inevitable. They happen at every level, with countless casualties wanting the ground to swallow them up every time a group of people get together to kick a ball around. Taking it from the friendly five-a-sides that we all know, now add several layers of consequence and ability on behalf of the opponents. Professional footballers are uniquely gifted in making their fellow pros look stupid. Entire teams have players whose whole game is built around creating – and then pouncing – on those errors. Unfortunately it then becomes a vicious cycle, with the knowledge of any discernible flaws being preyed upon again and again.

Titus Bramble became a punchline to a joke that didn't get funnier the longer it went on. Social media may have spread the unwanted legacy of Phil Jones and Harry Maguire in more recent years but it paled in comparison to the treatment and consensus regarding a player that at one time was seen as one of the biggest prospects in the country. Defenders of a certain age have to pay certain dues. It's understood that they will earn or acquire their imperviousness over time. What's more, the idea of making a big step up in dramatic circumstances always leads to wild conclusions about where a player's ceiling lies.

Bramble broke through into the Ipswich first team at the age of 19. If his performances weren't enough to get people talking, what the team as a whole was doing certainly did. Ipswich unlocked a secret code and found a particular formula off the back of the togetherness of their squad and George Burley's management to completely shatter all expectations when it came to their return to the Premier League. Nobody quite knew what was happening at the time and Ipswich were too busy enjoying themselves. It was like a house party where everyone in attendance had no idea how this stranger had been invited but they were too unique and cool to question.

Learning on the job is the same in any position but nowhere is it more of a crucible than at centre-half. All but a select few have gone through their careers without at least having to go through a certain something; before there was a recognisable fall it also is worth noting that in the beginning there was also a rise. Sir Bobby Robson saw enough to bring Bramble to St James' Park in the summer of 2002 to join a Newcastle side that had enough in the way of experience and promise to threaten the Arsenal–Manchester United duopoly that stood at the very top of English football. Not being able to break that particular stranglehold was no disgrace. But the opportunities that were spurned in that time and the way in which they were is a real blow to everyone involved. Looking for reasons is a lot harder than pointing at a scapegoat.

Football analysis has changed throughout the years and continues to evolve. Judgements reserved for a particular time and space grew with the spotlight. Mistakes could be dealt with in-house if for nothing else than for every era prior to this one, they weren't showcased on such a platform. The ever-growing culture of televised top-flight games doesn't in and of itself change anything. Filling in those gaps with vitriol disguised as criticism became inescapable. There's a word that wouldn't gain any larger prominence until later on but as the culture and scope around the game grew, so too did a particular concept. In the words of Richard Keys, it was just banter.

In much the same way that blame can be allocated disproportionately, to say that the programme *Soccer AM* is solely responsible for a shift in the way fans behaved is to give it too much weight. Between 9am and midday on a Saturday it was for some years appointment viewing, starting the weekend for so many and very much becoming a cultural touchpoint to those of a very particular demographic. Analysis was either too boring or barely scratched the surface and what's more, following the game to such a degree is meant to be fun. Fully tapping into the climate at the time paved the way for a much more contemporary take on everything that happens on a football pitch, which was to remove all context, empathy and understanding and not only relish failure but encourage everyone else to join in. It didn't take very long for Bramble to become the very centre of attention in exactly the wrong way.

Insight isn't to call out who was wrong, it's to identify why. Looking to individuals and highlighting their flaws is one-dimensional. How those players were put in those positions in the first place, either by the opposition or their team-mates, that's what matters. Bramble drew attention to himself initially for this very reason. The mistakes that were made tended to be completely apropos of nothing. These lapses in concentration made him an easy target. To some level it's a comfort mechanism, the overt nature of these errors and the simplicity with how they are understood. So many people watching on who never got their chance to play at a particular level, revelling in the false notion that this meant they could.

Giving any ammunition to critics enables them to continue to fire back all the same. Trying to justify a career while still growing into it again lends itself to the idea that in football there can be no room for nuance. Players are either this or that, with no room in the middle. Unfortunately, Bramble's misfortune was Newcastle's suffering but he wasn't alone in that. Sir Bobby Robson was in the midst of putting together a team that had the right amount of boundless energy from its youth contingent as well as a healthy mix of dependable experience. What that meant was that it had the quality to compete but also the propensity to self-destruct. Bramble epitomised that in the worst way. Years of being on the precipice of something, only to sabotage themselves as a club led to irrevocable damage. Out went Sir Bobby and in came Graeme Souness.

If things weren't precarious enough, there was another addition to the Newcastle team in 2005 that poured even more fuel on to an already combustible situation. Jean-Alain Boumsong had been linked to a move to the Premier League for a couple of years prior and proceeded to show nothing to warrant the interest that there had been in him. He and Bramble formed a partnership held in a very distinct regard, one that shone no light on either player. Their actual record together wasn't as terrible as the myth-making would suggest. In 32 games across all competitions they took part in 21 wins and conceded 27 goals. They were never going to be Paolo Maldini and Franco Baresi at the back and almost certainly suffered from their collective consideration as much as anything. Not quite at rock bottom but certainly in need of a lift and a lifeline, along came someone who knew a great deal about defending.

The idea of Steve Bruce looking over at what was happening at St James' Park, recognising some inherent ability and trying to help add some finishing touches, sounds like kismet. Things that sound too good to be true usually are. Titus Bramble was signed for Wigan Athletic by Chris Hutchings in the summer of 2007. When Bruce came in later in 2007/08 they were second from bottom of the Premier League and in need of some serious repair work. After some tactical switches that saw Wigan move to a back five during the latter part of that first season, it looked as though Bramble was about to be discarded before his career at the DW Stadium could even get going. The decision to go back to a more traditional flat back four in 2008 opened the door for the most consistent form of his Premier League career.

Wigan then enjoyed a season away from the drop zone, even challenging for a European place before settling down into the potentially disappointing security of mid-table. Scoring just 34 goals all season and conceding 45, this was as clamped down as a Steve Bruce side got. An earlier incarnation of Wigan had been free-flowing and vulnerable at the back; this was not that. There wasn't much Bramble could do in terms of repairing the way he was viewed on the whole but being named their player of the year will have been some vindication. On the whole, such was the recovery overseen at the club in a short space in time that Sunderland felt the need to take Bruce to the Stadium of Light. Roberto Martínez arrived and once more the floodgates opened.

Finding players to fit certain styles and moulds is part of a manager's remit. Let it not be said that it was a surprise to learn that Bramble wouldn't necessarily work so well in an open, passing system. It's not as though the evidence was already there. Wigan shipped 79 goals in 2009/10, yet it was a goal at the other end that allowed for another remarkable escape. At home to Arsenal, desperately needing the victory and down 2-0 with time running out, after all the highlighted errors that Bramble had been a part of here was one that finally went in his favour. Ben Watson had pulled one back with ten minutes left and when Łukasz Fabiański spilled a corner right in the middle of his goal all that was left was for Bramble to head into the net from a yard. Charles N'Zogbia completed the extraordinary comeback a few moments later and Wigan would live to play Premier League football for another season.

Leaving behind the exposure of a Roberto Martínez side for something much more beneficial in reuniting with Steve Bruce at Sunderland was an easy move for Bramble to make. What's more, the Black Cats were in the ascendancy. At the start of the 2010/11 season they were virtually unbeatable with one defeat in the first nine – albeit with far too many draws – before Newcastle and the Tyne–Wear derby that effectively ended it all. Already three goals behind and hopelessly outclassed, in the second half Bramble's reckless tackle on Andy Carroll resulted in a red card and being waved off by an unforgiving St James' Park crowd.

The two and a half years that followed were the very worst, almost as if he had reverted to a parody of himself. By this point the reputation completely dwarfed him as a player and there was no way back. To play at the top level for so long is to have that ability. Eight games shy of 300 in the Premier League doesn't happen by accident. Since Bramble retired it's a trend that's continued ever upward. Players are lambasted and harassed for less and less, not that any of them ever deserve it. As scrutiny has intensified and analysis becomes perpetual, the jeering voices have become less and less satisfied. It's all become a bit too personal.

39

Alisson

IT'S THE last minute. Everyone steels their resolve once more. There's a silent recognition among all the players; what follows next will potentially define the future and most certainly the 95 minutes that has come before. A million different things will all be contextualised following the actions of a solitary kick. Chaos theory suggests you can find a pattern inside the madness. There are signs of a design at least. A fully crowded penalty area disperses. Depending on the perspective, from here everything has to go right and wrong in the same action.

Sam Johnstone never stands a chance. As a goalkeeper all you can hope is to be able to be close enough to get something on it but the ball is beyond him with a ferocity that fully illustrates the futility of his position. The timing of this goal makes it beyond impressive, its circumstances consequently putting it beyond most realms of comprehension. Yet the structure of the goal itself is not its most significant feature, even with everything else to consider. Its magnificence lies not within the design but rather the architect itself: Alisson.

The celebrations are enough of a picture that paints more than a thousand words. A swarm of red shirts descend on the Brazilian goalkeeper, a mixture of joy and bewilderment all around. It's the sight of a side collectively letting out an emotion not just of competitive relief. Vision is only part of it, however. The sound of a goal of this magnitude should be visceral, guttural. From the deepest parts of the collective souls of everyone gathered together. No doubt houses up and down Merseyside would have reverberated with the kind of fervour that could power a million suns. Yet there's something more than haunting about the only noise in the ground coming from the players themselves. For as much as Liverpool have gained in this moment, it was also a stark reminder of what has been lost.

As far as 2020/21 was concerned, football could not take a break. Administratively there were all sorts of contractual and financial implications that ultimately mattered for absolutely nothing – the show would go on regardless. There were no definitive right answers at this stage for these were questions that had never previously been asked. Everyone involved did whatever was possible to carry on as normal in the most abnormal of circumstances as the Covid-19 pandemic continued. Safety was the prime concern, both in terms of the participants and also everyone who would have been cheering them on in the stands. This meant empty stadiums. At a time of such strong feelings, all of them were removed from the game. Football would not stop, this had been made clear. What was played out though didn't feel the same. Without the fans it was nothing. Very little mattered at that point. Those things that shone through did so with sobering clarity.

Post-match interviews are at best a tradition steeped in cliché. Requiring athletes to quantify all manner of emotions and circumstances in a way in which actual journalists struggle to let alone those involved seems like something of an exercise in futility. There are no words that could have sufficiently conveyed how Alisson felt at the time; there certainly was a feeling. In among the sheer weight of emotion on display that day professionally, there was something far more important internally being expressed. Tragedy had struck close to home and like so many at the time, Covid restrictions meant he would not be able to grieve properly. Not only to be unable to say goodbye and be in the presence of family but also to be on such a public stage when privacy will have been what was needed.

Football can be such a respite. The simplicity of a game in which a ball needs to be kicked into a very specific space versus an ever more complicated world. It's where restless minds can go to be at peace, having at least some time in the week to think about something else. Alisson's emotions that day brought all of that into focus and demonstrated that even though these players exist in a world beyond our own recognition, they were very much still going through the same things.

Covid changed everything so quickly. A year prior, Alisson watched from the sidelines as Atlético Madrid came out on top at Anfield in a Champions League match that shouldn't have been played. From handfuls of games being called off in Italy to the Premier League being interrupte, football was caught up to the same turmoil as the rest of the world in the blink of an eye. Unprecedented times asked a million different questions; the logistics of leagues continuing, if they should be able to at all. In the face of such horror football meant very little, but that did not mean that these people and their achievements meant nothing.

Finishing the season meant more than just the culmination of one campaign. For those playing it was the resumption of an effort that had been a few years in the making. A week before everything came screeching to a halt, Liverpool had gone to Watford and were torn to shreds. The home side won 3-0 with Alisson among others powerless to stop Ismaïla Sarr in particular. This was their first defeat in 44 games, on the back of a run that had only seen them drop two points in the entire season to that point. That point was in February and the elusive 19th title that had been so coveted by the Anfield faithful and so well-earned by Jürgen Klopp and his team was finally within touching distance. By the time they did get their hands on it, everything else seemed so far away.

So much had passed between Alan Hansen lifting the First Division title in 1990 and Jordan Henderson being handed the Premier League trophy. Now that the wait was over and Liverpool had got back their place at the top of English football, everything was in place for an epic celebration. Having seen off Chelsea 5-3 just moments before, the mood was one of completion. The trophy was handed over and fireworks were going off as far as the eye could see. Everything was there but one key ingredient. For the first time in 30 years the Reds were champions of England and there were no fans inside Anfield to see the coronation.

When the going is hard, it's only at the end that the path becomes clear, in so much as not going the quickest way doesn't matter if you got there in the end. There will always be one or two moments to look back on and see where everything veered off course altogether and possibly where it may have ended long before, in abject failure. For Liverpool the road to the 19th championship had been derailed many times previously, but in terms of Klopp's team and Alisson it is an odyssey with its roots in the European Cup.

Clubs with history are full of it. Whatever situation, there is almost inevitably a parallel. Not all of them are as immediate and direct as that which happened over the course of 2018, long before any of the trophies that were to follow became registered. What happened with Loris Karius and the potential after-effects of concussion in the Champions League Final do not change the record. Throwing the ball straight to Karim Benzema goes down as one of the most high-profile goalkeeping errors in a match of that magnitude that there has ever been. After Gareth Bale's second goal, which sealed Real Madrid's 3-1 victory, and the tears that followed after the final whistle led to the question of whether Karius would ever be the same again. Goalkeeping is such a volatile pursuit which is intricately tied to all those around them; Karius being openly mocked by a Chester forward in a friendly before the following season was but a mere taste of what was to come. Having attempted to back his man, Klopp would have to look elsewhere.

Lost among the endless scenarios in Premier League history that very nearly affected everything is the part that Thibaut Courtois and Kepa Arrizabalaga play in all of this. Real Madrid were among those batting eyelashes at Alisson, who had made significant progress at Roma over the past few years, but they baulked at the asking price. Bringing Courtois to the Bernabéu from Stamford Bridge instead left the path clear for Liverpool to get their man but put Chelsea in the market for a new goalkeeper themselves. When Alisson arrived at Anfield it was for the record fee paid for a goalkeeper, which was broken almost immediately as Kepa went to Chelsea. Irrespective of the price tag, not having that burden of being the costliest may have just allowed Alisson some more time to bed in. In another world it could even have been Kepa who had joined Liverpool, which again sets off another chain of events very distinct to what actually happened.

Goalkeeping is different today, even if the fundamentals have stayed the same. More progressive managers have made the decision that it's better to have 11 footballers on the pitch rather than ten, and as such goalkeepers are much more involved in the build-up play than they used to be. This clashes with certain old-school principles and mentalities in that watching those at the back pass the ball between themselves in an attempt to draw forwards out does certainly lead to some heart-in-mouth situations. Playing out from the back isn't something that could have been contemplated for even more aesthetic reasons previously. The pitches in the 1990s and even early 2000s were not conducive to such a style. It's only as the improvement in the playing surfaces themselves has gone on that this has become more of a possibility, rather than something more fundamentally tied to a brand new way of playing.

When Alisson arrived there was a real fervour for failure. After a mistake against Leicester in a game in which Liverpool won, there were question marks regarding his footwork and willingness to take on an opposition player. Though it may never look anything other than horrifying, it's proven to be a go-to strategy for those at the very top of European football. The harsh reality that some don't want to accept is that every now and then it's going to backfire.

One moment doesn't change it all. There's too much that happens either side to be sure that a single exchange is enough to set the course for the foreseeable future. When looking back though, there are instances that if removed from the timeline erase all that goes forth. The final group stage game of the Champions League in December 2018 saw Napoli visiting Anfield with the knowledge that this was effectively a winner-takes-all night. Not only that, a single Napoli goal would mean that the home side would need three. In the dying embers, with all the maths having been both checked and rechecked, Liverpool led the tie through a moment of magic from Mohammed Salah. As the game stretched into injury time, with absolutely no chance of a response, the ball fell to Arkadiusz Milik in front of goal. Alisson smothered the shot, making himself almost as big as the chance itself.

For a second everything stood still. There was no way of knowing that this one save would lead to a sixth European Cup for there was still so much work to do. Without it, however, there was no chance that the success could ever have happened. Remove it from the record and not only is the triumph in Madrid erased but so too potentially the momentum that carried the Reds to a 19th league title the following year. The difference between those two realities isn't down to the actions of one player alone, it's just that some people are called upon more than others. In that one moment, Alisson had the future of Liverpool in his hands. It was always going to be safe.

40

James Beattie

GOALS ARE an inevitability. Watching certain teams may not feel like that, and yet their weight can defy physics as well as the odds, for the significant ones have the ability to lift in a way that very few things can. Through a variation of different stakes, settings and skill they are the breadcrumbs that are left as clubs either find their way to glory or get lost in the process. Who is putting down those markers means nothing when compared with the enormity of them not being there in the first instance.

Because of the nature of football and especially as it has become ever more commoditised, identities of every kind begin to dissolve. Clubs move on to something new, the importance of which feels at odds with everything that has come before and the people involved take on greater significance. Through dint of nothing more than their career, these players became something else entirely. The Premier League did such a comprehensive job of erecting and placing so many on a pedestal that part of what was lost along the way was the humanity at the centre of it all.

Judged by a fraction of their being. Outlined by a series of abstract qualities. Representing something bigger than the singular and defined by the collective outcome. Putting on the shirt and wearing that badge, whichever one it may be, means something. Gives the bearer a higher purpose. There's a reason why goalscorers interviewed after the game always play down their own achievements in favour of 'getting the three points'. Cliched though it may be, what it adds to a sense of camaraderie it takes away from a very important distinction. Footballers are people too.

Kicking a ball around isn't rocket science. If anything, the delineation between athletes and academia has always been portrayed with complete antagonism. One cannot exist within the same space as the other, which is to say that football players are dumb and intellectuals can never be physically strong. At a professional level these cartoonish stereotypes are as exaggerated as they are exposed. Not everyone can be one thing or the other, nor should there ever be any pressure to be. Human beings are nuanced. Who knew?

More or less every interview James Beattie ever conducted either led with or shoehorned in the fact that he wanted to be a brain surgeon. Such a concept flies in the face of aforementioned typecasting. Either way, his path towards the pitch was far from conventional. Having been a proficient swimmer in his youth, moving from one sport to another was quite the switch. Shoulder injuries are rarely the foundation from which football careers are made and yet the teenage Beattie leaned into that choice. Far from the conventional route, it did lead to the chance to play at Ewood Park. Joining his boyhood team just after they had been crowned champions of England, circumstances again took a turn for the player and club.

Breaking from the youth team to make a smattering of appearances in the Premier League proved at the very least that Beattie was a prospect, which was the view Southampton took. As Kevin Davies was sent to Blackburn in the summer of 1998, part of the transfer was that Beattie would go the other way. Finally having found the opportunity for first-team football, any guarantee of a Premier League career was threatened by the events that transpired. The Saints had done more than flirt with relegation over the course of the early Premier League years, their survival more often than not spearheaded by the iconic Matt Le Tissier. Once again at the end of the 1998/99 season, a rescue effort was needed. Three wins from the last three games, inspired this time around by a combination of Le Tissier, cult hero Marians Parhars and Beattie himself, meant that he had firmly established himself as a top-flight player and endeared himself to the fanbase. This also enabled a much more important transition.

Saying goodbye to The Dell in 2001 was a moment for everyone. Home fans adored it, away fans were weary of it and everyone in between had no idea what they were missing out on. Moving stadium does not erase all that came before. Still, a new ground has a very different feel and flavour. So much of the identity of a club is based where they call home because for so many of those who travel there it's a journey that's been undertaken hundreds of times over. Changing that feels wrong, to the point where for some clubs it can feel like an entirely different entity. What's more, the structure of the ground pushes the energy in very different ways. It's a testament to the work that has been put in during those years since that St Mary's was never a millstone around the neck of Southampton. While it was different and people will always remember The Dell with a certain amount of fondness that can never be replicated, it was never to the detriment of the team.

There was more to move on from than just a stadium. Le Tissier was coming to the end of his playing days and that was always going to signify the end of an era. While no one could have possibly replaced what Le Tiss meant to the Southampton faithful, or even compared to the exceptional talent he possessed on the pitch, Beattie still found himself in possession of the baton that was passed. Change doesn't have to mean worse; at least at first it looked like a new dawn had arrived for a side that had spent far too long struggling in the bottom half of the table. The 2002/03 season was a breakout campaign with the Saints flying as high as fifth in the table before eventually finishing in a more than respectable eighth. Beattie led the way with a career-best 23 league goals. There was also the not so small matter of a trip to the Millennium Stadium and an FA Cup Final. Even though they went in as massive underdogs, in these kinds of games, all that's needed is one chance.

The beauty of cup football lies within a levelling of the playing field. Over the course of a season the teams with superior quality should overcome perceived lesser opponents. The one-off game, where spirits can be raised higher than even quality can account for at times, is at the very heart of sport as a contest. For those who are supposedly better, this is their chance to prove that superiority. For everyone else, the opportunity of a lifetime awaits. Southampton gave the very best account of themselves but it wasn't enough. Arsenal scored midway through the first half and held the Saints at arm's length throughout. Even then, it could all have been so different if Beattie's last-minute header hadn't been denied by Ashley Cole. As the final whistle blew, the ground was emptying. The Millennium Stadium remained chiefly populated by one set of fans – those from Southampton.

There's something to be said for being defiant and standing tall in defeat. It's the Rocky Balboa thing of just wanting to go the distance. There's no joy that comes with defeat, especially a close one that could have gone either way. When thinking about missed opportunities, it may be better to be beaten handily and not live with that regret. But to have that moment as a club, where players and fans alike are as close as they can be. It may not have been ideal but we gave it our all, especially when the opposition have shown a casual disregard. Certainly Arsenal have gone on to experience more finals than Southampton in the years that followed; they've also had to treat them with a lot more respect than this one. What goes around comes around.

Following up that kind of excitement and disappointment can be a grind. In order to make sure that the club positions itself to have another shot at glory simply involves getting the fundamentals right. For the teams that aren't blessed with an owner with endlessly deep pockets, stability comes before success. For Southampton that plan took a dramatic turn. Enjoying a straightforward season, far from danger and even pushing up towards the European places, out of nowhere in January 2004 news of manager Gordon Strachan's intention to leave the club at the end of the season was leaked to the press. His desire to take a break was expedited once it had been made public. Despite increased speculation that it would be Glenn Hoddle who would take his place, Paul Sturrock was plucked from Plymouth in the Second Division instead.

Players and managers don't always see eye to eye. For both, the other is a means to an end. Some divides can be bridged, others don't need to be. Those on the outside of the squad looking in are immediately replaceable but ultimately not influential enough to cause a real problem. When there's an issue between the one picking the team and the first name in it, that can get out of hand very quickly. Some can find a way to coexist, though the instances of it ever working well are few and far between. Beattie and Sturrock clashed to a degree that was never going to end well. From the very beginning, 2004/05 was something of a nightmare for Southampton fans, one that it might have been thought was well behind them.

Player unrest meant Sturrock was out the door just two games into the season. His immediate replacement, Steve Wigley, did little to improve either form or mood around the club. Just two wins in the first half of the season illustrated the seriousness of the situation. Southampton were in dire need of someone to come along and help and yet even then it was remarkable that they would turn to a former Portsmouth man to get them out of it. Harry Redknapp, fresh from walking out at Fratton Park, arrived at St Mary's and set about putting a squad together that could break free of the drop zone. As was ever the case, this meant a turnaround of transfers, signalling the end of Beattie's time at the club with a move away being sanctioned to raise funds. Despite Peter Crouch's best efforts there was finally no one left to save Southampton and six months later they sank into the Championship.

While his old club was on the way down, Beattie signed for Everton to find a team pushing towards new heights. Forcing a way into the so-called Big Four of Manchester United, Arsenal, Chelsea and Liverpool was the goal, which only one club during that period managed – Everton, this season. Everyone who comes into a new dressing room wants to make an impact, although they don't expect it to be quite like this. Half a dozen games into Beattie's time with the Toffees, would-be champions Chelsea came to town. Eight minutes in, Beattie received his first and only red card during his Premier League career for a headbutt on William Gallas. So soon into his Everton career, this inexplicable act left a mark on more than just the Chelsea defender. David Moyes – having initially defended the incident – never quite let it go. The two remained amicable throughout their time together, but you only get one chance to make a first impression.

Finishing in the top four was a significant achievement but it was also no guarantee. After all the effort that had been put into gaining access to the Champions League, there was still one more hurdle to overcome. Before one of many more changes to the rules over the years, the teams that finished third and fourth in the Premier League still had to go through a two-legged qualifying round in 2005/06 and due to the Blues being unseeded in this process that meant the possibility of coming up against some real heavy hitters. As it was, Villarreal of Spain were one of the worst-case scenarios, but still there was no doubt Moyes's team would give as much as they got. Beattie's goal in the game at Goodison gave them something to hope for in a 2-1 home defeat so all eyes were on El Madrigal for a night that Everton fans would never forget.

Referees make mistakes but some are more costly than others. With the weight of an entire season hinging on the outcome of one result, those kinds of decisions don't even themselves out, however. With ten minutes to go, the Spaniards very much on the back foot and everything still in the balance, Duncan Ferguson's wrongly disallowed goal let the hosts off the hook big time. With Everton denied the chance to take the tie into extra time, Diego Forlán finished them off once and for all. The result – especially the manner of it – knocked Everton back for some time. Defeats piled up to the point where they were bottom of the Premier League after the first ten games. Beattie led the recovery with ten league goals but the mood around the club had shifted.

As Moyes worked to get Everton back to where they were, playing time became more and more scarce. Other players arrived at the club, pushing Beattie further down the pecking order, and it came time to look elsewhere. Stepping down a division to lead the line for Sheffield United in 2007/08 meant getting back to basics and scoring plenty of goals. Joint second in the league with his old team-mate Kevin Phillips, after enough time playing a bit-part role, this was enough to allow for another run in the Premier League. Stoke and Tony Pulis had arrived in the top flight with a combative image already established and did not disappoint. No 90 minutes against them was ever going to be easy – they just needed someone to come along and add some finishing touches. Beattie answered the call in resounding fashion after signing midway through the 2008/09 season.

Without a win since late November and stuck in the relegation zone, whatever image Stoke were cultivating would have meant nothing if they weren't able to climb to safety. Scoring a consolation goal away at Tottenham was enough for Beattie to find his feet again, with seven goals in just half a season putting him behind only Ricardo Fuller in the striking charts at the Britannia. Goals against Manchester City, Bolton, West Brom and Wigan as well as a double against Portsmouth in a 2-2 draw saw the Potters finish comfortably mid-table and well away from any danger. Beattie's role the following season was much less impactful both in terms of playing time and an injury as 2009/10 progressed. There was also the time that, following a defeat to Arsenal at the Emirates, Tony Pulis angrily cancelled the Christmas party and ended up headbutting the striker while wearing no clothes. Perhaps the most preposterous aspect of that story was the lack of a baseball cap.

James Beattie's Premier League career drew to a close at Blackpool. His six months there started well enough but both the club and the player were on their way out. Fifteen seasons of top-flight football, all stemming from a shoulder issue as a teenager. Just eight shy of 150 goals in all competitions. It might not be brain surgery, but it's a living.

41

Ben Thatcher

LIFE-CHANGING CHOICES are forever made within too short a space and time as to quantify them. The space that exists between the before and after is so short that for the most part it cannot reasonably be calculated. Brain and body react in such a way that the unthinkable can become reality in less than a second. As such, consequences echo ever onward – sometimes permanently – for motions set into effect in a heartbeat.

In every game there is a moment that defines it. All it takes is one. Sometimes those instances resonate further and characterise entire seasons, while others reflect more on the team or individual. Most of the time these things are within the general scope of football itself, with goals being the ultimate example. Being synonymous with a specific event goes further than the confines of the game itself. In the limelight – with the whole world watching – a person can become indistinguishable from their lowest point.

Every conscious judgement that's ever made comes with the following caveat: what's the worst that could happen? That way, even if you get it wrong there are a multitude of ways in which it could have gone worse. Unfortunately, because of the sheer volume of both decisions that have to be made and the players making them, it becomes a mathematical certainty that we would end up at a particular point. A situation that is closer to any worst-case scenario than could have ever been imagined. The point in question? That of an elbow.

Goalless draws aren't often the source of particular infamy. If anything, both the game and its participants are consigned to the background. Premier League purgatory for Portsmouth who travelled to Manchester City, while judgement was to be forthcoming upon the villain of the piece. How exactly it happened is something of a blur, incomprehensible and foreseeable all at the same time.

The ball comes across from an over-hit corner so Glen Johnson and Pedro Mendes give chase. Ben Thatcher strides over and connects with an elbow of such force that very quickly Mendes, the injured party, begins to seize on the touchline. Perhaps what is the most surreal visual of this entire experience is how placid the scene is. Save for Johnson calling over for immediate medical assistance there are no Portsmouth players even gesticulating. What happens next adds another layer of surrealism to proceedings as referee Dermot Gallagher brandishes a card. Yellow.

Punishment from the FA was as swift as it was decisive. The referee in question would be demoted, while Thatcher in theory could face no action with the incident having been purportedly dealt with. Ultimately they would circumvent this rule to issue an eight-game suspension, underlining a six-game ban issued by Manchester City themselves. From here there are a multitude of repercussions and other facets that spiral outward, not least of which is that not only was this not the end of Thatcher's top-flight career but that there was room for another team still interested in his services afterwards. The only note of significance from the subsequent move to Charlton was in coming up once more against Portsmouth and Mendes, an occasion that the Addicks won 1-0 but was otherwise free of incident. In a different time it's hard to imagine that this would have played out in the same way.

In the days before social media, outrage sat on the windowsill, wafting through the neighbourhood. People still got upset – even justifiably so – but had nowhere to channel that indignity on a consistent basis and so it dissipated. That being said, even with no sustained online campaign there were enough calls of derision. A police investigation was mooted and even talk of criminal charges being filed was enough to highlight how seriously it was being taken.

Away from the furore, there is still a need to understand that remains. Thatcher himself disclosed in an interview with Manchester City's official YouTube channel that he meant no real malice; in fact there wasn't even a thought process of any kind. This kind of explanation does hold for certain isolated transgressions, but not necessarily someone with a history. Some years prior, an elbow on Sunderland's Nicky Summerbee was enough for Kevin Keegan to close the door on an England call-up for Thatcher. There was another flare-up during a pre-season friendly in China that resulted in a collapsed lung for the recipient. This is all casting aside the fact that Thatcher's account of apologising to Mendes in the moment doesn't fit with that of the Portsmouth team and you have a very specific picture painted. The question then becomes, how did we get to this point?

What determines whether to create or destroy always comes down to circumstance. In spite of the fact one is seen as morally superior to the other, it rarely looks that way from the dugout. Make no mistake, no matter what the manager's preference may be, the best teams have always had the ability to do both when it mattered. Problem is, the scales of integrity will always be weighted in favour of the wealthy. For those at the bottom, simply having a choice is a luxury in itself. The beautiful game. Where beauty might have to poke the eye of the beholder.

Imagine going to work, going about the daily routine and every time you got up, someone would come along and spoil everything you had done over the last hour or so. Not only that, they were cheered on for their efforts in ruining everything you might want to accomplish. It might even be their actual job. Such is team sports.

The dark arts. The line between stopping someone and outright assault. Defending has always struggled to walk down a particular path with this line because idealistically it doesn't exist. When the ends justify the means, so long as it doesn't end up as a goal what does it matter? This particular grey area has always existed and is even widely accepted. So long as the tactical foul exists, this brand of cynicism will thrive. Additionally, this spoke to a balancing act that was forever tilted. An acceptance of a certain type of aggression sowed the seeds. The hypocrisy here being that if you had the right face or were doing it for supposedly justifiable reasons then none of it mattered.

Compare Thatcher's elbow to Roy Keane's challenge on Alf-Inge Haaland. For one there has always remained a plausible – albeit flimsy – ambiguity on behalf of the challenge on Mendes. The same cannot be said for an act of premeditated violence that has been rehabilitated in myth for as much as it was devastating. Ignoring the obvious culpability connections and subsequent punishment be it either morally or literally, fundamentally there was a very different culture surrounding on-field brutality at the time. Consider, also, an intentionally harsh David Beckham challenge on Thatcher himself during a game between England and Wales that would allow the Manchester United man to ride out an international suspension at the same time as being injured. Not withstanding the severity of the challenge Thatcher put forth on to Mendes, there has always been a hierarchy of contempt and castigation.

The 1990s was a somewhat broken and misguided period for football, led away from the fans both in terms of price and product. A forced period of reflection as the decade began would induce wholesale changes, of which the Premier League was but a part. As far as the powers that be were concerned, football had an image problem. It was a sport for savages and it needed to be treated as such. Modern policing by comparison to other sports still very much reflects this.

On the field, progression meant a move away from the adages of old. Practically this meant more of a gravitation towards attackers rather than defenders. Both still had their job but as the seasons ticked over, there became very little room for defence by intent alone. Ability was always destined to triumph regardless of how it was being channelled. Unfortunately it left a generation of players behind, those who had grown up in a different age. As this process accelerated, so too did the dissonance between those playing and supporting. The game can change for good and for ill at the same moment.

At the same time as trying to sanitise the action as it played out, there was a simultaneous push to do something similar to those in the stands. Making a more family oriented experience has over the years created a very different experience to which certain clubs aren't quite the same. As more and more at the top move away from their roots and gravitate towards corporate sponsorships more so than the match-going fan, this in turn goes too far away from what unites a community in such a way. Paying for a ticket to support the team fell by the wayside in favour of something that had no connection to the game itself. Whatever was gained in gentrifying football both on and off the pitch, there was always going to be a disconnect.

The way that football has been offered to the public over the last 30 years versus how football fans themselves are treated is something that will continue to drive that wedge. Modern Premier League audiences are a world away from those who filled the stands during the early to mid-1990s. With ever-extortionate ticket prices at the heart of those in charge and corporate box owners being more of the focus than the everyday match-going fan, it's an entirely different experience from what was. If any side epitomised what was given in terms of structure and ability but also taken away in terms of a connection it's the side that Ben Thatcher made his initial top-flight breakthrough with. Wimbledon were and always will be an anomaly for so many reasons.

The Crazy Gang were a family. Throughout their rise and their fall, what mattered more than quality was commitment. Winning was a by-product of doing whatever it took. As a perennial underdog, there's a perceived leeway involved that makes for a great leveller. On top of this there was the off-field culture, which took on a life of its own. The line between Wimbledon as it was and football as it is now is far from a straight one. But as one way of life changed completely, so too did another. Improving the standard of the football on show was a good idea. Perhaps it came at the expense of those watching in the stands.

There's a lot that gets swept under the rug when it comes to certain principles. This holistic idea that those who commit such egregious acts are doing so in complete isolation. When it's all boiled down, football ignores the person. They are an irrelevance, a means to an end. Part of something bigger for better or worse. All the second-hand stories about Thatcher are of someone who had some really serious issues off the pitch; coming into training under the influence, throwing himself into slide tackles on plant pots and climbing on to bars. For someone who has had more than his fair share of controversy, it might not be a question of who they were but rather the circumstances of when they were.

In another life, during another era, Thatcher is transferred to Tottenham at the age of 25 and is able to carve out a credible career within the game. As it was, being cast aside by Glenn Hoddle only compounded his problems. Scoring his solitary Premier League goal during a 4-4 draw for a doomed Leicester side in 2004 proved little in the way of anything. Regardless of any kind of judgement, having amassed over 200 Premier League appearances made for the backbone of a solid top-flight career. All of that time, all of that work and all of that effort, all to be distilled down to a single moment. A single, horrifying moment.

42

Patrick Vieira

RIVALRY EXAMINES in a way that camaraderie cannot. On a sporting level, those looking to exploit weakness can push an individual further than whatever unity can offer. Adversity reveals the truth, pulling the curtain down over comfort. Direct opposition nurtures and moulds both character and talent. Their biased assessments add broader strokes to a picture, even if their brush is being used to paint in an intentionally unflattering light.

The word 'nemesis' evokes both an inescapable contest and this idea of a counterbalance. Roy Keane certainly radiated the aura of a vengeful spirit. The hostility that was wrought between Manchester United and Arsenal during the late 1990s carried with the clubs the kind of intensity and significance that has yet to be equalled in the Premier League era. As far as Keane and Patrick Vieira were concerned, what stood before them was a singular goal; what stood between them was each other.

It's very telling and also completely understandable that Keane saw Arsenal and Vieira as bullies. Projectional protestations aside, the inescapable reality is that the assumption was correct. Manchester United had their way with the Premier League, all but unopposed for the better part of a decade, save for one instance at Upton Park when they were made to feel mortal and Blackburn walked away with the trophy. Given what one team had done to the rest of the league there was no other choice. The only way to usurp a side that had laid waste to the very top of English football was to beat it down further.

The road to immortality had a familiar beginning before an unexpected turn. From the streets of Dakar to Cannes and then onwards to Milan. The kind of prodigious rise befitting the reputation his career would take. The assumed heir to Frank Rijkaard at the San Siro could not find the chance to take this particular crown. A year and two league starts later, with other players above him in the pecking order it was time to look for a different path. Destiny beckoned at Highbury; London calling.

Bruce Rioch might not be the biggest name to come out of the 1990s, even restricting that criteria solely to Arsenal. He is though cast in a meaningful role during the summer of 1996 which began with him entangled with the boardroom regarding transfers and also the directors' growing frustration in him signing a new deal. Of those who put pen to paper that summer, it would turn out that Rioch's signature would be the least important.

Arsène Wenger's transfer record throughout his Arsenal career was something that would play heavily into the circumstances of his latter years. Such was his early success rate, it seems fitting that he could make such a monumental signing before even being appointed at the club. Convincing Vieira to reject a move to Ajax in favour of joining the Gunners as part of Wenger's own foreword started a compelling chapter in Premier League history. Like a post-credit scene at the end of a Marvel movie, Arsenal were coming.

For a country so infatuated and a league largely constructed with a focus on pace and power, it had never seen the likes of Vieira. Even beyond the lazy commentary stereotypes, he was so much more than that. Vieira could do it all, blessed with immaculate timing and a technique that defied his frame; a spatial awareness capped off with the ability to either find or be on the end of any given pass; the aggressiveness of a combative midfielder and the finesse of someone who could finish. As contemporary analysis began to evolve, so too did the play. The term 'box-to-box midfielder' may not have originated in north London but it was very close to being perfected there.

No one man could take on the might of Manchester United alone. It was an assault on all fronts, a gamble that paid off long after any initial success. The likes of David Platt, Paul Merson and Ian Wright were augmented by Vieira and Dennis Bergkamp, all the while being marshalled by that notorious Arsenal defensive line. At the end of that inaugural Wenger season there was still plenty of work to do, however. Missing out on Champions League football by goal difference at the first time of it being offered to second place might have been seen as a setback to Arsenal. It most certainly wasn't.

Conquering the world isn't for everyone. As the World Cup in France drew to an emphatic and yet surprising conclusion, Vieira had laid waste to two empires within one season. Coming off the bench to assist Emmanuel Petit in the dying embers to put an exclamation point over Les Blues' victory over Brazil would have been enough to fulfil any kind of wildest dreams. Preceding it with a domestic double and stopping Manchester United from claiming a fifth title in six years was yet another. By the time David Trezeguet scored the winner in Amsterdam to claim the European Championship in 2000, Vieira stood tall. More than just a midfield general but highly decorated all the same. For all he had won domestically, for all he was a part of internationally, still there was a fight to be had. Manchester United would not go quietly into the night. They would not go in any way, shape or form.

One of the things that solidified this particular match-up was not just their league form, it was the ferocity of their in-season encounters as the conflicts continued. Very few things loom as large as the image of Martin Keown engulfing Ruud van Nistelrooy; as iconic a visual as exists within the anthology of the Premier League. To say this moment is a boiling point is to undersell it, for the whole game was a culmination of animosity. Neither side could be separated, underlined by the penalty miss that animated Keown so. A goalless stalemate so early on in the 2003/04 season meant very little to either side. After all, nobody could possibly gain notoriety for simply not losing.

What happened in the months afterwards confirmed both invincibility and immortality. Going through a full campaign without tasting defeat was a flight of fancy. A preposterous carrot to dangle, given how many great sides in the past had never done it. Anyone can beat anyone. That was – and still remains – the clichéd bedrock that ostensibly holds together the equilibrium up and down the leagues. Each week came a revolving cast of potential spoilers. Some were more qualified to play the role than others. None could break Arsenal down and so on to a particular hallowed plinth they went, the Preston North End side of 1888/89 finally happy to have some company.

Vieira and his team-mates had planted a flag, asking a question of the rest of the league and daring them to stand up to the challenge. The problem with this kind of demand is that it's only ever going to end one way. Defeat is assured. Defeat is inescapable. The only uncertainties were when it would arrive and who would herald it. After having taken Manchester United's crown, the stage was set for revenge. All roads lead back to Old Trafford.

There are ways to lose, none of which make the end result any better, but some at the very least make it easier to take. At the end of a remarkable run the likes of which Arsenal were on at the time, the hope is only that however it happens is deserved. That's not to say that Manchester United weren't on their level on the day in October 2004; far from it. There had been too much evidence on display that these two sides were more than a match for each other. Both United's 2-0 win and the contest itself were administered – from an Arsenal perspective – incorrectly. Of all those out on the pitch that day, it shouldn't be the referee making the headlines. If the game was contentious then the afters were even more infamous. Post-match tunnel confrontations aren't unheard of and especially in the circumstances it would almost have been more mystifying if things hadn't spilled out. It's not every day a manager puts an end to his opponent's 49-game unbeaten streak. It's not every day that the same manager is accosted by an airborne pizza.

According to the honours board, the margherita mugging isn't even the most significant game the two teams played that season. The Millennium Stadium in Cardiff was to be the venue for yet another heavyweight encounter between Manchester United and Arsenal, significant if for nothing else that this was the first FA Cup Final decided on penalty kicks. Not for the first time the outcome was decided by the boot of Vieira, in what would be the last kick of a hall of fame-worthy Arsenal career. Talk of his exit followed him on an almost annual basis with the rumour mill perpetually in motion. This time there was more to it than just paper talk and the Arsenal captain called time on his Highbury career. What happened next for both the man and the club he left behind was something of a roller coaster.

The connective tissue of the Venn diagram between Vieira moving back to Italy and Arsenal getting left behind may be flimsy at worst, but they do touch. From the top there is only one direction of travel and yet their descent into madness doesn't happen overnight. Just as they had altered the power structure of the Premier League in the late 1990s, another force had emerged. Endowed by Roman Abramovich and fuelled by José Mourinho's all-encompassing presence, Chelsea airlifted themselves to the summit. It is bittersweet and yet somewhat telling that in the season in which the streak was broken and ended with Vieira lifting the FA Cup, it was the Londoners in blue who stood tallest. With the power balance at the top now broken, it was to be Arsenal who were left in an increasingly precarious position as the 2000s rolled on.

As Arsenal would face questions over their fragility, Juventus were to be presented with questions of a very different kind. Following on from the Calciopoli scandal that saw the club relegated, Vieira moved to Inter Milan after just 12 months and returned to the San Siro a much more rounded and experienced player than in his earlier time with AC Milan, helping himself to two further Serie A titles following the power vacuum that Juventus's departure created. In spite of all that, his playing minutes were dwindling and opportunities lessened. Time, it seemed, had done what very few opposition players had been able to in bringing Vieira to a standstill. Contributions come in many forms, however.

Statistically speaking, Vieira's time at Manchester City represents a further regression very firmly in his twilight years. This is why you shouldn't speak to statistics, nor trust anyone who converses with them alone. Twenty-eight games in just two years represents very little from a footballing perspective, yet the job involves much more than the end result after 90 minutes. Sometimes it's more theoretical than practical. Learning how to win on a consistent basis with a given group of players is like cultivating a garden. First the seeds have to be planted. As far as Manchester City were concerned, Vieira would teach them via osmosis. The effect – mentally if nothing more – of having a player like that in training would do much more to add to a collective culture, especially of a side so desperate to blossom from out of the shadow of their cross-city neighbours.

Even the greatest of players find themselves hauled off stage unceremoniously. Some are barely even able to find one which to be thrown. That the whistle blew at Wembley as Vieira's curtain call feels rather fitting, even if he had to be rather rushed on to the pitch at the last moment to ensure it. The 2011 FA Cup was the first trophy for Manchester City for 35 years. They would not have to wait as long for many others.

After a decade of playing within the Premier League and growing to become one of its most iconic players, returning as a manager felt like something of an inevitability for Vieira. Selhurst Park and Crystal Palace were in need of a refresh. Although things hadn't gone smoothly for him during his time at Nice or in New York, his dynamic young Eagles side have definitely shaken the cobwebs off and are giving fans new hope. It's just a shame that Roy Keane appears to have retired from management, just to rekindle that old conflict one last time.

43

Les Ferdinand

EVERY GENERATION has its own plot points and protagonists, all of whom are passed down as the years go on. People and proceedings that take on a larger significance to even those who were too young to have been present at the time. While there is no changing the past, yesterday shapes what today brings. Unfinished business means something very different in a football context. Not everything has the chance to be seen through until the end. When it comes to a success that never was, time might not necessarily heal all wounds.

Destiny doesn't belong to anyone. Glory isn't given, it's taken. The things that seem predetermined are only ever seen through the eyes of those who end up on the winning side. Every victor by proxy creates a loser, yet some on either side are undeserving. Fates become intertwined – even if you don't believe in that sort of thing. Everyone has a role to play, which is to say that a player of Les Ferdinand's ability should have more in his trophy haul than the reality that stands as is. One domestic trophy from his time in Turkey followed by the 1999 League Cup. It could have been more, it should have been more. Such is football.

Team games are the aggregation of work among a group of players. Whether one of them shines above the rest can become painfully immaterial at times. Part of the process in making it at all is about standing out even at the expense of those on the same side. Ferdinand's initial elevation came at a time when the idea of taking someone up through the divisions was more rationalised, even if not prevalent. Playing across a variety of non-league teams before moving from Hayes all the way up to the top flight at Queens Park Rangers in 1987, although it took a couple of years to be established in the first team, it was clear from the outset that Ferdinand was someone who had all the tools to make a name for himself.

The process of going from the bottom to the top did take one small diversion, by way of a season on loan in Istanbul for Beşiktaş. The Turkish Cup may not have been Ferdinand's primary goal when he was playing in south London as a teenager, but both securing it and scoring 14 goals in 24 games pushed him to the brink of first-team football at Loftus Road. In the 1990s and wearing those famous hoops, Ferdinand delivered a reliable 18 goals in 41 games across two years as QPR had been solidly mid-table. Going into the inaugural Premier League season, nobody could have expected what was about to happen.

What made the whirlwind start to those initial 11 games of the 1992/93 season even more remarkable is that QPR didn't sign a single player during that summer. Rather than attacking the newly rebranded First Division with a raft of new faces, Gerry Francis went with the tried and tested. Ferdinand repaid that faith by finishing second in the goalscoring charts and the team as a whole performed admirably throughout to end up in fifth place. Not only was this a thumb in the face of more conventional sides but it also – however briefly – rendered QPR front and centre as far as London was concerned.

The capital city of the home of football. There isn't a region of England that doesn't live and breathe the beautiful game but as far as London goes, all the clubs are on top of one another. If it were sibling rivalry, the R's would have been forced to have been quiet in the face of some of their more prominent peers.

Sixty goals in those first three Premier League years would not go unnoticed. What's more, during that period QPR had never finished outside of the top ten, so it wasn't to say that removing one piece should see the whole club come tumbling down, but that's exactly what happened. Ferdinand signed for Newcastle in 1995 and the following season would see QPR fall away. There's no scenario in which finishing 19th would be preferable to coming second, yet the heartache that was to come for his old team paled in comparison to the agony which was about to play out.

Part of the reason why hope kills is that there's a moment when an alternate – much more preferable – reality plays out. While QPR went down in 1995/96, that window never really happened. For Newcastle and their ambitions it was open the entire time, only to slam shut in the most dramatic way imaginable. Ferdinand was a revelation for the Magpies, 25 league goals more than repaying the £6m that was laid out. Their runaway start to the season saw only two defeats before Christmas, closely followed by a pivotal third during a visit to Old Trafford. Not that anyone would ever know what happened between Manchester United and Newcastle that season. All of the scrutiny of how the 1995/96 Premier League title was won boiled down to nothing that happened on the pitch and instead focused on the words that were said off it.

If history is written by the winners, Kevin Keegan wrote comparatively little between his days as a player and a manager. Even within the rewriting of the events that were to follow, what he managed to accomplish with Newcastle from the moment he was appointed was remarkable. Arriving with the club in the second tier of English football in February 1992 to find them on the verge of dropping even further, to even be in such a position four years later would have been unthinkable. In terms of distance travelled, it wasn't so much how far Newcastle had come. What mattered and the reason why this season became so important, was how little they had left to go.

Whatever the lead, titles aren't decided in January. Twelve points is such a cushion that it never should have become an issue. Hindsight has a way of altering all that which came before, especially when it comes to an ending of this sort. Not that it will ever be seen as such due to all that came after, but the Newcastle side that was put together that year enthralled the Premier League. Supplementing Ferdinand's arrival were David Ginola and then Faustino Asprilla to join up with a still productive Peter Beardsley and Rob Lee, who was having the season of his career. The goals flowed but so too did the chaos.

A stumble can become a fall. Before Keegan said what he said, there was a pivotal home game against Manchester United. Hypothetical history usually assumes that changing the moment will have no effect on all that follows. Manchester United came out on top that day but it did not stop Newcastle. For all the shouts of fragility that are closely associated with this season, the Magpies recovered to beat West Ham – something that a mentally broken team wouldn't have done. At this point as the games ticked down and the gap became smaller, it was all about pressure. Newcastle could apply none for they were already ahead, while Manchester United turned the heat up week after week. The dynamic that Alex Ferguson preferred – or at least the narrative – was one of chasing rather than leading outright. With no other option than to look ahead, the Red Devils kept winning. Trips to Highbury and Anfield were just that for Newcastle; two defeats in a row were the stumble.

Some players take a long time to be popular among a fanbase. For whatever reason, others never make that leap. Les Ferdinand only spent two years on Tyneside yet it was enough for him to get an honorary knighthood from the St James' Park faithful. Joining him in that second season was one of their own as an incredible homecoming became an astounding partnership. Keegan took in all that had happened during that fateful run-in and decided to double down. The purchase of Alan Shearer shattered the world transfer record and set down a marker that Newcastle would be back, but another kind of agony awaited.

A one-off result would never be able to make up for what came before, especially given Manchester United had already dished out their own beating in the Charity Shield at the start of the season. Even so, Newcastle 5 Manchester United 0 felt earth-shattering. Philippe Albert chipping Peter Schmeichel to cap off the victory that Sunday evening could have easily been a tipping point for a changing of the guard. And then Keegan resigned. Kenny Dalglish coming in on paper seemed like a good fit. He even had the credibility in having taken down Alex Ferguson some years before, and at first the signs were good. Shearer and Ferdinand stormed the goalscoring charts with a tally of over 40 between them. Once again Newcastle finished in second place but beating Arsenal to a Champions League place having been down in fifth was enough of an upturn to have hope for the following season. It was a future Ferdinand would not be a part of.

That summer saw mass upheaval. The board at Newcastle were purportedly so keen on cashing in on a now 30-year-old Ferdinand that it was among the reasons for Keegan's departure. In July they would get their wish. Football has always had a strange relationship with players' ages but even in 1997 to discard someone just as they were entering their 30s seemed unwise to put it mildly, not least because it gave off the impression that those at the club didn't want him there. With his boyhood club in Spurs waiting for a signature, an opportunity arose for Ferdinand to stay at St James' Park. Shearer had been injured and the worst was being feared. It wasn't easy but because of the way he felt he had been treated by the club, the decision was made to go to White Hart Lane.

Things were happening at Tottenham in the late 1990s. Hardly a season went by without some kind of chaos, from the departure of Gerry Francis to the memorably ridiculous arrival of Christian Gross. In a world where perception becomes reality so quickly, holding up a Tube ticket and likening it to a golden future, Gross became a laughing stock almost immediately. The truth of his failure had more to do with his inability to get the right coaching staff brought in and no doubt a myriad of other problems that arose but his die had long been cast before he eventually got the boot. George Graham brought with him an air of wariness due to his former ties with Arsenal but this was at least initially offset by the addition of the League Cup to the Tottenham trophy cabinet in 1999.

A turnover at boardroom level led to yet another displacement in the dugout. Alan Sugar selling the club to ENIC and Daniel Levy preceded Graham being removed from his position for an alleged breach of contract in disclosing private information to the media. By the time Glenn Hoddle took over in 2001, Ferdinand was on his fourth manager as well as a boardroom power switch in just four years. In all that time a tenth-place finish was the highest they could manage.

With time came a succession of bit-part roles. Robbie Keane's arrival at White Hart Lane signalled the end of Ferdinand's time there. It's probably for the best that he isn't remembered for going from Spurs to being a part of the West Ham side that went down in 2003. Leicester followed them down the following season but at least this time Ferdinand managed to hit double figures and was named player of the year at Filbert Street for his efforts. His final spell in the Premier League with Bolton featured – in what was his only goal for the club – the last goal he ever scored in the top flight: a 90th-minute potential winner against Manchester United. Bitterly fitting then, that a side against whom he had fought his greatest battles went up the other end and cancelled the goal out a minute later.

After retirement came coaching and then taking an even wider handle on club affairs, closing the loop on a stellar career at Tottenham and then back to where it all began at Queens Park Rangers. Being a part of something and being responsible for it are inextricably linked but not the same. Les Ferdinand had been a part of changing the course of what the team was capable of as a player, then some 20 years later returned to Loftus Road as director of football. The ties between certain people and who they represent go far beyond what they can do on the pitch. Every generation has its own plot points and protagonists. For some clubs, they can be the same people.

44

Robert Huth

TIME TRAVELS on a curve, not a straight line. As far as football is concerned, history repeats itself on a regular basis. What provokes a reaction tomorrow will in turn be forgotten about days later, allowing for it to come back around. Déjà vu is but a disciple to recognition. That feeling of it all coming back on itself.

The first all-English Champions League semi-final, between Liverpool and Chelsea in 2005, had enough plots and sub-plots to fill years of soap opera storylines. In the dying embers of the second leg and down 1-0 with ten minutes to play, a choice was made. José Mourinho was very much a man of the moment. Yet turning to a promising defender and deploying him up front, he was taking a tried and tested page out of tactics gone by.

This is significant not for what immediately happened next. It could very well have worked. There is something to be said for this incarnation of Chelsea who had that year looked unconquerable suddenly being that desperate. In such circumstances anything will do. What could have been so very different, wasn't. Scoring goals wasn't part of Robert Huth's remit. A second life as an emergency striker was put on hold for now in the pursuit of his primary career.

So much had transformed in the four years that Huth had been at Chelsea. The club as a whole made so many breakthroughs into the upper echelons of the Premier League all while Huth was trying to establish himself. A chance then to work with Mourinho over the coming few years may have felt like the perfect marriage. Chelsea were moulded into one of the best containing and dominating defensive setups ever seen in England. They were an intense blend of defence and attack. The problem was not in Huth trying to establish his own credentials, it was in those ahead of him. John Terry and Ricardo Carvalho were not only one the more dominant partnerships in the Premier League but also two players who very rarely missed any games. The problem with moving on is that there are still so many other things that can hinder.

After a staggered four years at Stamford Bridge, moving to Middlesbrough was to be a fresh start all around. With England insistent on having a domestic candidate replace Sven-Göran Eriksson, Boro's Steve McClaren was the man chosen to fill the role. This in turn allowed Gareth Southgate to step into the dugout at the Riverside before making a move for Huth. Despite the German failing the medical, Boro were insistent on getting their man. It definitely set the tone for what was to come.

Two torrid years playing just 30 games as his body broke down and a simple diagnosis wasn't enough. Scans of Huth's muscles made a startling discovery; his constant injuries were the result of one of his legs being slightly larger than the other. This led to disproportionate strain across both of them and as a result made him susceptible to more lengthy periods on the sidelines. A pair of custom insoles later meant he was finally ready to make a proper impact. Twenty-eight appearances in 2008/09 underlined a much better development in one sense but unfortunately there were very few signs of progression anywhere else. Huth was able to play certainly but he was unable to stop Middlesbrough from being relegated in 19th place. Finally fixed and ready to function, it was time for another move, to a team and a process all but built in his image.

Certain combinations work better together, whether it's personality from a playing perspective or for how they conduct themselves off the pitch in accordance with the wider consensus of the fanbase as a whole. Every player arrives at a new club as an outsider. A select few of them are welcomed with open arms, as if they had been a part of the family all along. Stoke and Robert Huth were made for each other in that he was an extension of their passion and solidarity. Tony Pulis had put together a footballing nightmare. A side that played with dogged determination that would never under any circumstances give an inch to the opponent. Huth very quickly became another bolt in an already locked door.

Establishing yourself in the Premier League is about more than winning games and avoiding relegation. Teams can go up and back down again without ever really leaving a mark, but Stoke made it very clear from the off that – win or lose – in every game at the Britannia, no side would leave having enjoyed their afternoon. The notorious reputation developed even before Huth had ever kicked a ball for the Potters remained until the bitter end of their Premier League era. After having gained a proper foothold within the top flight their ambition and hunger remained strong. The 2011 FA Cup Final pitted two clubs both desperate for a trophy for very different reasons. Manchester City wanted to kick-start a dynasty; Stoke were looking for one day in the sun. Hard-fought though it was, the closeness of the scoreline betrayed what was a comfortable enough 1-0 victory for the team in blue. Missing out had become a theme for Huth.

Parallel to his efforts in the Premier League, there was an international career that fell foul of misfortune and disappointment. German football was in a state of flux from the very start of the century. Their failure at Euro 2000 prompted big changes within their setup and approach to their youth teams. Going in this direction reaped rewards with a reinvigorated team that got to the semi-finals of the World Cup in 2010 and won the following tournament in Brazil. Before all that, there were still places to be played for with Germany hosting in 2006.

The Confederations Cup in 2005 was to be Huth's audition. Even before he got a real chance to compete for a starting place at Chelsea, this was a testament to how highly regarded he was in terms of his potential. Losing to Brazil in the semi-final wasn't a disgrace in its own right. That was how it ended. Even before it, nothing went right for Huth. Being sent off against Northern Ireland in a friendly and blamed for goals conceded against Australia in their opening game, coupled with the emergence of both Per Mertesacker and Christoph Metzelder, meant that while he was part of the Germany squad in 2006 his international career was all but over before it had even started.

Before, during and after Huth's time at Stoke, the Potters persisted within the Premier League for a decade. That amount of time in the top tier for anyone is worth celebrating, let alone a club that was unfancied and unliked. Everything they had they earned through grit and determination, annoying as many of the traditional big teams as possible along the way. Their demise is often associated with the departure of Tony Pulis, so close were the two related. It's a little more complicated than that.

Mark Hughes's managerial career, if nothing else, placed him in very different places at particularly interesting times in their history. By the time he was appointed at the Britannia Stadium, Stoke had done enough in terms of building a foundation to look further forward. A particular set of tactics – or at the very least the perception of how that style of play was prevalent – coloured the view of what was to come. Huth had moved on three years prior to the Potters' relegation in 2018, injury once again taking him out of contention and forcing a decision in regard to his future. No longer a talked-about prospect, with a disrupted career and time very much not on his side, going on loan to relegation-threatened Leicester in 2015 seemed like part of a natural regression and fading into insignificance. Everything that had happened before, every disappointment and setback, all of it had led to this.

The Foxes sat bottom of the Premier League when Huth signed on the dotted line for them. On 10 February 2015 they suffered a 2-1 defeat to Arsenal at the Emirates. Some 369 days later Huth would return and Leicester would lose by the same scoreline having just fallen to a 95th-minute Danny Welbeck winner. The Arsenal celebrations were wild after what was very much a statement result. One of these two would be league champions come the end of the season, however, and it wasn't the home side.

During that time, a lot happened. Saving Leicester from relegation was just the beginning. There have been more celebrated escapes, teams who whether through tradition or the lateness with which they were liberated are heralded in such a way, but none more important than how Nigel Pearson and the Foxes pulled to safety in 2014/15. It took until April for them to register just their fifth win of the season. At the time they were cut off at the bottom of the table and some seven points away from safety. A late Andy King winner over West Ham at the King Power Stadium sparked a run of form that would see them pick up more points than anyone in the league during the last stretch of the season. A visit to The Hawthorns saw another last-gasp reprieve with Jamie Vardy scoring in added time after Huth's 80th-minute equaliser. Five more victories in the remaining seven games of the season were enough to see Leicester finish four places and six points above the drop zone. This feat alone could easily have been called a miracle, but by comparison it was just the appetiser.

Everything had led to what happened. Not just for Huth but for everyone involved at Leicester City. For all the moments earlier on in his career, the stuttered start at the top to being eventually written off altogether, to come back around like this was just a part of the story. A face from Huth's past came forth to define the future. Claudio Ranieri was the manager who gave him his Chelsea debut over a decade prior. Even despite his amiable reputation within the Premier League, there were doubts as to whether the Italian would be able to keep the Foxes out of danger. The game in England had moved on since he last took charge. Tactically there are differences emerging all the time but there should still be room for some romance, something that shocks the system and stirs the heart all at the same time. At a time when it was thought impossible, football made it possible.

It began as a quest for individual glory. Vardy's goalscoring run during the early months of the season gave Leicester an unexpected presence towards the top of the table. By the time November arrived and Manchester United came to town, there was a real sense of anticipation. Vardy's strike to take the Premier League record for scoring in ten straight games was something of an inevitability. Something else was happening throughout the rest of the squad too. After having been involved in a few reckless encounters earlier on in the season, the defence was starting to clamp down. Ranieri openly came out in the press and challenged his team to keep just one clean sheet, with their charming reward being the boss would get them all a pizza if they did. When one came, more and more began to follow. Huth and captain Wes Morgan, with Kasper Schmeichel behind them, were soon a resolute force at the back. N'Golo Kanté grew more and more into his role ahead of them. All the while the attack was becoming increasingly sharpened as Riyad Mahrez and Shinji Okazaki joined in with the Vardy party. Heading into the Christmas period, it had been a wild ride. The serious business was about to begin.

The idea that the stars aligned for Leicester fails to recognise their actual achievements. In December they took on Chelsea, Liverpool and Manchester City within quick succession of one another. Even for those teams with much more in terms of resources, getting through a period like this was going to be difficult. Falling at this hurdle would have been understandable;

there would still have been plenty of plaudits and still there was a sense of overachievement. Four points from nine represented enough of a return to encourage, especially with another impressive victory at Everton wedged in the middle. Halfway through the season with only two defeats to their name, the thought process began to turn. Instead of it being about how they couldn't possibly win it because eventually things would catch up with them, belief began to build.

If the run in December was enough to make the impossible now possible, the early part of 2016 brought it closer still. At both ends it was Huth's time to shine; from being punted up front all those years ago to becoming the unlikeliest hero in a team full of them. It started in January at White Hart Lane. With ten minutes left to go, Huth found himself unmarked from a corner to bullet a header beyond Hugo Lloris in the Tottenham goal. The next time he would find himself on the scoresheet was in yet another milestone a couple of weeks later. Going to the Etihad and taking on Manchester City was another big test of Leicester's credentials. After just two minutes they were in front courtesy of a well-worked set-piece routine and Huth escaping his marker to slot home. Mahrez doubled their lead immediately after the restart and when it came time for the third they emphatically defied whatever doubters still remained. Another powerful header from the German centre-half after a corner led to him running away to celebrate with the ecstatic Leicester fans by the goal. Arsenal's late victory over the Foxes in the following game may have racked up the tension but by now the end was in sight.

Those last few weeks weren't easy. One mistake could have undone all that hard work and denied Leicester the fairy-tale ending that so many were waiting for. That first half of the season was so carefree; in March it really mattered. A series of 1-0 victories was the order of the day, each one getting them closer and closer to the finish line as Huth and Morgan became rocks at the heart of the defence. By the time Leicester headed to Manchester United at the start of May the margins were achingly thin. A 1-1 draw wasn't enough to secure the title and subsequently Huth himself would be forced to sit out what remained of the season after clashing with Marouane Fellaini. As it turned out, the entire squad would be sitting on and watching as their wildest dreams came true. Huth became a Premier League champion after what happened at Stamford Bridge the following day, when Chelsea drew with Spurs.

Not everyone has their career tied up in a bow. This wasn't even the end, as fitting as it might have been. Leicester soaked up the plaudits, cherished their moment and the subsequent adventure that came in the Champions League. Events and circumstances moved as quickly downward as they had gone up previously. Ranieri was sacked, the club narrowly avoided relegation and Huth's playing days drew to a close. His retirement announcement was typical of the man who had been a no-nonsense defender for a new generation. Replying on Twitter to speculation regarding him moving from Leicester to Derby with the simple phrase 'I've retired!' was followed up in typical fashion with, 'I just haven't done an interview and cried about it.'

Football is forever in a state of flux. The constant movement away from the present, headed in an unspecified direction for an unknown length of time. Some things don't change though. Eventually everything will come back around. This means that there will always be a place for someone that does the simple things right. A space for the hard-working defenders who maybe never quite get their plaudits. Above all else, with an increasing sense of cynicism around the game as a whole, there should always be scope for an underdog. The dream that – like Leicester – anything is possible.

45

Paolo Di Canio

NO ONE is either entirely one thing nor the other when it comes to questions of character. These are more personal truths than universal. They may be ugly, projecting an image that others find repugnant. What people see in themselves can be very different to that which the rest of the world looks upon. As such, being authentic matters much more than what anyone does or says. Being true to who they are, regardless of any sense of righteousness.

That line. That theoretical line. If the question to cross it in order to have success was to be asked of many clubs and fans alike, how many would say no? For most, the answer to that question is even more depressingly cynical than the premise. Too often it isn't about what is or isn't acceptable – it's about their status within the squad. The higher the talent, the more the moral line disappears completely.

Morality is meant to be about very simple boundaries. Good or bad, right and wrong. The game itself – as in life – has very clearly defined rules. The problem, as ever, lies within interpretation. So much of what is seen as corrupt or rotten revolves around choices being made that others simply could not. The term 'modern football', often used in disgust, will likely continue to do so as whatever standards remain inevitably erode.

Greed has driven both institutions and communities to the brink and will continue to put the foot down, perhaps until there is nothing left. But it doesn't stop there.

The politicisation of football is at once a process that those in a higher office are happy to manipulate when it suits them and simultaneously a pointless endeavour. Something cannot become political, it can only be used in such a way. Footballers have a platform. Through and after the game, they speak to everyone in a way that few other voices are ever capable of reaching. Yet when that message is bigger than who wins and who loses, listening becomes much harder. Binary truths are easily digestible. Which is why their place as role models, even sincerely, is often misguided. They are people. Their lows are as much a reflection on humanity as their highs are a reflection on what they can do for it.

Paolo Di Canio was complicated. Adored by his fans, reviled by others and when it came to his time as manager of both Swindon and Sunderland, there was a little mixture of both. Something about the fiery Italian gelled with the English culture and game in a way that very few coming from foreign shores have ever been able to. His ability was unquestionable. He scored arguably the greatest goal in Premier League history when he redefined the scissor kick against Wimbledon in 2000 with a moment of true footballing artistry. There was no denying he had another side to him, however. More than just a temper that would get him into trouble.

Sheffield Wednesday might have had more dutiful players, those much more grounded in the area and connected with the supporters. Certainly in the Premier League era they have not had any better than Paolo Di Canio. Being able to attract a player who a year prior had been winning Serie A for AC Milan was certainly a coup. Of course it came with complications, which went with the territory. Before moving to England in August 1997, Di Canio spent an eventful season in Scotland with Celtic, packing in the PFA Scotland Players' Player of the Year award along with multiple on-field incidents that brought into focus the duality of his ability and attitude. Unbridled passion spilled over into outright recklessness, all the while at odds with the refinement and elegance he possessed on the ball. Between the beauty of his goals and the violent nature that lay beneath it all, he had set the stall out early for what would be the rest of his career.

Sheffield Wednesday needed a boost. Having been relegated at the end of the 1980s, to bounce back so emphatically enabled them to establish themselves as one of the more reliable teams within the middle of the Premier League. Earlier on in the decade they had even managed to savour some cup runs, losing both domestic finals in 1992/93 to Arsenal only two years after winning the League Cup as a Second Division side. By the mid-1990s, however, just as that impetus was beginning to fade, narrowly missing out on European football saw the need to bring in something a little extra. Di Canio was definitely that.

He was only at Hillsborough for two years. Aside from an 'of its time' publicity shoot with Benito Carbone and a very bland-looking pizza, he is only ever remembered for one game. Some incidents are so isolated from the football matches they are contained within, they become inexorably bigger than the scoreline itself. On 26 September 1998, Sheffield Wednesday beat Arsenal 1-0. This was a fantastic early season result for the Owls given that their opponents would go on to finish second and that Wednesday themselves were hotly tipped for relegation. Very much in defiance of that tag, they would later go on to beat Manchester United, who themselves were having a stellar 1998/99 campaign. But all of that was overlooked because of Paolo Di Canio.

Being sent off in that victory over Arsenal didn't hit the headlines. Even having gone wildly into a collection of Arsenal players looking to get a hold of firstly Patrick Vieira and then Martin Keown seemed like standard behaviour. From a fan perspective it could even be applauded, running to the defence of a team-mate after they had been shoved to the floor. What came next floored everyone; those in the stadium figuratively, referee Paul Alcock literally. Pushing the referee to the ground is about as far over the line as a player can go without causing any major damage to anyone. As serious as it was, the outrageous way Alcock fell backward, off balance and in stages, lent an air of farce to the whole proceedings but this was no joke.

An exceptional punishment was due for an inconceivable act. Di Canio maintained in his autobiography that the push wasn't meant to be violent. Though there was very little in the way of force behind it, that was not the point. Banned for 11 games and fined £10,000, the punishment satisfied no one. He felt it should have been lighter; the referees' association believed the opposite. The Italian had crossed a line and now found himself all alone. His Sheffield Wednesday career was effectively over and whatever his capacity for greatness on the pitch, there was already a long list of reasons as to why any manager would be put off. Harry Redknapp was not just any manager.

Looking to redress the balance is something that players have to do on a week-to-week basis. It's a lot harder to come back from a place of honour and shame than it is a simple lack of form, yet therein lies the key. West Ham finished fifth in the immediate aftermath of Di Canio's arrival. The following season wasn't quite as successful for the team as a whole but Di Canio's assimilation into relative anonymity over time was complete. The thing with players of a certain ability – let alone someone with his kind of temperament – is that they will never stay quiet for long.

Great goals out of context should always have an element of artistry to them. The last-minute winner or a strike that becomes integral to a trophy-winning campaign will always have a separate and deeper aura. Stripped of all that, goals that exist outside of a bigger purpose must have something special to be remembered. Against Wimbledon in March 2000, the game had barely begun before those inside Upton Park and watching at home on TV were treated to what would go on to be voted the greatest goal scored in the ground's history. Trevor Sinclair looped a standard high ball forward from right to left and all appeared normal. Di Canio met it in the air well before it had a chance to bounce and swivelled his feet. Given the power and accuracy of the strike, very few footballs in any ground have ever been struck more sweetly. In terms of percentage football this was the exact opposite. The kind of scenario that goes wrong for so many players so often that some don't even dare to try it. Audacious at a baseline level and almost impossible to recreate. Few would be able to conceive it; Di Canio did it.

Being unpredictable makes things so much more complicated. For Di Canio that applied multiple times over. The possibilities were endless, in both good and bad senses of the word. Still, there was more to come. After having scored the goal of the season in 1999/2000 there was an incident in December 2000 that once again left everyone watching on speechless. With the game on the line against Everton at Goodison Park, goalkeeper Paul Gerrard raced out to meet Frédéric Kanouté as he was running through on goal. Having won the ball, any attempt to clear it further was hampered by a serious injury that saw Gerrard pull up and leave the goal unattended. With the cross swung in and an empty net beckoning, scoring would have been inevitable. Except it wasn't. Rather than convert the cross, Di Canio picked it out of the sky with his arms and allowed Gerrard to get medical attention.

It was one of the ultimate shows of sportsmanship and of course the internal reaction was initially one of fury. Among the coaching staff, Stuart Pearce reportedly was quoted as saying he wanted to 'rip his head off'. This is why common sense doesn't make sense. Part of the ethos that will always see the ends justify the means. How players can come back from abhorrent acts off the pitch to open arms. Why fans don't care where the money comes from so long as it leads to success. FIFA awarded Di Canio a fair play honour for his actions. Here was a player seemingly magnetised towards controversy, instead being held up as an example of virtue. It's not hypocrisy, nor does it make a mockery of a game built on double standards. It's life.

Whatever charges there are to bring against Paolo Di Canio, he cared, particularly about West Ham. Having once rejected a move to Manchester United so much was the strength of feeling he had for the club, how his time there ended was visibly painful. Once Redknapp moved on and Glenn Roeder took over, the Hammers went from a position of some strength to an incredible struggle in the blink of an eye. A public disagreement between Di Canio and Roeder lasted right up until the point the manager of them was taken ill. The very concept of recovery held an additional meaning. Trevor Brooking came in to halt an impossibility. Coming back into the fold for the final two games of the season, Di Canio played his part.

Feelings draw the blueprints for a fight. Emotion builds something, even if it is to inevitably fall away. More often than not, post-match interviews offer little insight. Tactically or personality-wise they are nothing more than a formality. Being cornered by the television cameras immediately following his late winner against Chelsea in the Hammers' penultimate game of 2002/03, there were no words. With tears in his eyes and hope still left, West Ham had given themselves one last chance at a reprieve. The following week they travelled to face Birmingham City. Last-minute goals are primed to matter but Di Canio's effort at St Andrew's ranks among the more agonisingly insignificant. The Hammers were too good to go down no more.

An oft-forgotten year at The Valley and helping Charlton to finish seventh in the Premier League followed. Part of the stigma that comes with such a reputation lies within nobody paying attention in terms of just getting on with the job. Much more notorious was Di Canio's return to Italy. Going back to wrap up his career with Lazio after having come through the ranks there barely scratches the surface as to how deep Di Canio's connection with that club and its culture goes. Problematic ties that can be ignored or written off become even more difficult to swallow in the face of a specific image.

The question is not what happened to integrity within football, it's whether it was ever there in the first place. If the game ever had a purity, over the years people corrupted it on and off the field. It's hard to digest the top-level corruption, to see over the grotesque sums of money used to mould and shape the game even further away from its roots. The players themselves have become so far removed from public life it's essentially a different existence. All the while, so long as they're scoring or the team is winning everyone is happy. The dilemma of Di Canio is one at the centre of that hypocrisy. A talent beyond compare; a genius with the ball at his feet. His passion and authenticity are enamouring. Yet behind it all there is a bitter aftertaste. Fans have over the years defended all sorts of things much worse than anything Di Canio ever did, and they will likely continue to do so. Regimes even. Whatever the cost of football's soul in the future, let's hope the price was worth it.

Also available at all good book stores

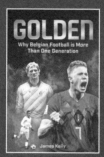

9781801501057

9781801500999

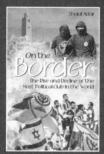

9781801500951

9781801500920

9781801501019

9781801501026

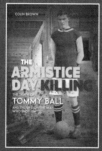

9781801501071

9781801501323

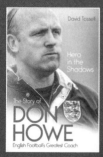

9781801500876